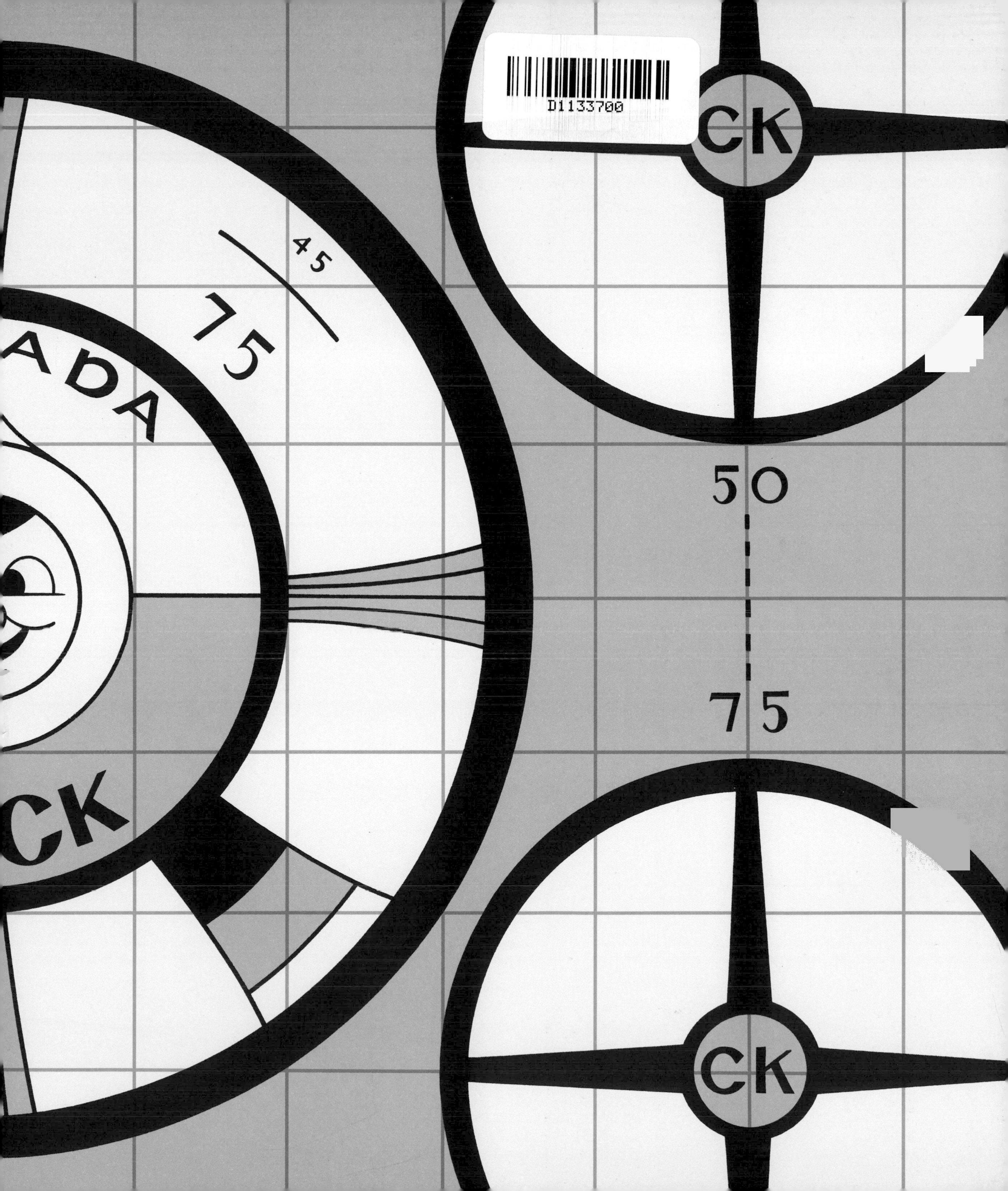
45
75
ADA
CK
CK
50
75
CK

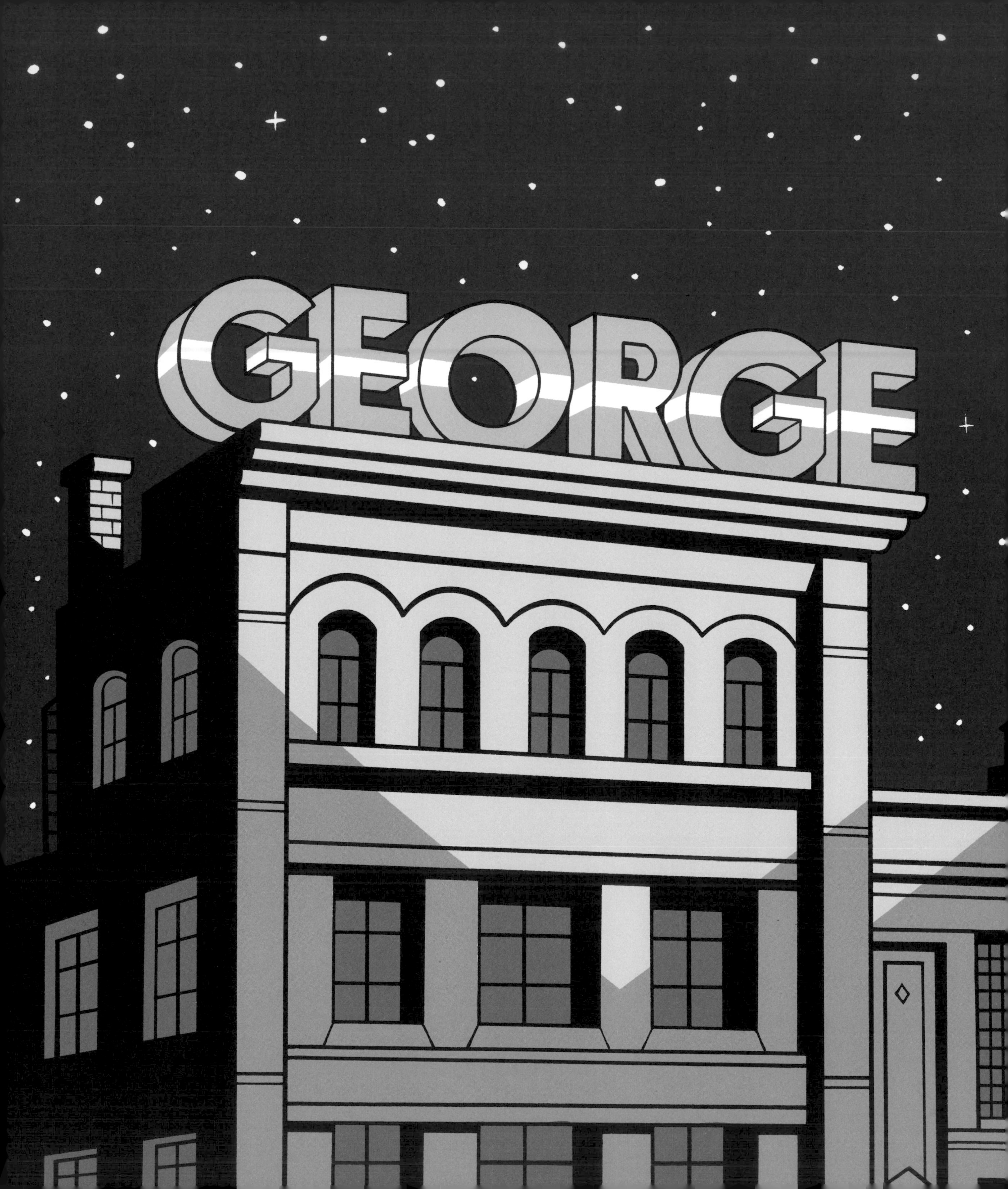
GEORGE

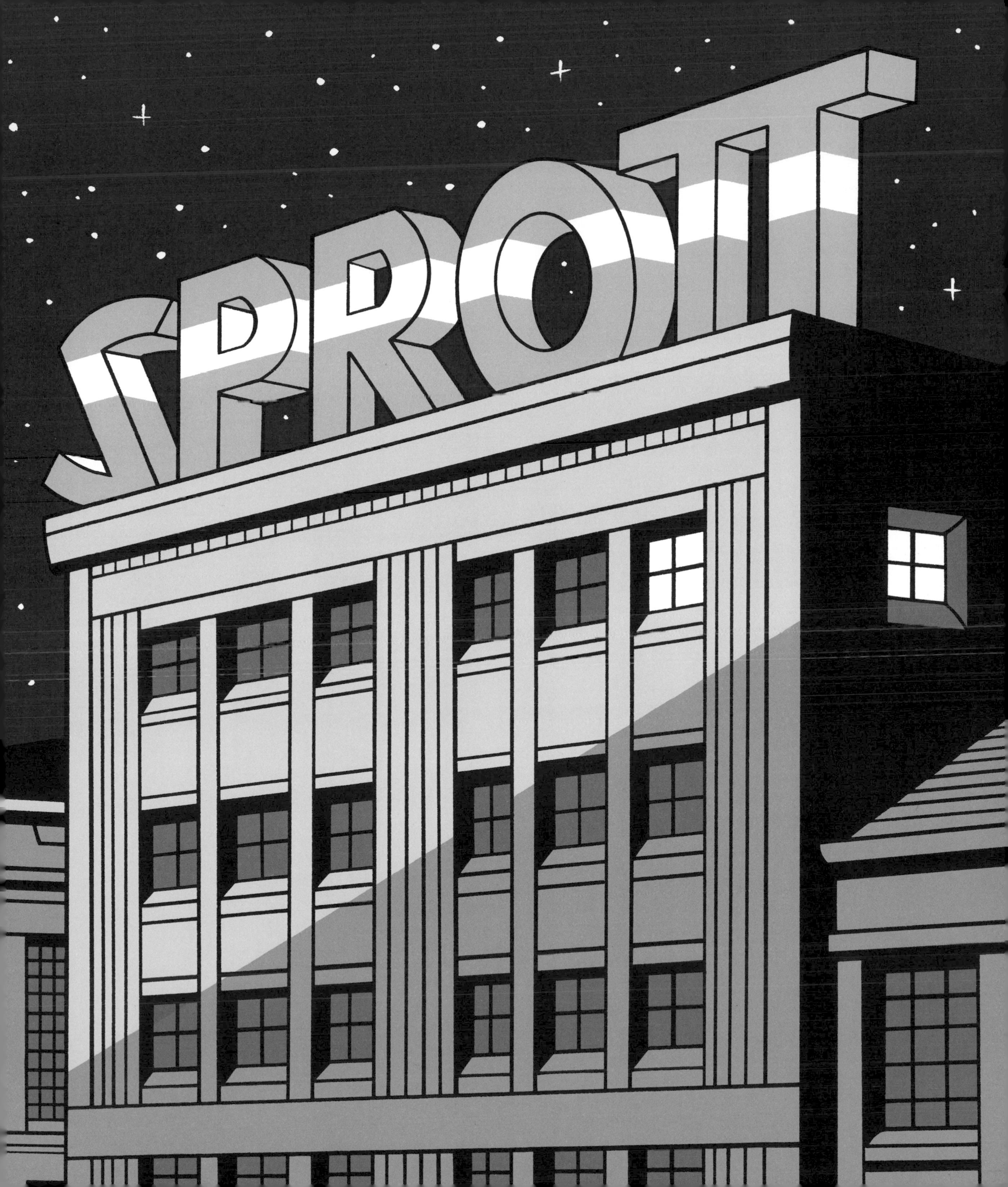
SPROTT

1894

1975

The Stars of CKCK—1966

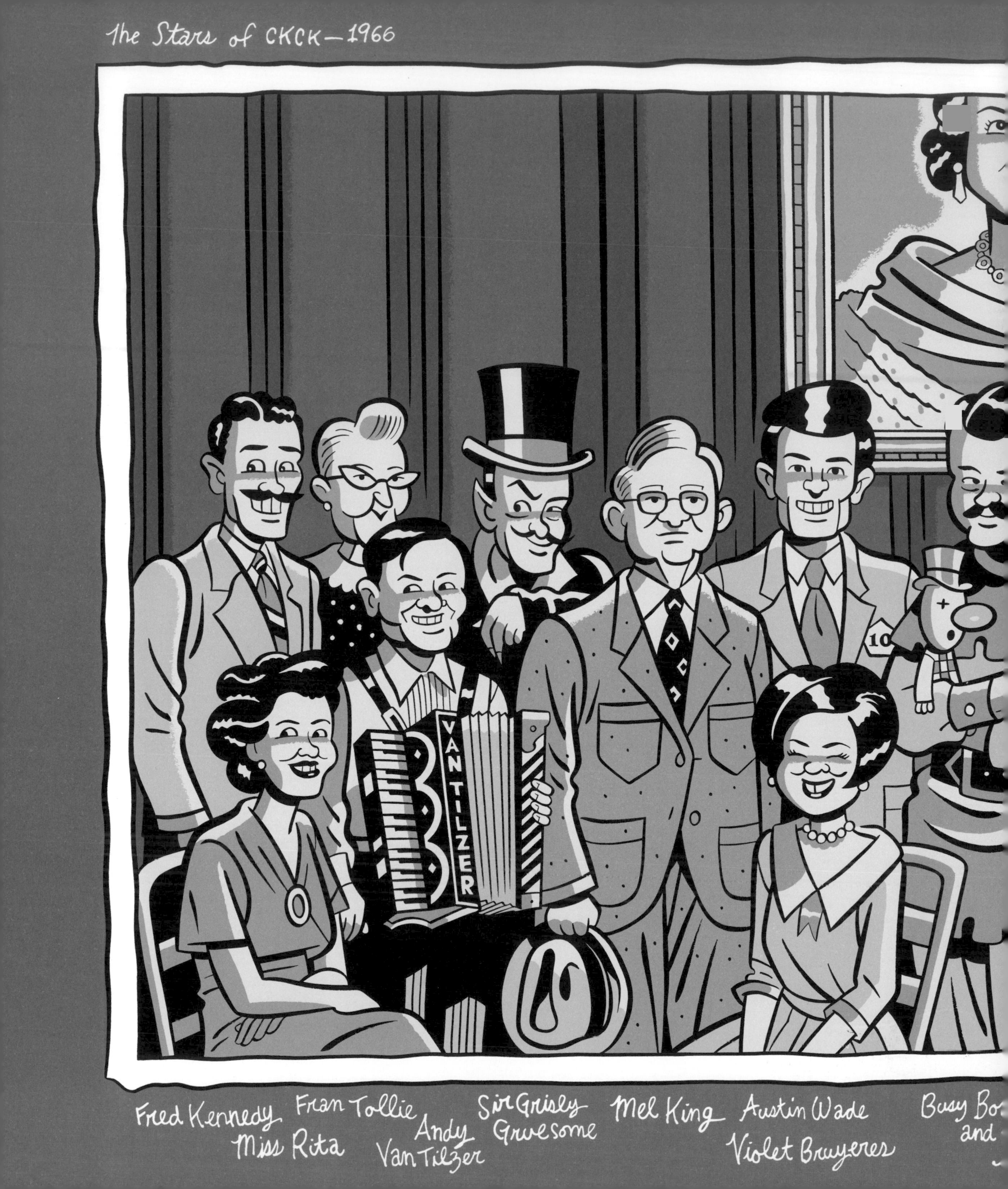
VAN TILZER
10

Fred Kennedy Fran Tollie Sir Grisly Gruesome Mel King Austin Wade Busy Bo
Miss Rita Andy Van Tilzer Violet Bruyeres and

From the Collection of Mr. O. Trade.

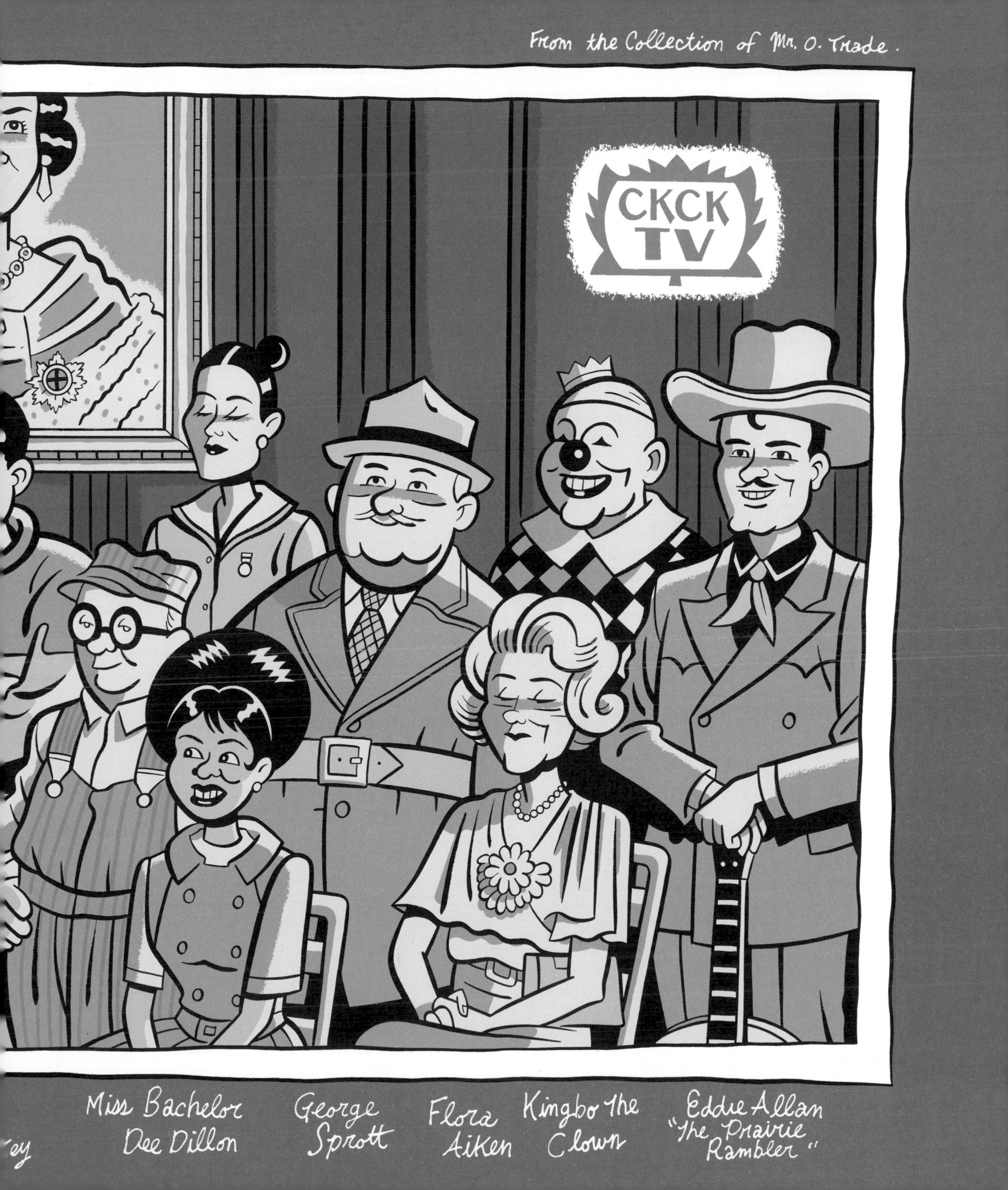
CKCK
TV

...ey

Miss Bachelor Dee Dillon

George Sprott

Flora Aiken

Kingbo the Clown

Eddie Allan "The Prairie Rambler"

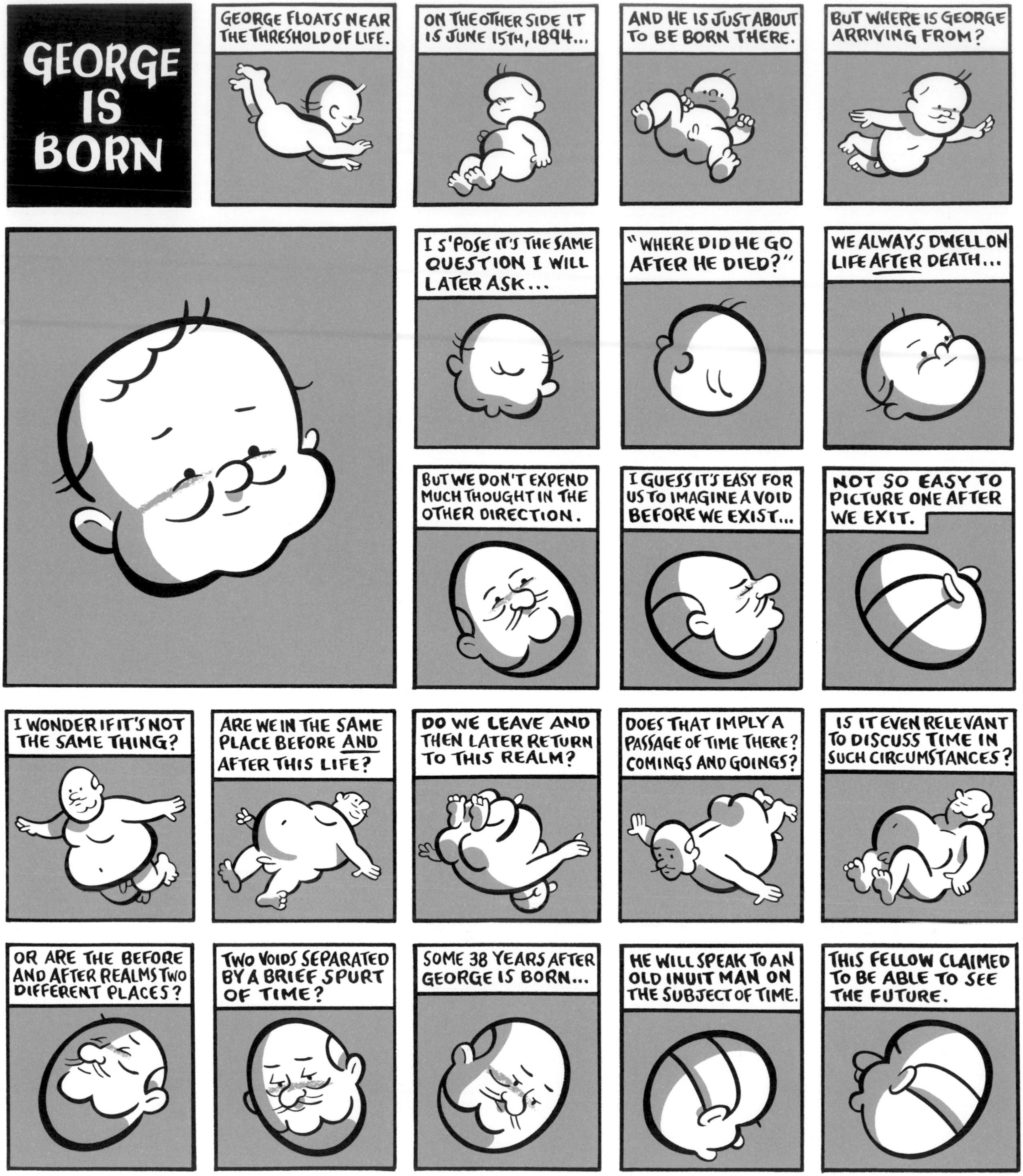
GEORGE IS BORN
GEORGE FLOATS NEAR THE THRESHOLD OF LIFE.
ON THE OTHER SIDE IT IS JUNE 15TH, 1894...
AND HE IS JUST ABOUT TO BE BORN THERE.
BUT WHERE IS GEORGE ARRIVING FROM?
I S'POSE IT'S THE SAME QUESTION I WILL LATER ASK...
"WHERE DID HE GO AFTER HE DIED?"
WE ALWAYS DWELL ON LIFE AFTER DEATH...
BUT WE DON'T EXPEND MUCH THOUGHT IN THE OTHER DIRECTION.
I GUESS IT'S EASY FOR US TO IMAGINE A VOID BEFORE WE EXIST...
NOT SO EASY TO PICTURE ONE AFTER WE EXIT.
I WONDER IF IT'S NOT THE SAME THING?
ARE WE IN THE SAME PLACE BEFORE AND AFTER THIS LIFE?
DO WE LEAVE AND THEN LATER RETURN TO THIS REALM?
DOES THAT IMPLY A PASSAGE OF TIME THERE? COMINGS AND GOINGS?
IS IT EVEN RELEVANT TO DISCUSS TIME IN SUCH CIRCUMSTANCES?
OR ARE THE BEFORE AND AFTER REALMS TWO DIFFERENT PLACES?
TWO VOIDS SEPARATED BY A BRIEF SPURT OF TIME?
SOME 38 YEARS AFTER GEORGE IS BORN...
HE WILL SPEAK TO AN OLD INUIT MAN ON THE SUBJECT OF TIME.
THIS FELLOW CLAIMED TO BE ABLE TO SEE THE FUTURE.

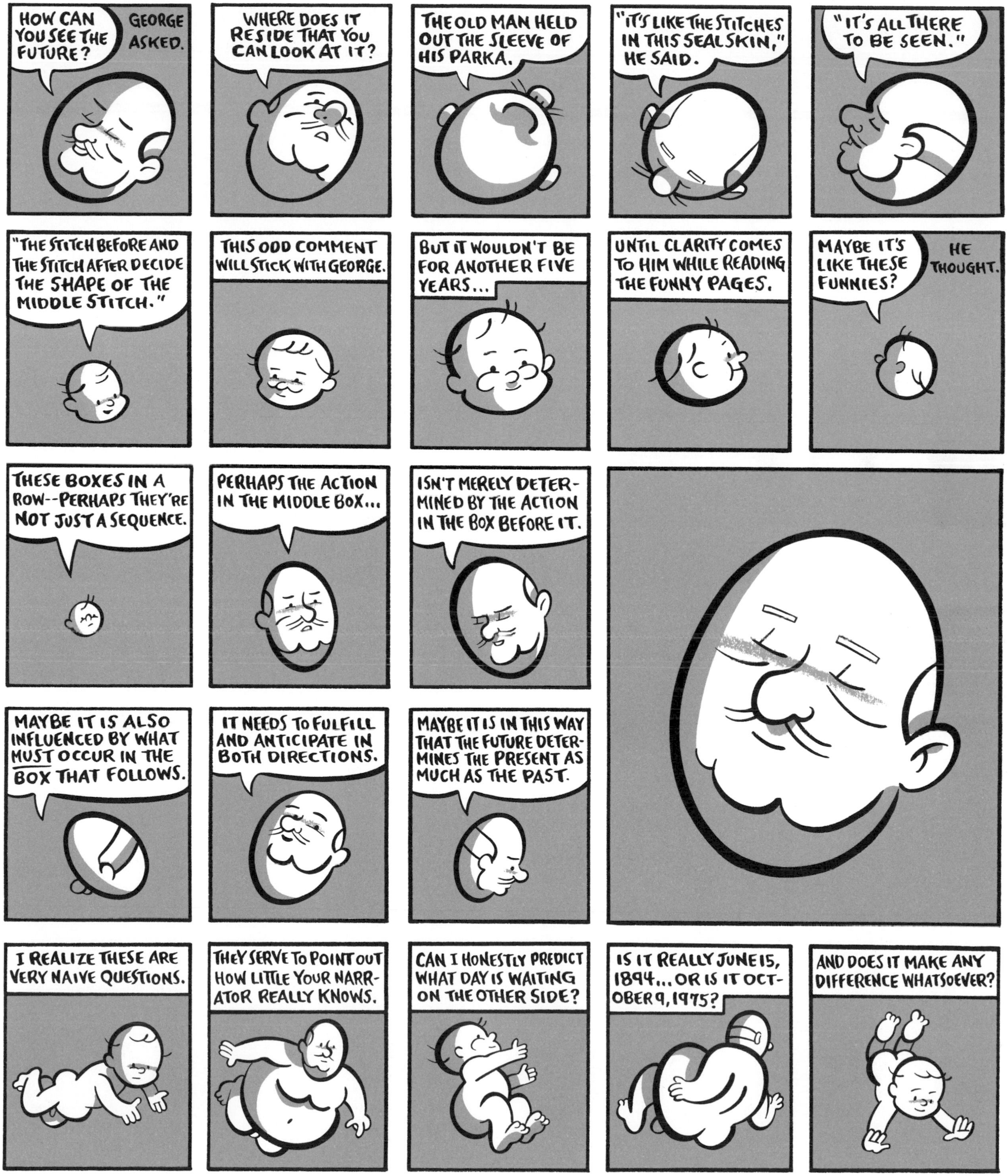
HOW CAN YOU SEE THE FUTURE?
GEORGE ASKED.
WHERE DOES IT RESIDE THAT YOU CAN LOOK AT IT?
THE OLD MAN HELD OUT THE SLEEVE OF HIS PARKA.
"IT'S LIKE THE STITCHES IN THIS SEALSKIN," HE SAID.
"IT'S ALL THERE TO BE SEEN."
"THE STITCH BEFORE AND THE STITCH AFTER DECIDE THE SHAPE OF THE MIDDLE STITCH."
THIS ODD COMMENT WILL STICK WITH GEORGE.
BUT IT WOULDN'T BE FOR ANOTHER FIVE YEARS...
UNTIL CLARITY COMES TO HIM WHILE READING THE FUNNY PAGES.
MAYBE IT'S LIKE THESE FUNNIES?
HE THOUGHT.
THESE BOXES IN A ROW--PERHAPS THEY'RE NOT JUST A SEQUENCE.
PERHAPS THE ACTION IN THE MIDDLE BOX...
ISN'T MERELY DETERMINED BY THE ACTION IN THE BOX BEFORE IT.
MAYBE IT IS ALSO INFLUENCED BY WHAT MUST OCCUR IN THE BOX THAT FOLLOWS.
IT NEEDS TO FULFILL AND ANTICIPATE IN BOTH DIRECTIONS.
MAYBE IT IS IN THIS WAY THAT THE FUTURE DETERMINES THE PRESENT AS MUCH AS THE PAST.
I REALIZE THESE ARE VERY NAIVE QUESTIONS.
THEY SERVE TO POINT OUT HOW LITTLE YOUR NARRATOR REALLY KNOWS.
CAN I HONESTLY PREDICT WHAT DAY IS WAITING ON THE OTHER SIDE?
IS IT REALLY JUNE 15, 1894... OR IS IT OCTOBER 9, 1975?
AND DOES IT MAKE ANY DIFFERENCE WHATSOEVER?

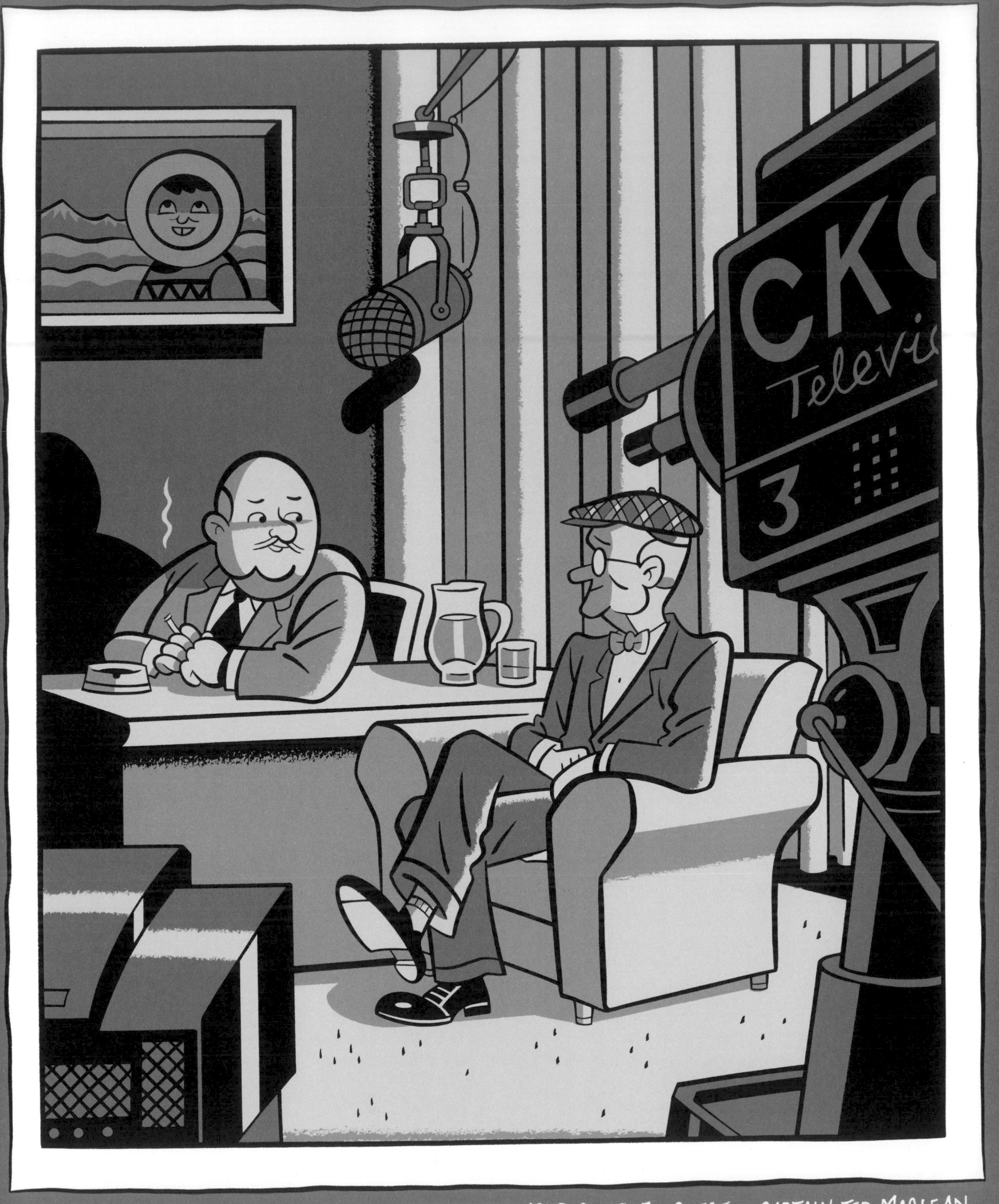

NORTHERN HI-LIGHTS with GEORGE SPROTT ~ THURSDAY, NOVEMBER 9, 1967. GUEST -- CAPTAIN TED MACLEAN

GEORGE SPROTT

1894
1975

A PICTURE NOVELLA by SETH

ARCTOS SECRETUM ARCTOS

JONATHAN CAPE
LONDON

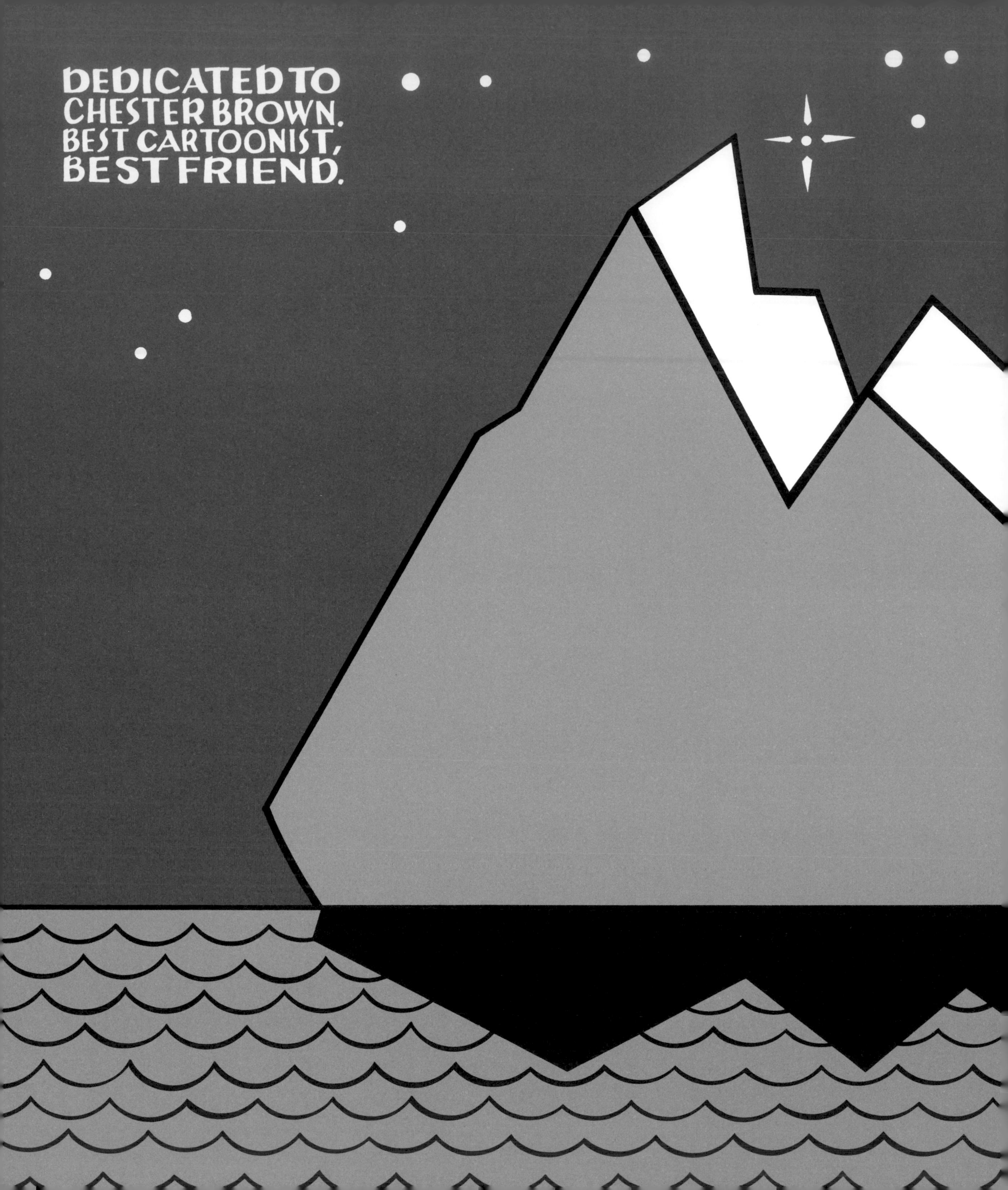
DEDICATED TO
CHESTER BROWN.
BEST CARTOONIST,
BEST FRIEND.

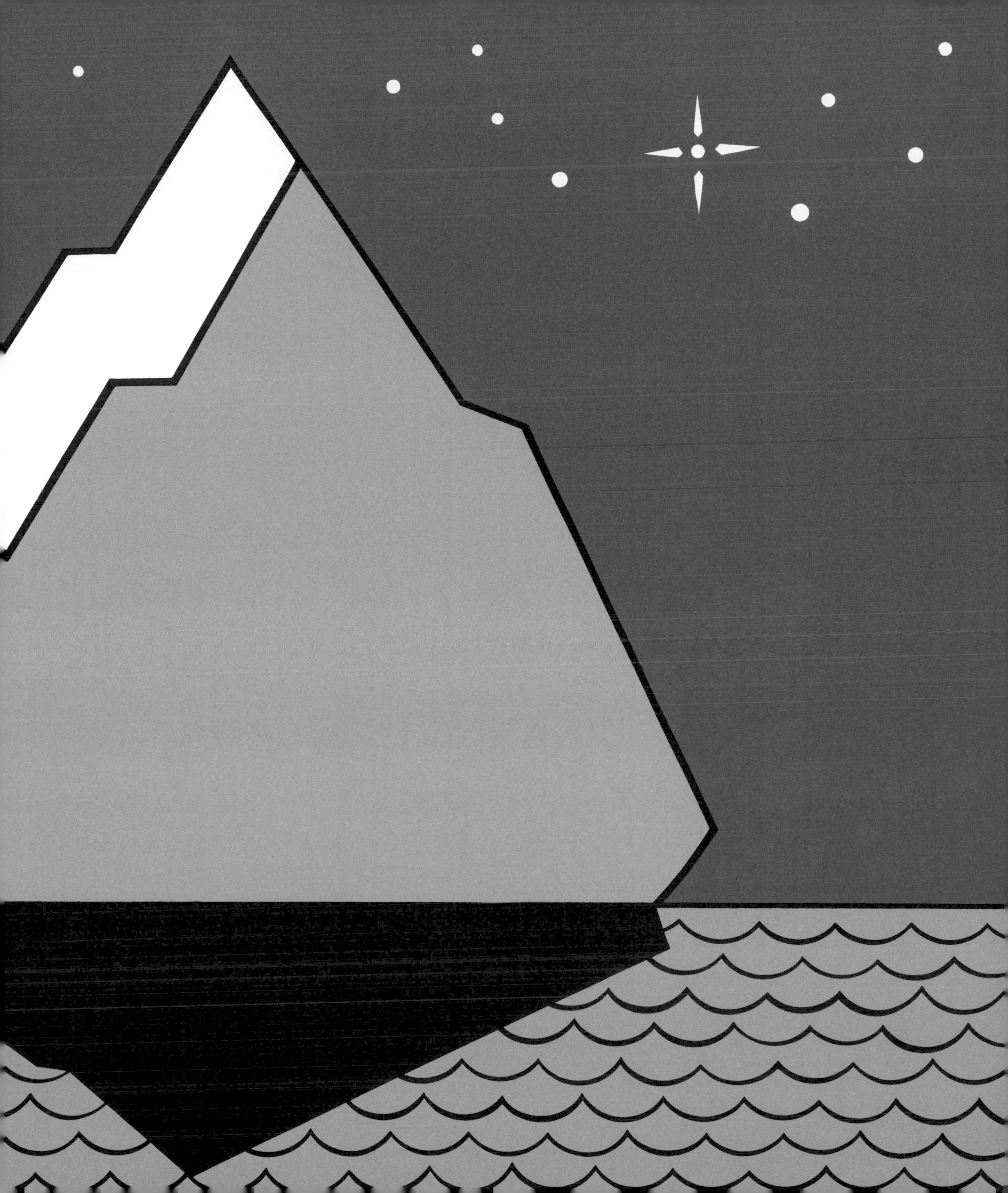

PROLOGUE

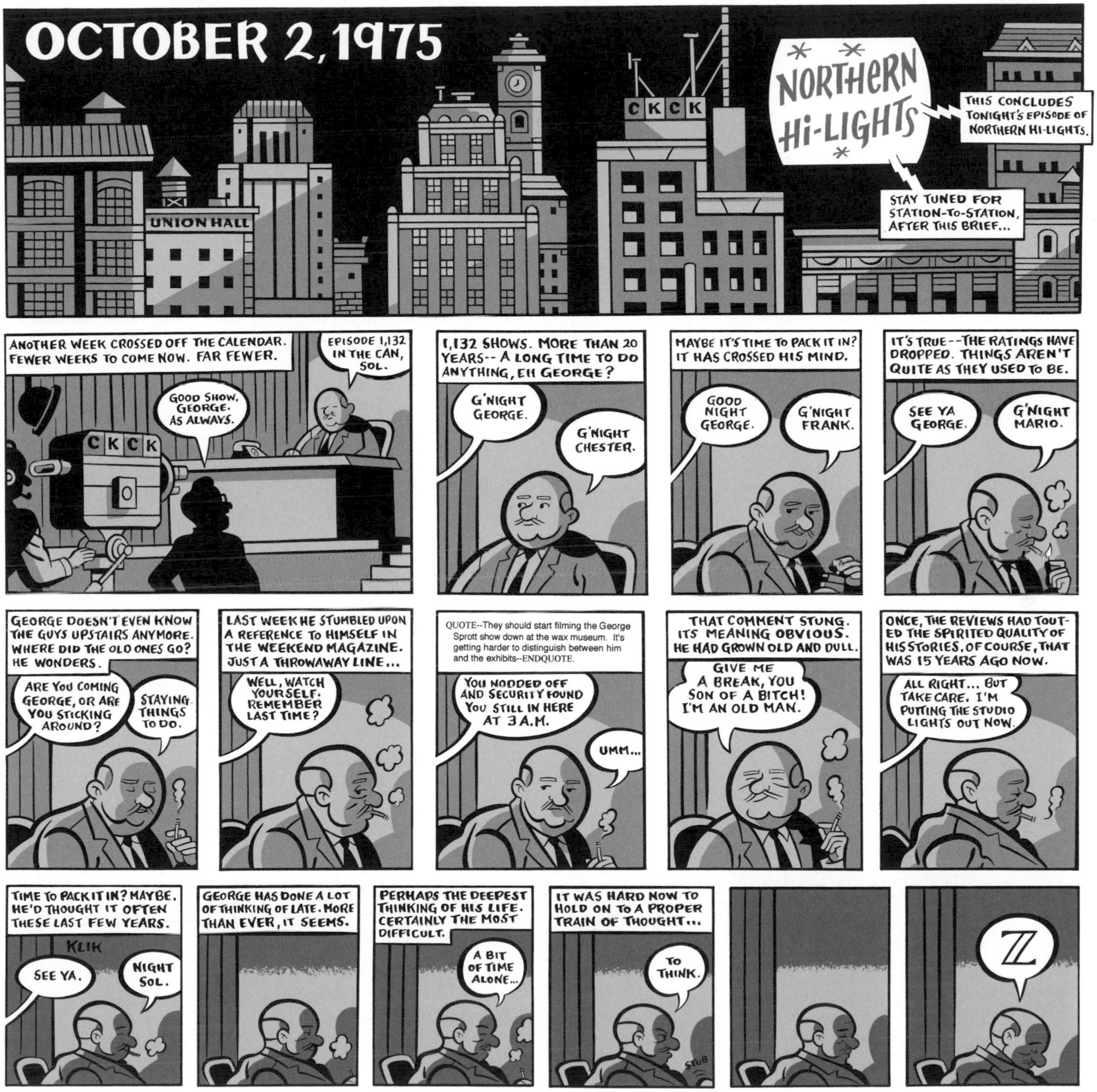

OCTOBER 2, 1975
CKCK
UNION HALL
NORTHERN HI-LIGHTS
THIS CONCLUDES TONIGHT'S EPISODE OF NORTHERN HI-LIGHTS.
STAY TUNED FOR STATION-TO-STATION, AFTER THIS BRIEF...
ANOTHER WEEK CROSSED OFF THE CALENDAR. FEWER WEEKS TO COME NOW. FAR FEWER.
EPISODE 1,132 IN THE CAN, SOL.
GOOD SHOW, GEORGE. AS ALWAYS.
CKCK
1,132 SHOWS. MORE THAN 20 YEARS-- A LONG TIME TO DO ANYTHING, EH GEORGE?
G'NIGHT GEORGE.
G'NIGHT CHESTER.
MAYBE IT'S TIME TO PACK IT IN? IT HAS CROSSED HIS MIND.
GOOD NIGHT GEORGE.
G'NIGHT FRANK.
IT'S TRUE--THE RATINGS HAVE DROPPED. THINGS AREN'T QUITE AS THEY USED TO BE.
SEE YA GEORGE.
G'NIGHT MARIO.
GEORGE DOESN'T EVEN KNOW THE GUYS UPSTAIRS ANYMORE. WHERE DID THE OLD ONES GO? HE WONDERS.
ARE YOU COMING GEORGE, OR ARE YOU STICKING AROUND?
STAYING. THINGS TO DO.
LAST WEEK HE STUMBLED UPON A REFERENCE TO HIMSELF IN THE WEEKEND MAGAZINE. JUST A THROWAWAY LINE...
WELL, WATCH YOURSELF. REMEMBER LAST TIME?
QUOTE--They should start filming the George Sprott show down at the wax museum. It's getting harder to distinguish between him and the exhibits--ENDQUOTE.
YOU NODDED OFF AND SECURITY FOUND YOU STILL IN HERE AT 3 A.M.
UMM...
THAT COMMENT STUNG. ITS MEANING OBVIOUS. HE HAD GROWN OLD AND DULL.
GIVE ME A BREAK, YOU SON OF A BITCH! I'M AN OLD MAN.
ONCE, THE REVIEWS HAD TOUTED THE SPIRITED QUALITY OF HIS STORIES. OF COURSE, THAT WAS 15 YEARS AGO NOW.
ALL RIGHT... BUT TAKE CARE. I'M PUTTING THE STUDIO LIGHTS OUT NOW.
TIME TO PACK IT IN? MAYBE. HE'D THOUGHT IT OFTEN THESE LAST FEW YEARS.
KLIK
SEE YA.
NIGHT SOL.
GEORGE HAS DONE A LOT OF THINKING OF LATE. MORE THAN EVER, IT SEEMS.
PERHAPS THE DEEPEST THINKING OF HIS LIFE. CERTAINLY THE MOST DIFFICULT.
A BIT OF TIME ALONE...
IT WAS HARD NOW TO HOLD ON TO A PROPER TRAIN OF THOUGHT...
TO THINK.
STUB
Z

MERRILY WE ROLL ALONG

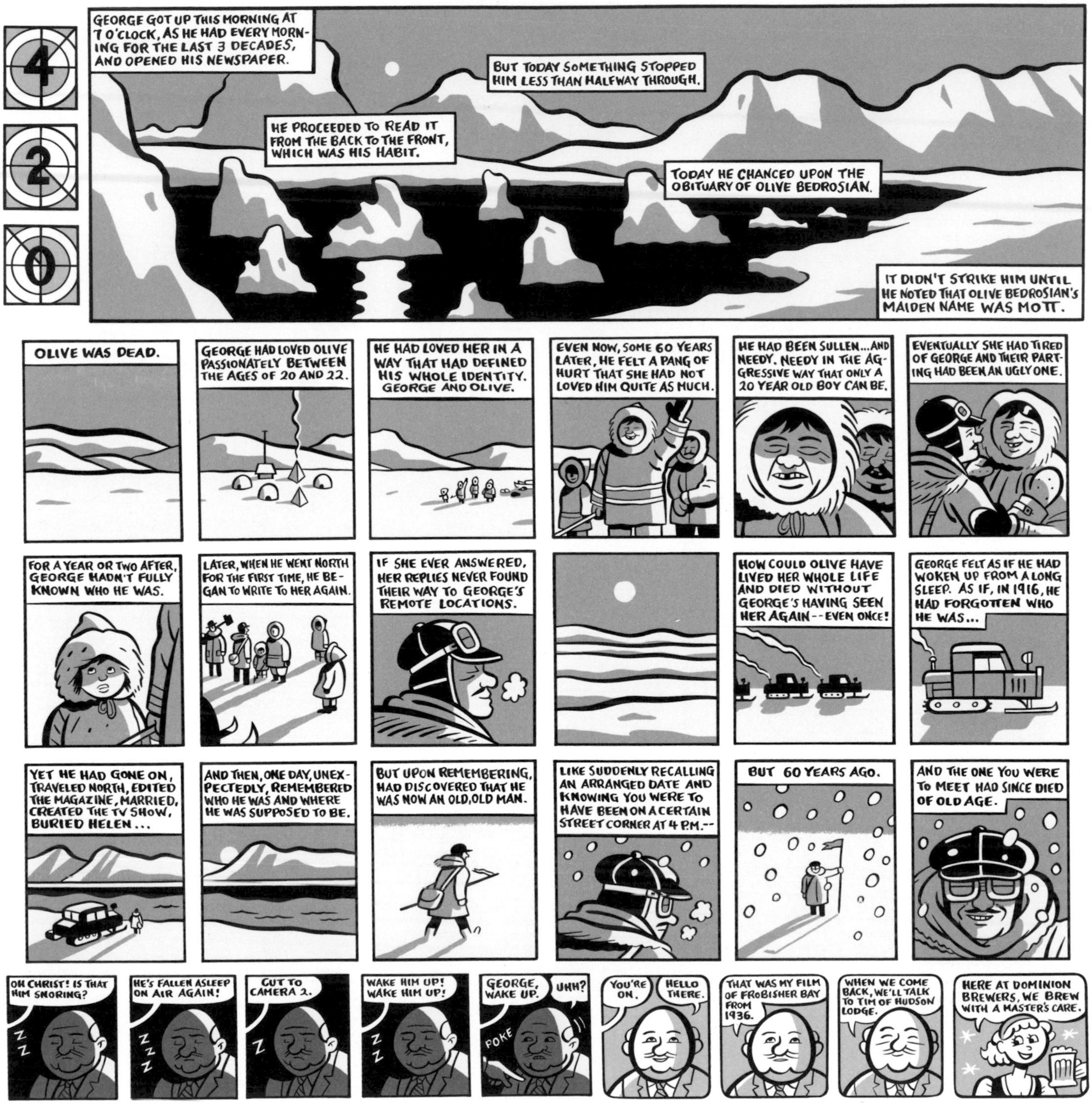

4
2
0
GEORGE GOT UP THIS MORNING AT 7 O'CLOCK, AS HE HAD EVERY MORNING FOR THE LAST 3 DECADES, AND OPENED HIS NEWSPAPER.
HE PROCEEDED TO READ IT FROM THE BACK TO THE FRONT, WHICH WAS HIS HABIT.
BUT TODAY SOMETHING STOPPED HIM LESS THAN HALFWAY THROUGH.
TODAY HE CHANCED UPON THE OBITUARY OF OLIVE BEDROSIAN.
IT DIDN'T STRIKE HIM UNTIL HE NOTED THAT OLIVE BEDROSIAN'S MAIDEN NAME WAS MOTT.
OLIVE WAS DEAD.
GEORGE HAD LOVED OLIVE PASSIONATELY BETWEEN THE AGES OF 20 AND 22.
HE HAD LOVED HER IN A WAY THAT HAD DEFINED HIS WHOLE IDENTITY. GEORGE AND OLIVE.
EVEN NOW, SOME 60 YEARS LATER, HE FELT A PANG OF HURT THAT SHE HAD NOT LOVED HIM QUITE AS MUCH.
HE HAD BEEN SULLEN... AND NEEDY. NEEDY IN THE AGGRESSIVE WAY THAT ONLY A 20 YEAR OLD BOY CAN BE.
EVENTUALLY SHE HAD TIRED OF GEORGE AND THEIR PARTING HAD BEEN AN UGLY ONE.
FOR A YEAR OR TWO AFTER, GEORGE HADN'T FULLY KNOWN WHO HE WAS.
LATER, WHEN HE WENT NORTH FOR THE FIRST TIME, HE BEGAN TO WRITE TO HER AGAIN.
IF SHE EVER ANSWERED, HER REPLIES NEVER FOUND THEIR WAY TO GEORGE'S REMOTE LOCATIONS.
HOW COULD OLIVE HAVE LIVED HER WHOLE LIFE AND DIED WITHOUT GEORGE'S HAVING SEEN HER AGAIN -- EVEN ONCE!
GEORGE FELT AS IF HE HAD WOKEN UP FROM A LONG SLEEP. AS IF, IN 1916, HE HAD FORGOTTEN WHO HE WAS...
YET HE HAD GONE ON, TRAVELED NORTH, EDITED THE MAGAZINE, MARRIED, CREATED THE TV SHOW, BURIED HELEN...
AND THEN, ONE DAY, UNEXPECTEDLY, REMEMBERED WHO HE WAS AND WHERE HE WAS SUPPOSED TO BE.
BUT UPON REMEMBERING, HAD DISCOVERED THAT HE WAS NOW AN OLD, OLD MAN.
LIKE SUDDENLY RECALLING AN ARRANGED DATE AND KNOWING YOU WERE TO HAVE BEEN ON A CERTAIN STREET CORNER AT 4 P.M.--
BUT 60 YEARS AGO.
AND THE ONE YOU WERE TO MEET HAD SINCE DIED OF OLD AGE.
OH CHRIST! IS THAT HIM SNORING?
Z Z
HE'S FALLEN ASLEEP ON AIR AGAIN!
Z Z Z
CUT TO CAMERA 2.
Z
WAKE HIM UP! WAKE HIM UP!
Z Z
GEORGE, WAKE UP.
UHH?
POKE
YOU'RE ON.
HELLO THERE.
THAT WAS MY FILM OF FROBISHER BAY FROM 1936.
WHEN WE COME BACK, WE'LL TALK TO TIM OF HUDSON LODGE.
HERE AT DOMINION BREWERS, WE BREW WITH A MASTER'S CARE.

A FRESH START

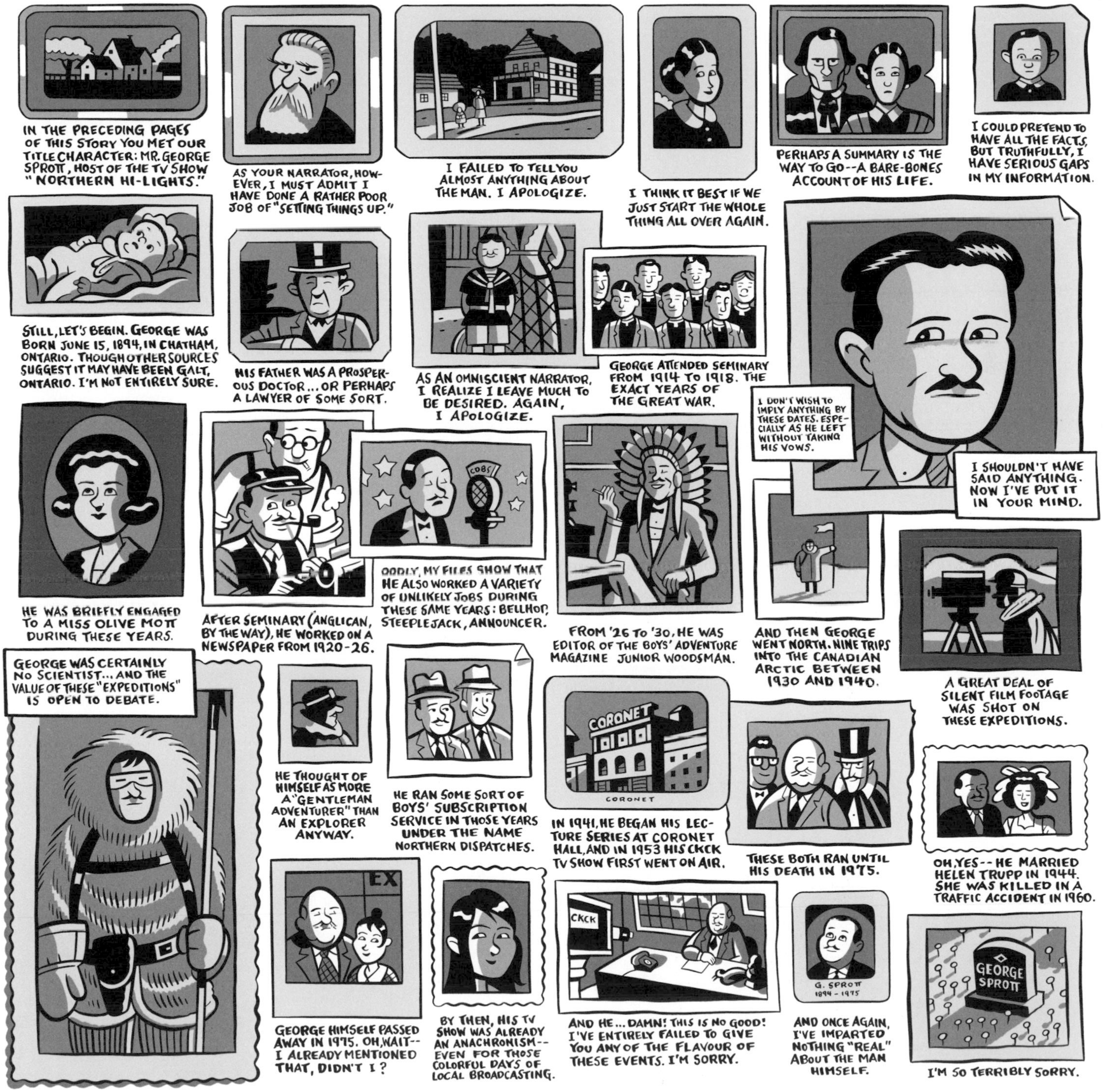

IN THE PRECEDING PAGES OF THIS STORY YOU MET OUR TITLE CHARACTER: MR. GEORGE SPROTT, HOST OF THE TV SHOW "NORTHERN HI-LIGHTS."
AS YOUR NARRATOR, HOWEVER, I MUST ADMIT I HAVE DONE A RATHER POOR JOB OF "SETTING THINGS UP."
I FAILED TO TELL YOU ALMOST ANYTHING ABOUT THE MAN. I APOLOGIZE.
I THINK IT BEST IF WE JUST START THE WHOLE THING ALL OVER AGAIN.
PERHAPS A SUMMARY IS THE WAY TO GO--A BARE-BONES ACCOUNT OF HIS LIFE.
I COULD PRETEND TO HAVE ALL THE FACTS, BUT TRUTHFULLY, I HAVE SERIOUS GAPS IN MY INFORMATION.
STILL, LET'S BEGIN. GEORGE WAS BORN JUNE 15, 1894, IN CHATHAM, ONTARIO. THOUGH OTHER SOURCES SUGGEST IT MAY HAVE BEEN GALT, ONTARIO. I'M NOT ENTIRELY SURE.
HIS FATHER WAS A PROSPEROUS DOCTOR... OR PERHAPS A LAWYER OF SOME SORT.
AS AN OMNISCIENT NARRATOR, I REALIZE I LEAVE MUCH TO BE DESIRED. AGAIN, I APOLOGIZE.
GEORGE ATTENDED SEMINARY FROM 1914 TO 1918. THE EXACT YEARS OF THE GREAT WAR.
I DON'T WISH TO IMPLY ANYTHING BY THESE DATES. ESPECIALLY AS HE LEFT WITHOUT TAKING HIS VOWS.
I SHOULDN'T HAVE SAID ANYTHING. NOW I'VE PUT IT IN YOUR MIND.
HE WAS BRIEFLY ENGAGED TO A MISS OLIVE MOTT DURING THESE YEARS.
AFTER SEMINARY (ANGLICAN, BY THE WAY), HE WORKED ON A NEWSPAPER FROM 1920-26.
CBS
ODDLY, MY FILES SHOW THAT HE ALSO WORKED A VARIETY OF UNLIKELY JOBS DURING THESE SAME YEARS: BELLHOP, STEEPLEJACK, ANNOUNCER.
FROM '26 TO '30, HE WAS EDITOR OF THE BOYS' ADVENTURE MAGAZINE JUNIOR WOODSMAN.
AND THEN GEORGE WENT NORTH. NINE TRIPS INTO THE CANADIAN ARCTIC BETWEEN 1930 AND 1940.
A GREAT DEAL OF SILENT FILM FOOTAGE WAS SHOT ON THESE EXPEDITIONS.
GEORGE WAS CERTAINLY NO SCIENTIST... AND THE VALUE OF THESE "EXPEDITIONS" IS OPEN TO DEBATE.
HE THOUGHT OF HIMSELF AS MORE A "GENTLEMAN ADVENTURER" THAN AN EXPLORER ANYWAY.
HE RAN SOME SORT OF BOYS' SUBSCRIPTION SERVICE IN THOSE YEARS UNDER THE NAME NORTHERN DISPATCHES.
CORONET
CORONET
IN 1941, HE BEGAN HIS LECTURE SERIES AT CORONET HALL, AND IN 1953 HIS CKCK TV SHOW FIRST WENT ON AIR.
THESE BOTH RAN UNTIL HIS DEATH IN 1975.
OH, YES-- HE MARRIED HELEN TRUPP IN 1944. SHE WAS KILLED IN A TRAFFIC ACCIDENT IN 1960.
EX
GEORGE HIMSELF PASSED AWAY IN 1975. OH, WAIT-- I ALREADY MENTIONED THAT, DIDN'T I?
BY THEN, HIS TV SHOW WAS ALREADY AN ANACHRONISM-- EVEN FOR THOSE COLORFUL DAYS OF LOCAL BROADCASTING.
CKCK
AND HE... DAMN! THIS IS NO GOOD! I'VE ENTIRELY FAILED TO GIVE YOU ANY OF THE FLAVOUR OF THESE EVENTS. I'M SORRY.
G. SPROTT 1894 - 1975
AND ONCE AGAIN, I'VE IMPARTED NOTHING "REAL" ABOUT THE MAN HIMSELF.
GEORGE SPROTT
I'M SO TERRIBLY SORRY.

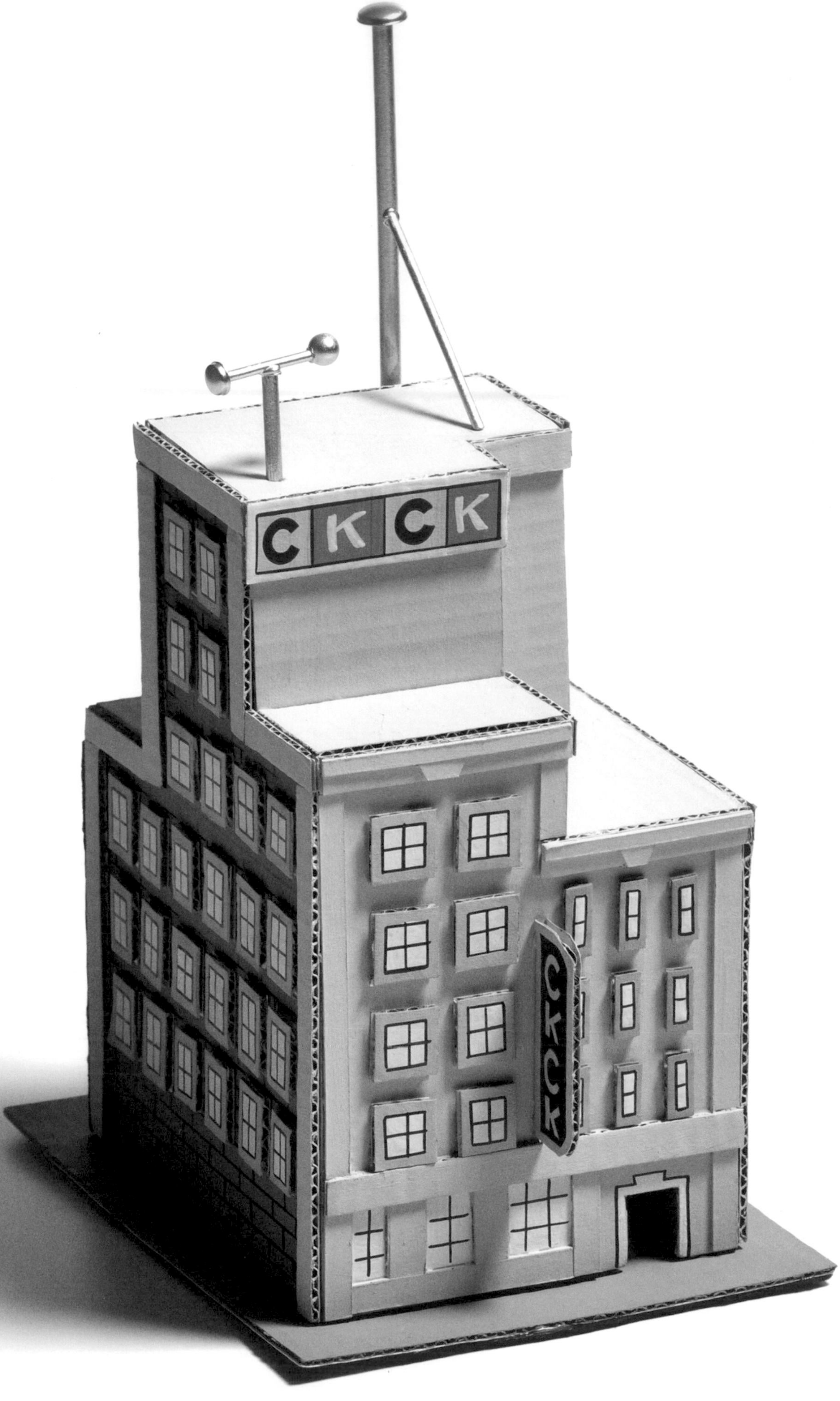
CKCK
CKCK

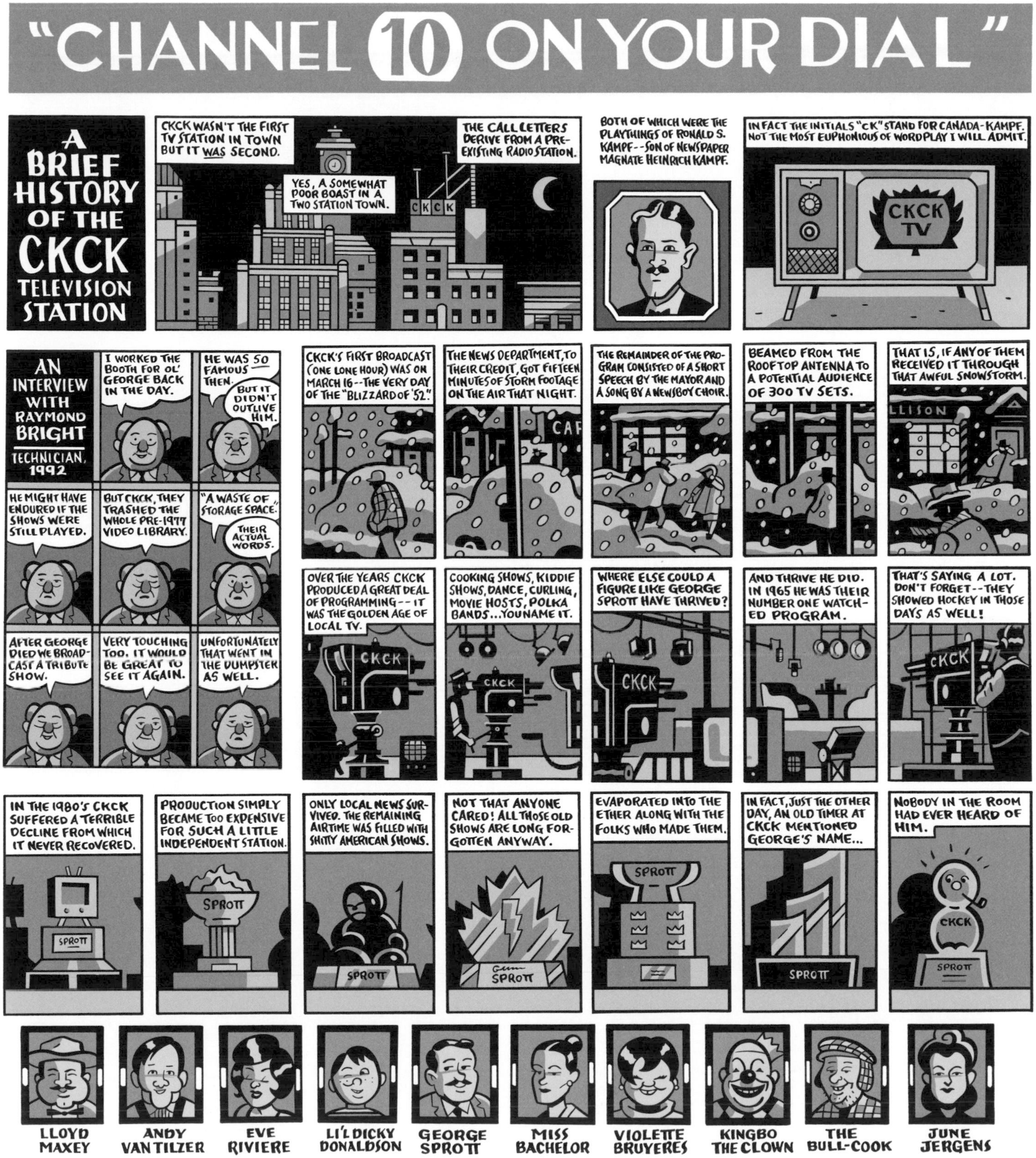
"CHANNEL 10 ON YOUR DIAL"
A BRIEF HISTORY OF THE CKCK TELEVISION STATION
CKCK WASN'T THE FIRST TV STATION IN TOWN BUT IT WAS SECOND.
YES, A SOMEWHAT POOR BOAST IN A TWO STATION TOWN.
THE CALL LETTERS DERIVE FROM A PRE-EXISTING RADIO STATION.
CKCK
BOTH OF WHICH WERE THE PLAYTHINGS OF RONALD S. KAMPF--SON OF NEWSPAPER MAGNATE HEINRICH KAMPF.
IN FACT THE INITIALS "CK" STAND FOR CANADA-KAMPF. NOT THE MOST EUPHONIOUS OF WORDPLAY I WILL ADMIT.
CKCK TV
AN INTERVIEW WITH RAYMOND BRIGHT
TECHNICIAN, 1992
I WORKED THE BOOTH FOR OL' GEORGE BACK IN THE DAY.
HE WAS SO FAMOUS — THEN.
BUT IT DIDN'T OUTLIVE HIM.
HE MIGHT HAVE ENDURED IF THE SHOWS WERE STILL PLAYED.
BUT CKCK, THEY TRASHED THE WHOLE PRE-1977 VIDEO LIBRARY.
"A WASTE OF STORAGE SPACE."
THEIR ACTUAL WORDS.
AFTER GEORGE DIED WE BROADCAST A TRIBUTE SHOW.
VERY TOUCHING TOO. IT WOULD BE GREAT TO SEE IT AGAIN.
UNFORTUNATELY THAT WENT IN THE DUMPSTER AS WELL.
CKCK'S FIRST BROADCAST (ONE LONE HOUR) WAS ON MARCH 16--THE VERY DAY OF THE "BLIZZARD OF '52."
THE NEWS DEPARTMENT, TO THEIR CREDIT, GOT FIFTEEN MINUTES OF STORM FOOTAGE ON THE AIR THAT NIGHT.
THE REMAINDER OF THE PROGRAM CONSISTED OF A SHORT SPEECH BY THE MAYOR AND A SONG BY A NEWSBOY CHOIR.
BEAMED FROM THE ROOFTOP ANTENNA TO A POTENTIAL AUDIENCE OF 300 TV SETS.
THAT IS, IF ANY OF THEM RECEIVED IT THROUGH THAT AWFUL SNOWSTORM.
OVER THE YEARS CKCK PRODUCED A GREAT DEAL OF PROGRAMMING-- IT WAS THE GOLDEN AGE OF LOCAL TV.
CKCK
COOKING SHOWS, KIDDIE SHOWS, DANCE, CURLING, MOVIE HOSTS, POLKA BANDS... YOU NAME IT.
CKCK
WHERE ELSE COULD A FIGURE LIKE GEORGE SPROTT HAVE THRIVED?
CKCK
AND THRIVE HE DID. IN 1965 HE WAS THEIR NUMBER ONE WATCHED PROGRAM.
THAT'S SAYING A LOT. DON'T FORGET--THEY SHOWED HOCKEY IN THOSE DAYS AS WELL!
CKCK
IN THE 1980'S CKCK SUFFERED A TERRIBLE DECLINE FROM WHICH IT NEVER RECOVERED.
SPROTT
PRODUCTION SIMPLY BECAME TOO EXPENSIVE FOR SUCH A LITTLE INDEPENDENT STATION.
SPROTT
ONLY LOCAL NEWS SURVIVED. THE REMAINING AIRTIME WAS FILLED WITH SHITTY AMERICAN SHOWS.
SPROTT
NOT THAT ANYONE CARED! ALL THOSE OLD SHOWS ARE LONG FORGOTTEN ANYWAY.
SPROTT
EVAPORATED INTO THE ETHER ALONG WITH THE FOLKS WHO MADE THEM.
SPROTT
IN FACT, JUST THE OTHER DAY, AN OLD TIMER AT CKCK MENTIONED GEORGE'S NAME...
SPROTT
NOBODY IN THE ROOM HAD EVER HEARD OF HIM.
CKCK
SPROTT
LLOYD MAXEY
ANDY VANTILZER
EVE RIVIERE
LI'L DICKY DONALDSON
GEORGE SPROTT
MISS BACHELOR
VIOLETTE BRUYERES
KINGBO THE CLOWN
THE BULL-COOK
JUNE JERGENS

JULY
10
1904

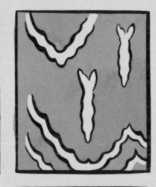

HEY SMELLY!

YOU'D BEST GO HOME...

YER MOTHER NEEDS TO WIPE YER ASS!

GO TO HELL, TOMMY!

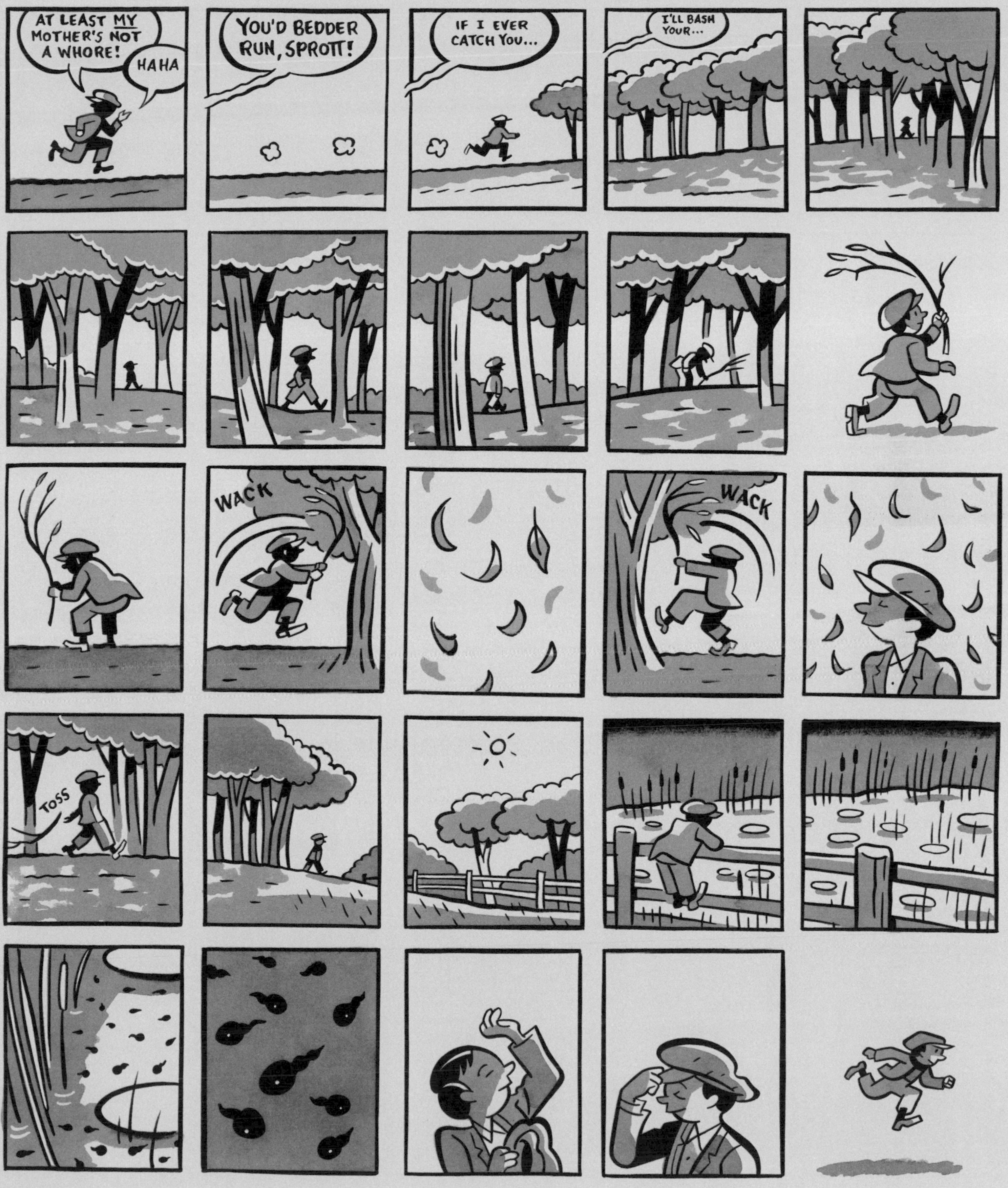
AT LEAST MY MOTHER'S NOT A WHORE!
HAHA
YOU'D BEDDER RUN, SPROTT!
IF I EVER CATCH YOU...
I'LL BASH YOUR...
WACK
WACK
TOSS

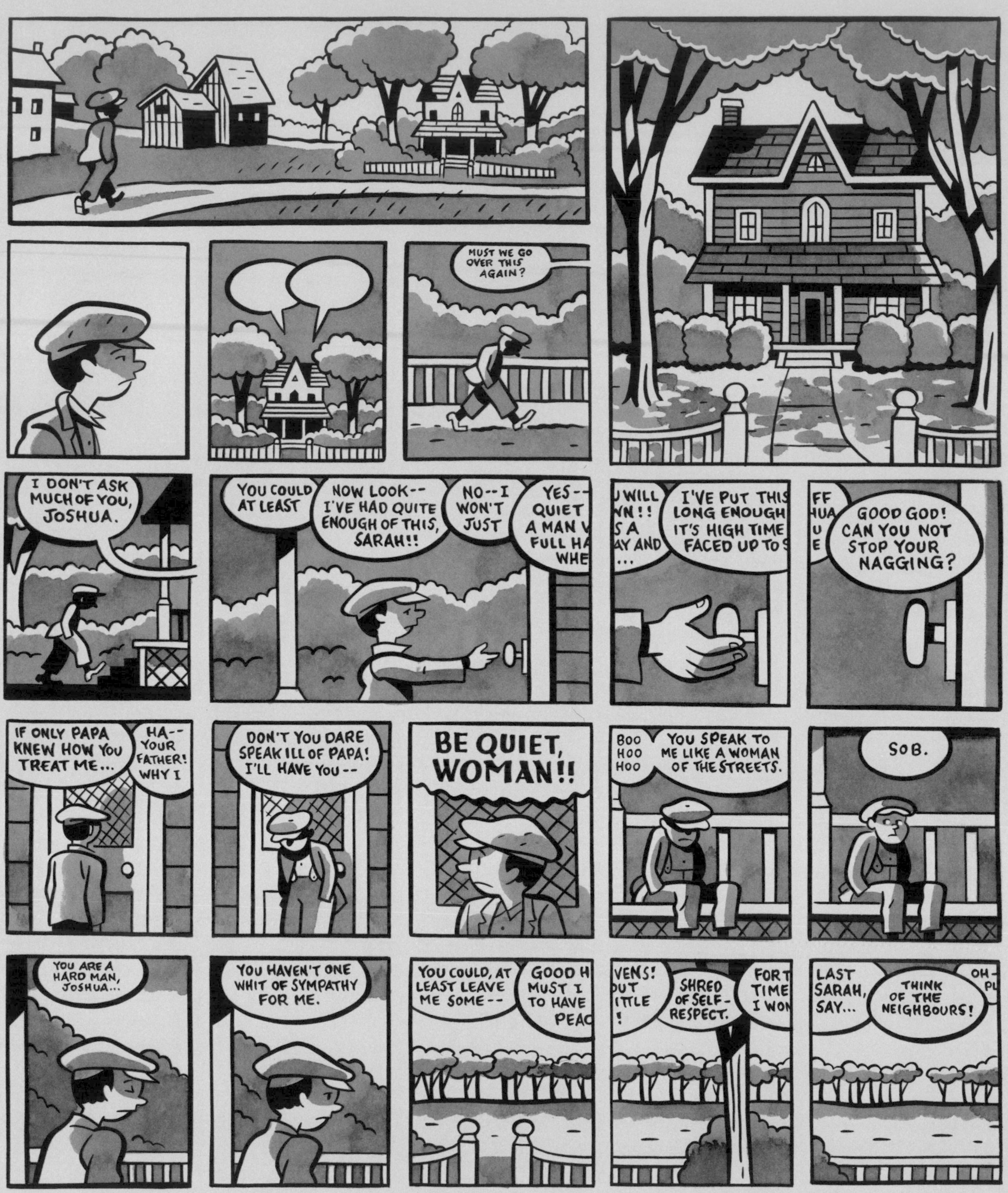
MUST WE GO OVER THIS AGAIN?
I DON'T ASK MUCH OF YOU, JOSHUA.
YOU COULD AT LEAST
NOW LOOK-- I'VE HAD QUITE ENOUGH OF THIS, SARAH!!
NO--I WON'T JUST
YES-- QUIET A MAN V FULL HA WHE
U WILL WN!! S A AY AND ...
I'VE PUT THIS LONG ENOUGH IT'S HIGH TIME FACED UP TO S
FF HUA U E
GOOD GOD! CAN YOU NOT STOP YOUR NAGGING?
IF ONLY PAPA KNEW HOW YOU TREAT ME...
HA-- YOUR FATHER! WHY I
DON'T YOU DARE SPEAK ILL OF PAPA! I'LL HAVE YOU--
BE QUIET, WOMAN!!
BOO HOO HOO
YOU SPEAK TO ME LIKE A WOMAN OF THE STREETS.
SOB.
YOU ARE A HARD MAN, JOSHUA...
YOU HAVEN'T ONE WHIT OF SYMPATHY FOR ME.
YOU COULD, AT LEAST LEAVE ME SOME--
GOOD H MUST I TO HAVE PEAC
VENS! UT ITTLE !
SHRED OF SELF-RESPECT.
FOR T TIME I WON
LAST SARAH, SAY...
THINK OF THE NEIGHBOURS!
OH- P

FRIDAY FRIGHT NIGHT

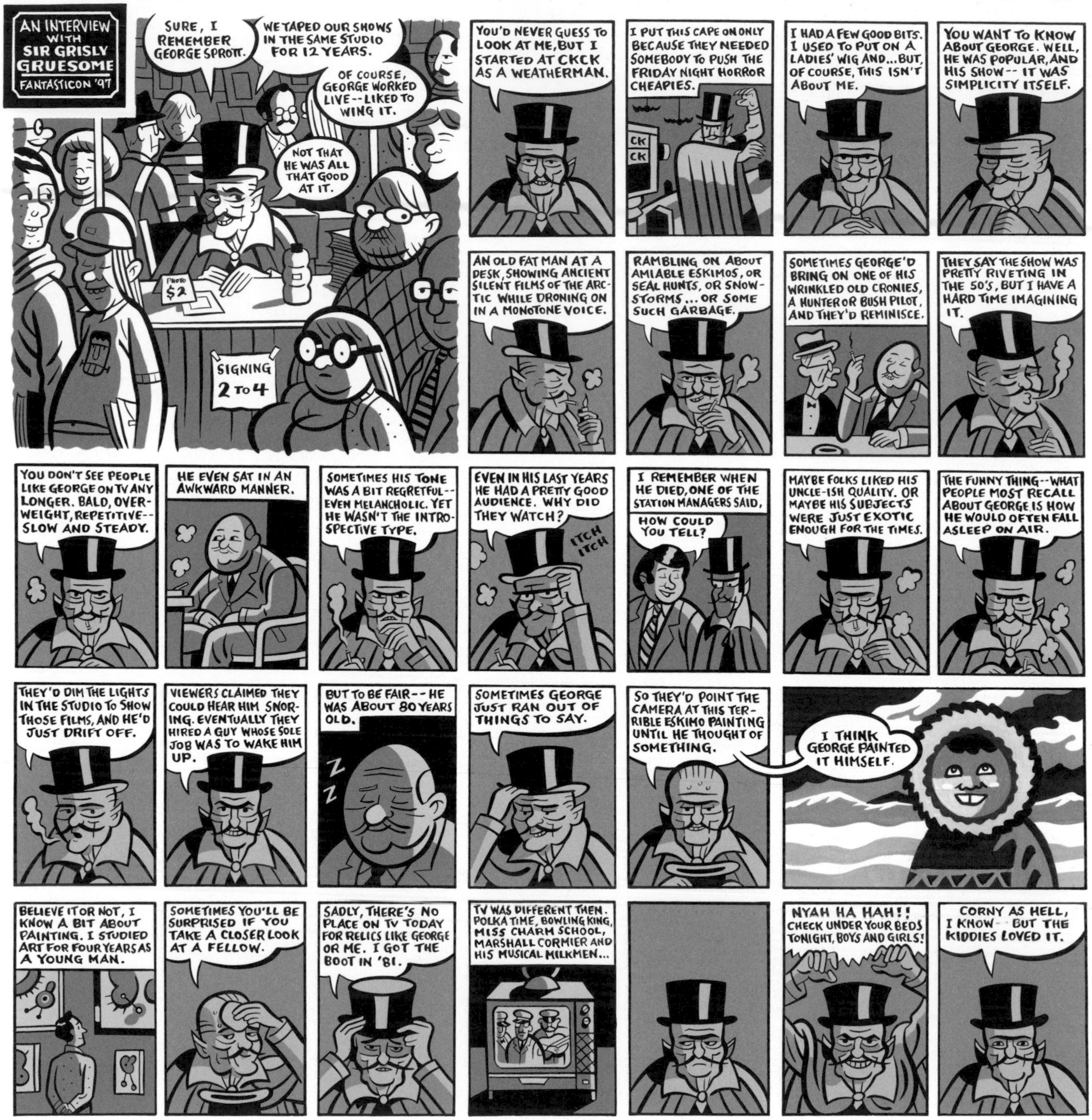

AN INTERVIEW WITH SIR GRISLY GRUESOME FANTASTICON '97
SURE, I REMEMBER GEORGE SPROTT.
WE TAPED OUR SHOWS IN THE SAME STUDIO FOR 12 YEARS.
OF COURSE, GEORGE WORKED LIVE--LIKED TO WING IT.
NOT THAT HE WAS ALL THAT GOOD AT IT.
PHOTO $2
SIGNING 2 TO 4
YOU'D NEVER GUESS TO LOOK AT ME, BUT I STARTED AT CKCK AS A WEATHERMAN.
I PUT THIS CAPE ON ONLY BECAUSE THEY NEEDED SOMEBODY TO PUSH THE FRIDAY NIGHT HORROR CHEAPIES.
I HAD A FEW GOOD BITS. I USED TO PUT ON A LADIES' WIG AND... BUT, OF COURSE, THIS ISN'T ABOUT ME.
YOU WANT TO KNOW ABOUT GEORGE. WELL, HE WAS POPULAR, AND HIS SHOW-- IT WAS SIMPLICITY ITSELF.
AN OLD FAT MAN AT A DESK, SHOWING ANCIENT SILENT FILMS OF THE ARCTIC WHILE DRONING ON IN A MONOTONE VOICE.
RAMBLING ON ABOUT AMIABLE ESKIMOS, OR SEAL HUNTS, OR SNOWSTORMS... OR SOME SUCH GARBAGE.
SOMETIMES GEORGE'D BRING ON ONE OF HIS WRINKLED OLD CRONIES, A HUNTER OR BUSH PILOT, AND THEY'D REMINISCE.
THEY SAY THE SHOW WAS PRETTY RIVETING IN THE 50'S, BUT I HAVE A HARD TIME IMAGINING IT.
YOU DON'T SEE PEOPLE LIKE GEORGE ON TV ANY LONGER. BALD, OVERWEIGHT, REPETITIVE-- SLOW AND STEADY.
HE EVEN SAT IN AN AWKWARD MANNER.
SOMETIMES HIS TONE WAS A BIT REGRETFUL-- EVEN MELANCHOLIC. YET HE WASN'T THE INTROSPECTIVE TYPE.
EVEN IN HIS LAST YEARS HE HAD A PRETTY GOOD AUDIENCE. WHY DID THEY WATCH?
ITCH ITCH
I REMEMBER WHEN HE DIED, ONE OF THE STATION MANAGERS SAID,
HOW COULD YOU TELL?
MAYBE FOLKS LIKED HIS UNCLE-ISH QUALITY. OR MAYBE HIS SUBJECTS WERE JUST EXOTIC ENOUGH FOR THE TIMES.
THE FUNNY THING--WHAT PEOPLE MOST RECALL ABOUT GEORGE IS HOW HE WOULD OFTEN FALL ASLEEP ON AIR.
THEY'D DIM THE LIGHTS IN THE STUDIO TO SHOW THOSE FILMS, AND HE'D JUST DRIFT OFF.
VIEWERS CLAIMED THEY COULD HEAR HIM SNORING. EVENTUALLY THEY HIRED A GUY WHOSE SOLE JOB WAS TO WAKE HIM UP.
BUT TO BE FAIR-- HE WAS ABOUT 80 YEARS OLD.
Z Z
SOMETIMES GEORGE JUST RAN OUT OF THINGS TO SAY.
SO THEY'D POINT THE CAMERA AT THIS TERRIBLE ESKIMO PAINTING UNTIL HE THOUGHT OF SOMETHING.
I THINK GEORGE PAINTED IT HIMSELF.
BELIEVE IT OR NOT, I KNOW A BIT ABOUT PAINTING. I STUDIED ART FOR FOUR YEARS AS A YOUNG MAN.
SOMETIMES YOU'LL BE SURPRISED IF YOU TAKE A CLOSER LOOK AT A FELLOW.
SADLY, THERE'S NO PLACE ON TV TODAY FOR RELICS LIKE GEORGE OR ME. I GOT THE BOOT IN '81.
TV WAS DIFFERENT THEN. POLKA TIME, BOWLING KING, MISS CHARM SCHOOL, MARSHALL CORMIER AND HIS MUSICAL MILKMEN...
NYAH HA HAH!! CHECK UNDER YOUR BEDS TONIGHT, BOYS AND GIRLS!
CORNY AS HELL, I KNOW-- BUT THE KIDDIES LOVED IT.

7:01 PM, OCTOBER 9, 1975

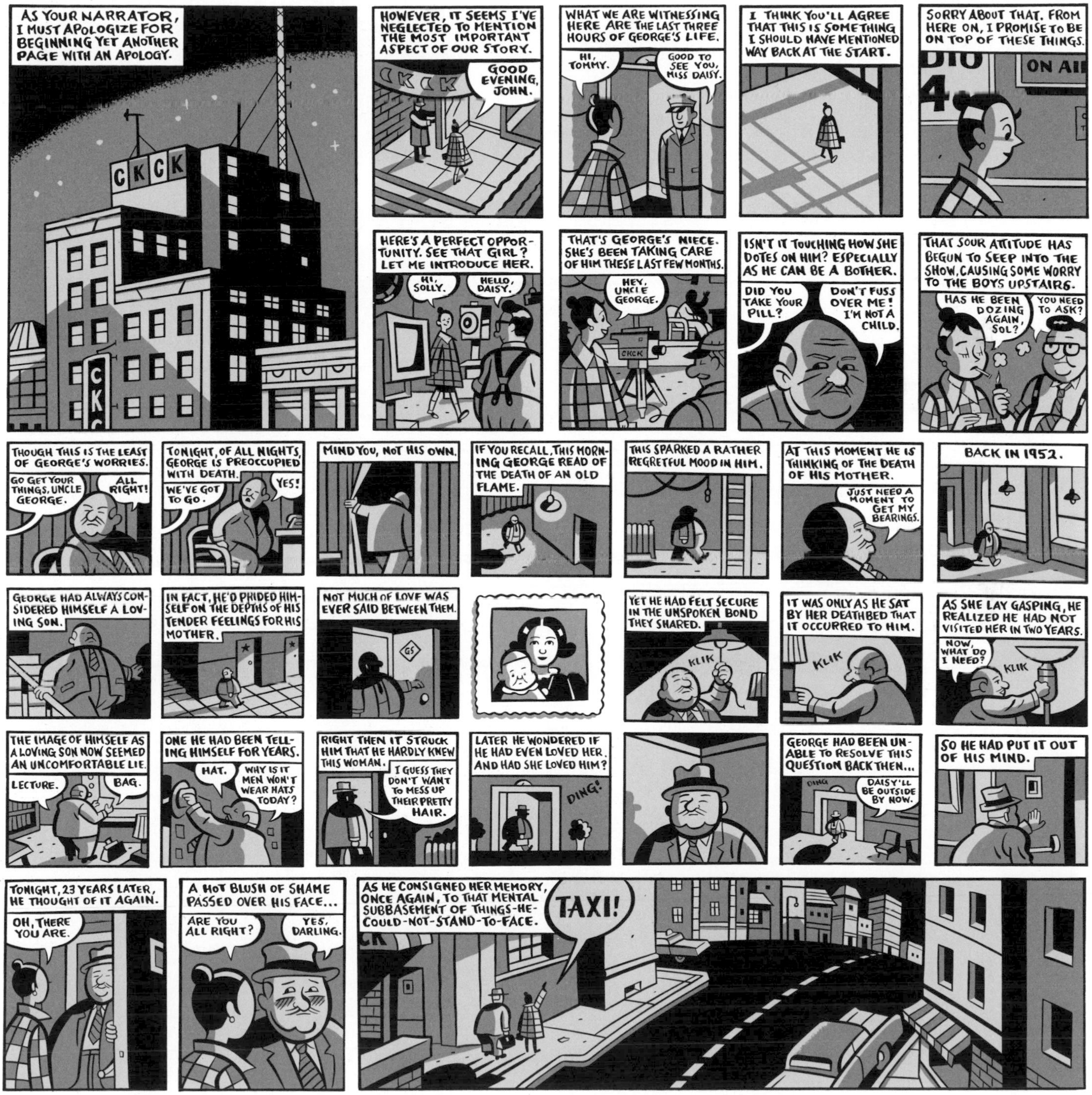
AS YOUR NARRATOR, I MUST APOLOGIZE FOR BEGINNING YET ANOTHER PAGE WITH AN APOLOGY.
CKCK
HOWEVER, IT SEEMS I'VE NEGLECTED TO MENTION THE MOST IMPORTANT ASPECT OF OUR STORY.
GOOD EVENING, JOHN.
WHAT WE ARE WITNESSING HERE ARE THE LAST THREE HOURS OF GEORGE'S LIFE.
HI, TOMMY.
GOOD TO SEE YOU, MISS DAISY.
I THINK YOU'LL AGREE THAT THIS IS SOMETHING I SHOULD HAVE MENTIONED WAY BACK AT THE START.
SORRY ABOUT THAT. FROM HERE ON, I PROMISE TO BE ON TOP OF THESE THINGS.
HERE'S A PERFECT OPPORTUNITY. SEE THAT GIRL? LET ME INTRODUCE HER.
HI, SOLLY.
HELLO, DAISY.
THAT'S GEORGE'S NIECE. SHE'S BEEN TAKING CARE OF HIM THESE LAST FEW MONTHS.
HEY, UNCLE GEORGE.
CKCK
ISN'T IT TOUCHING HOW SHE DOTES ON HIM? ESPECIALLY AS HE CAN BE A BOTHER.
DID YOU TAKE YOUR PILL?
DON'T FUSS OVER ME! I'M NOT A CHILD.
THAT SOUR ATTITUDE HAS BEGUN TO SEEP INTO THE SHOW, CAUSING SOME WORRY TO THE BOYS UPSTAIRS.
HAS HE BEEN DOZING AGAIN, SOL?
YOU NEED TO ASK?
THOUGH THIS IS THE LEAST OF GEORGE'S WORRIES.
GO GET YOUR THINGS, UNCLE GEORGE.
ALL RIGHT!
TONIGHT, OF ALL NIGHTS, GEORGE IS PREOCCUPIED WITH DEATH.
WE'VE GOT TO GO.
YES!
MIND YOU, NOT HIS OWN.
IF YOU RECALL, THIS MORNING GEORGE READ OF THE DEATH OF AN OLD FLAME.
THIS SPARKED A RATHER REGRETFUL MOOD IN HIM.
AT THIS MOMENT HE IS THINKING OF THE DEATH OF HIS MOTHER.
JUST NEED A MOMENT TO GET MY BEARINGS.
BACK IN 1952.
GEORGE HAD ALWAYS CONSIDERED HIMSELF A LOVING SON.
IN FACT, HE'D PRIDED HIMSELF ON THE DEPTHS OF HIS TENDER FEELINGS FOR HIS MOTHER.
NOT MUCH OF LOVE WAS EVER SAID BETWEEN THEM.
GS
YET HE HAD FELT SECURE IN THE UNSPOKEN BOND THEY SHARED.
KLIK
IT WAS ONLY AS HE SAT BY HER DEATHBED THAT IT OCCURRED TO HIM.
KLIK
AS SHE LAY GASPING, HE REALIZED HE HAD NOT VISITED HER IN TWO YEARS.
NOW, WHAT DO I NEED?
KLIK
THE IMAGE OF HIMSELF AS A LOVING SON NOW SEEMED AN UNCOMFORTABLE LIE.
LECTURE.
BAG.
ONE HE HAD BEEN TELLING HIMSELF FOR YEARS.
HAT.
WHY IS IT MEN WON'T WEAR HATS TODAY?
RIGHT THEN IT STRUCK HIM THAT HE HARDLY KNEW THIS WOMAN.
I GUESS THEY DON'T WANT TO MESS UP THEIR PRETTY HAIR.
LATER HE WONDERED IF HE HAD EVEN LOVED HER. AND HAD SHE LOVED HIM?
DING!
GEORGE HAD BEEN UNABLE TO RESOLVE THIS QUESTION BACK THEN...
DING
DAISY'LL BE OUTSIDE BY NOW.
SO HE HAD PUT IT OUT OF HIS MIND.
TONIGHT, 23 YEARS LATER, HE THOUGHT OF IT AGAIN.
OH, THERE YOU ARE.
A HOT BLUSH OF SHAME PASSED OVER HIS FACE...
ARE YOU ALL RIGHT?
YES, DARLING.
AS HE CONSIGNED HER MEMORY, ONCE AGAIN, TO THAT MENTAL SUBBASEMENT OF THINGS-HE-COULD-NOT-STAND-TO-FACE.
TAXI!

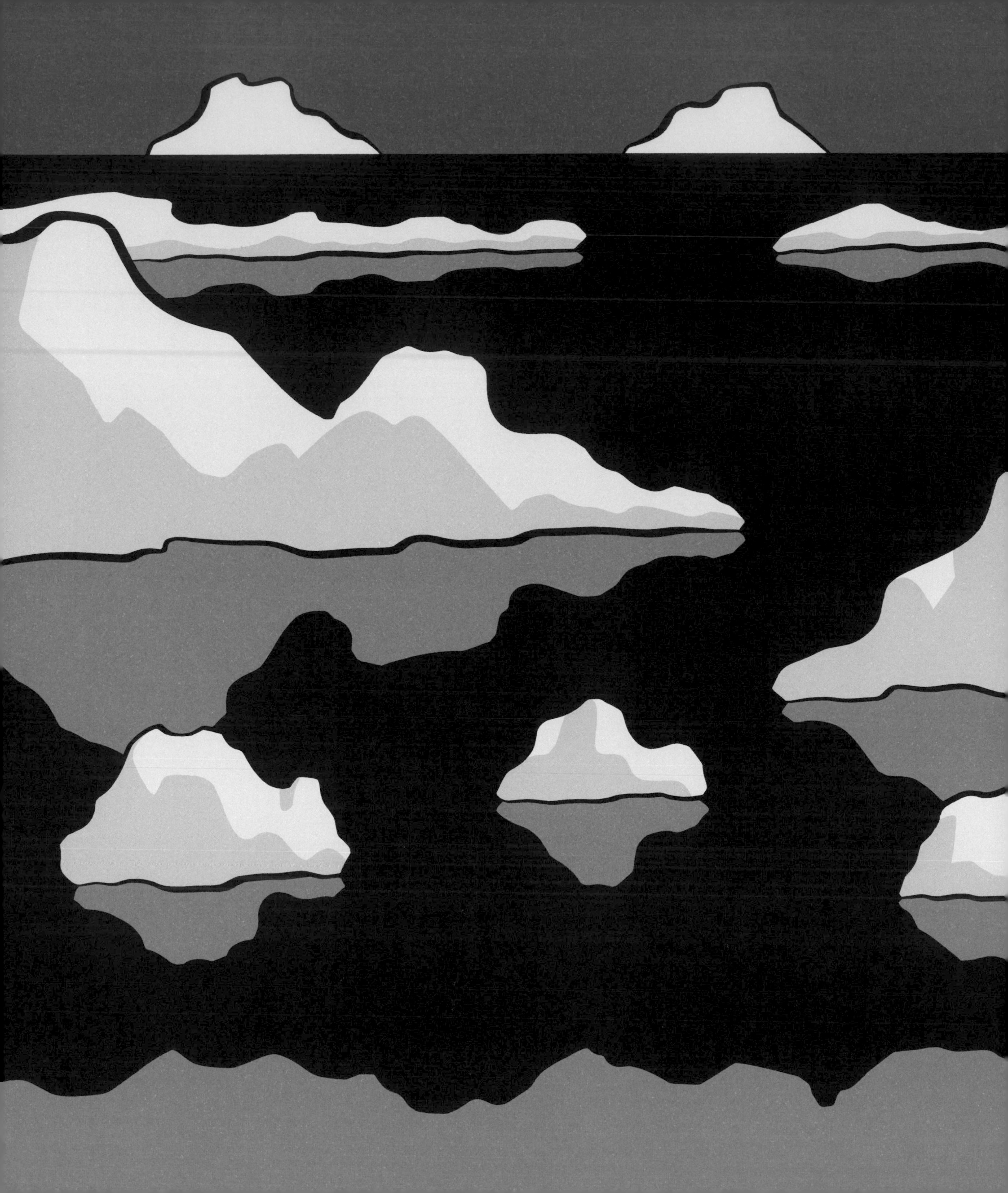

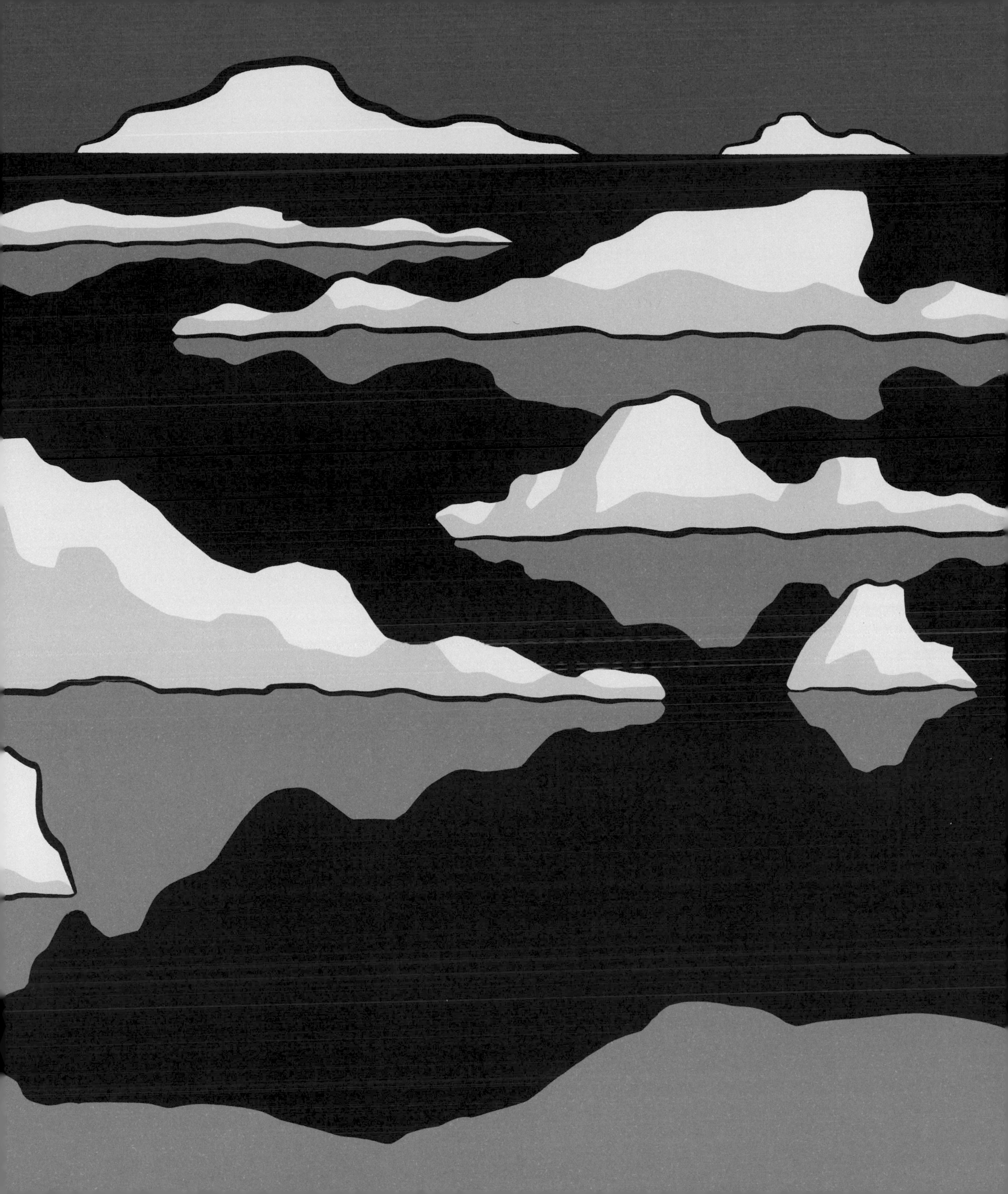

THE GENTLEMAN ADVENTURER

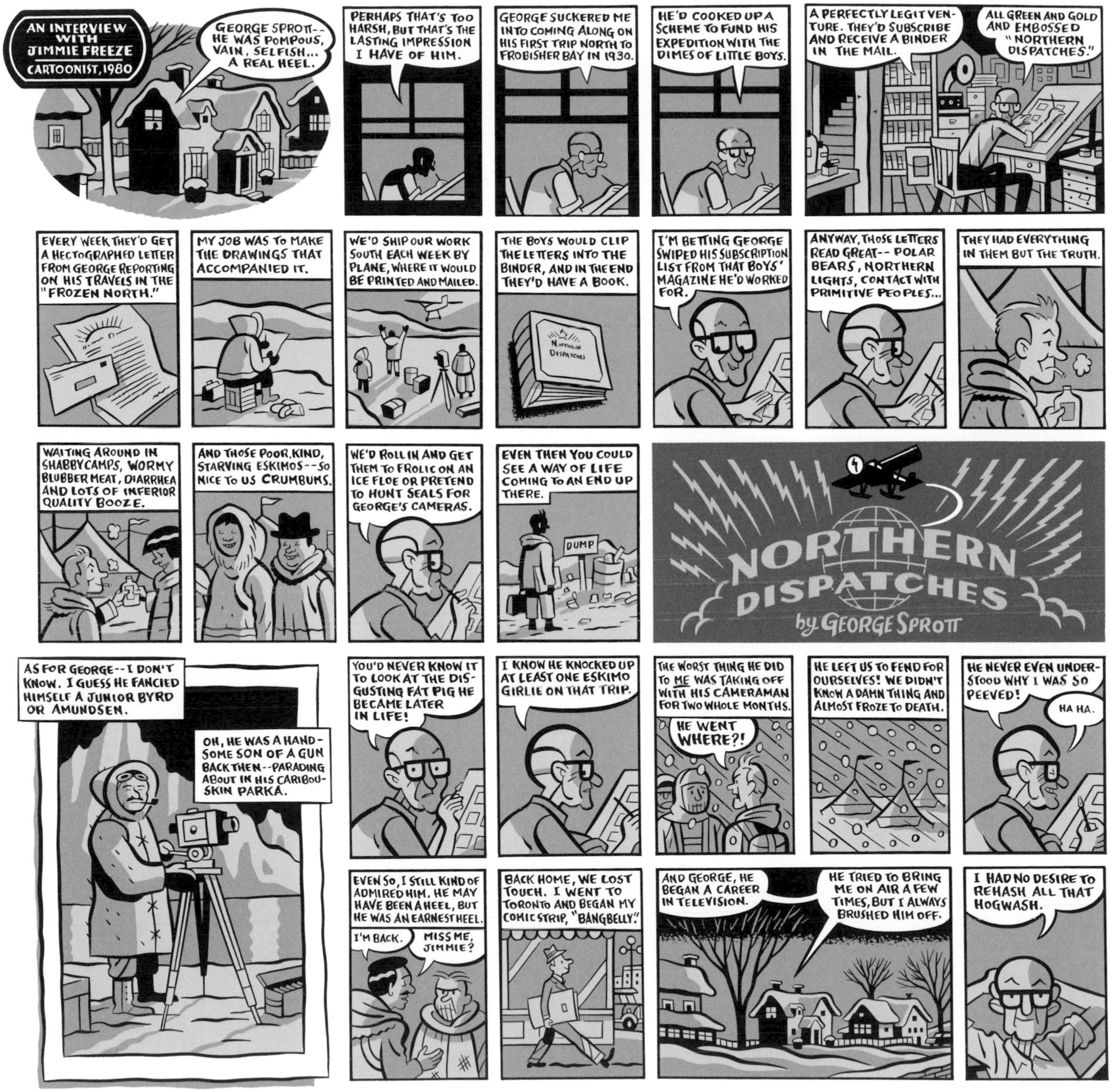

AN INTERVIEW WITH JIMMIE FREEZE
CARTOONIST, 1980
GEORGE SPROTT--HE WAS POMPOUS, VAIN, SELFISH... A REAL HEEL.
PERHAPS THAT'S TOO HARSH, BUT THAT'S THE LASTING IMPRESSION I HAVE OF HIM.
GEORGE SUCKERED ME INTO COMING ALONG ON HIS FIRST TRIP NORTH TO FROBISHER BAY IN 1930.
HE'D COOKED UP A SCHEME TO FUND HIS EXPEDITION WITH THE DIMES OF LITTLE BOYS.
A PERFECTLY LEGIT VENTURE. THEY'D SUBSCRIBE AND RECEIVE A BINDER IN THE MAIL.
ALL GREEN AND GOLD AND EMBOSSED "NORTHERN DISPATCHES."
EVERY WEEK THEY'D GET A HECTOGRAPHED LETTER FROM GEORGE REPORTING ON HIS TRAVELS IN THE "FROZEN NORTH."
MY JOB WAS TO MAKE THE DRAWINGS THAT ACCOMPANIED IT.
WE'D SHIP OUR WORK SOUTH EACH WEEK BY PLANE, WHERE IT WOULD BE PRINTED AND MAILED.
THE BOYS WOULD CLIP THE LETTERS INTO THE BINDER, AND IN THE END THEY'D HAVE A BOOK.
NORTHERN DISPATCHES
I'M BETTING GEORGE SWIPED HIS SUBSCRIPTION LIST FROM THAT BOYS' MAGAZINE HE'D WORKED FOR.
ANYWAY, THOSE LETTERS READ GREAT-- POLAR BEARS, NORTHERN LIGHTS, CONTACT WITH PRIMITIVE PEOPLES...
THEY HAD EVERYTHING IN THEM BUT THE TRUTH.
WAITING AROUND IN SHABBY CAMPS, WORMY BLUBBER MEAT, DIARRHEA AND LOTS OF INFERIOR QUALITY BOOZE.
AND THOSE POOR, KIND, STARVING ESKIMOS--SO NICE TO US CRUMBUMS.
WE'D ROLL IN AND GET THEM TO FROLIC ON AN ICE FLOE OR PRETEND TO HUNT SEALS FOR GEORGE'S CAMERAS.
EVEN THEN YOU COULD SEE A WAY OF LIFE COMING TO AN END UP THERE.
DUMP
NORTHERN DISPATCHES
by GEORGE SPROTT
AS FOR GEORGE--I DON'T KNOW. I GUESS HE FANCIED HIMSELF A JUNIOR BYRD OR AMUNDSEN.
OH, HE WAS A HANDSOME SON OF A GUN BACK THEN--PARADING ABOUT IN HIS CARIBOU-SKIN PARKA.
YOU'D NEVER KNOW IT TO LOOK AT THE DISGUSTING FAT PIG HE BECAME LATER IN LIFE!
I KNOW HE KNOCKED UP AT LEAST ONE ESKIMO GIRLIE ON THAT TRIP.
THE WORST THING HE DID TO ME WAS TAKING OFF WITH HIS CAMERAMAN FOR TWO WHOLE MONTHS.
HE WENT WHERE?!
HE LEFT US TO FEND FOR OURSELVES! WE DIDN'T KNOW A DAMN THING AND ALMOST FROZE TO DEATH.
HE NEVER EVEN UNDERSTOOD WHY I WAS SO PEEVED!
HA HA.
EVEN SO, I STILL KIND OF ADMIRED HIM. HE MAY HAVE BEEN A HEEL, BUT HE WAS AN EARNEST HEEL.
I'M BACK.
MISS ME, JIMMIE?
BACK HOME, WE LOST TOUCH. I WENT TO TORONTO AND BEGAN MY COMIC STRIP, "BANGBELLY."
AND GEORGE, HE BEGAN A CAREER IN TELEVISION.
HE TRIED TO BRING ME ON AIR A FEW TIMES, BUT I ALWAYS BRUSHED HIM OFF.
I HAD NO DESIRE TO REHASH ALL THAT HOGWASH.

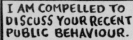

MAY 7 1916

MR. G. SPROTT

RIP

DEAR GEORGE:

AS A FRIEND OF YOUR FATHER I TRUST YOU WILL PARDON MY FRANKNESS...

I AM COMPELLED TO DISCUSS YOUR RECENT PUBLIC BEHAVIOUR.

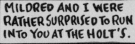

MILDRED AND I WERE RATHER SURPRISED TO RUN INTO YOU AT THE HOLT'S.

WE WERE UNAWARE THAT YOU WERE VISITING IN TORONTO.

I MUST SAY, I WAS UNPREPARED FOR YOUR ADVANCED STATE OF INTOXICATION.

HA

I WILL ASSUME THE ALCOHOL EXPLAINS THE COMMONNESS OF YOUR MANNER.

FRANKLY, YOUR CONVERSATION THAT EVENING WAS SHOCKING.

DOUBLY SO FOR A YOUNG MAN STUDYING IN THE MINISTRY.

SCRATCH

I CERTAINLY UNDERSTAND ABOUT "YOUTH AND HIGH SPIRITS..."

I BET!

SO I TRUST THAT THIS WAS AN ABERRATION, MY BOY.

OUT OF RESPECT FOR YOUR FATHER--

WHO WAS THANKFULLY SPARED WITNESSING THIS SHAMEFUL SPECTACLE--

I WILL KEEP THIS MATTER TO MYSELF.

GEORGE, I TRUST YOU WILL TAKE THIS LETTER TO HEART.

OH, I SHALL.

I REMAIN, YOURS, MR. THOMAS YORK

CRUNCH

THE OLD PRIG.

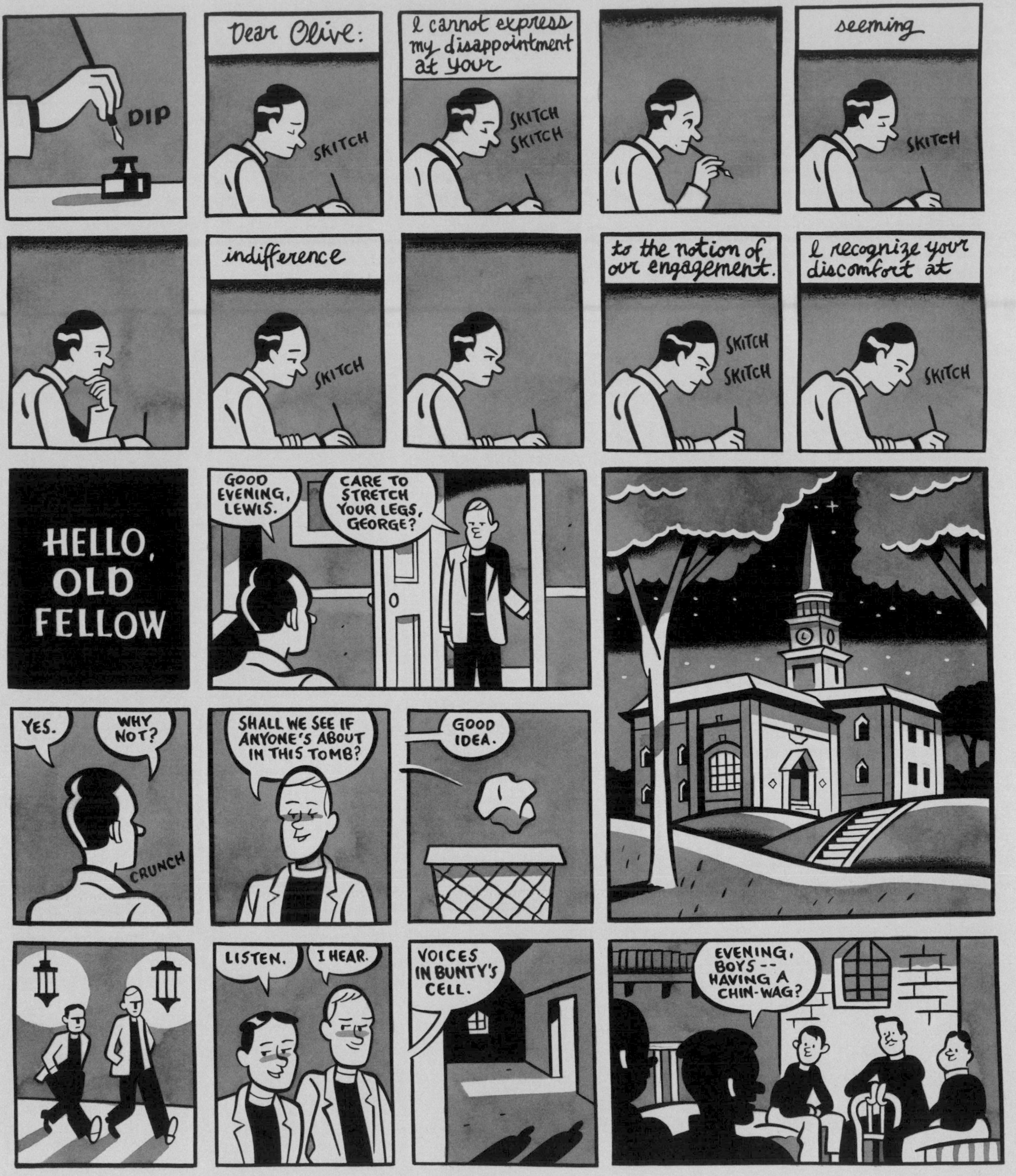
DIP
Dear Olive:
SKITCH
I cannot express my disappointment at your
SKITCH SKITCH
seeming
SKITCH
indifference
SKITCH
to the notion of our engagement.
SKITCH SKITCH
I recognize your discomfort at
SKITCH
HELLO, OLD FELLOW
GOOD EVENING, LEWIS.
CARE TO STRETCH YOUR LEGS, GEORGE?
YES.
WHY NOT?
CRUNCH
SHALL WE SEE IF ANYONE'S ABOUT IN THIS TOMB?
GOOD IDEA.
LISTEN.
I HEAR.
VOICES IN BUNTY'S CELL.
EVENING, BOYS -- HAVING A CHIN-WAG?

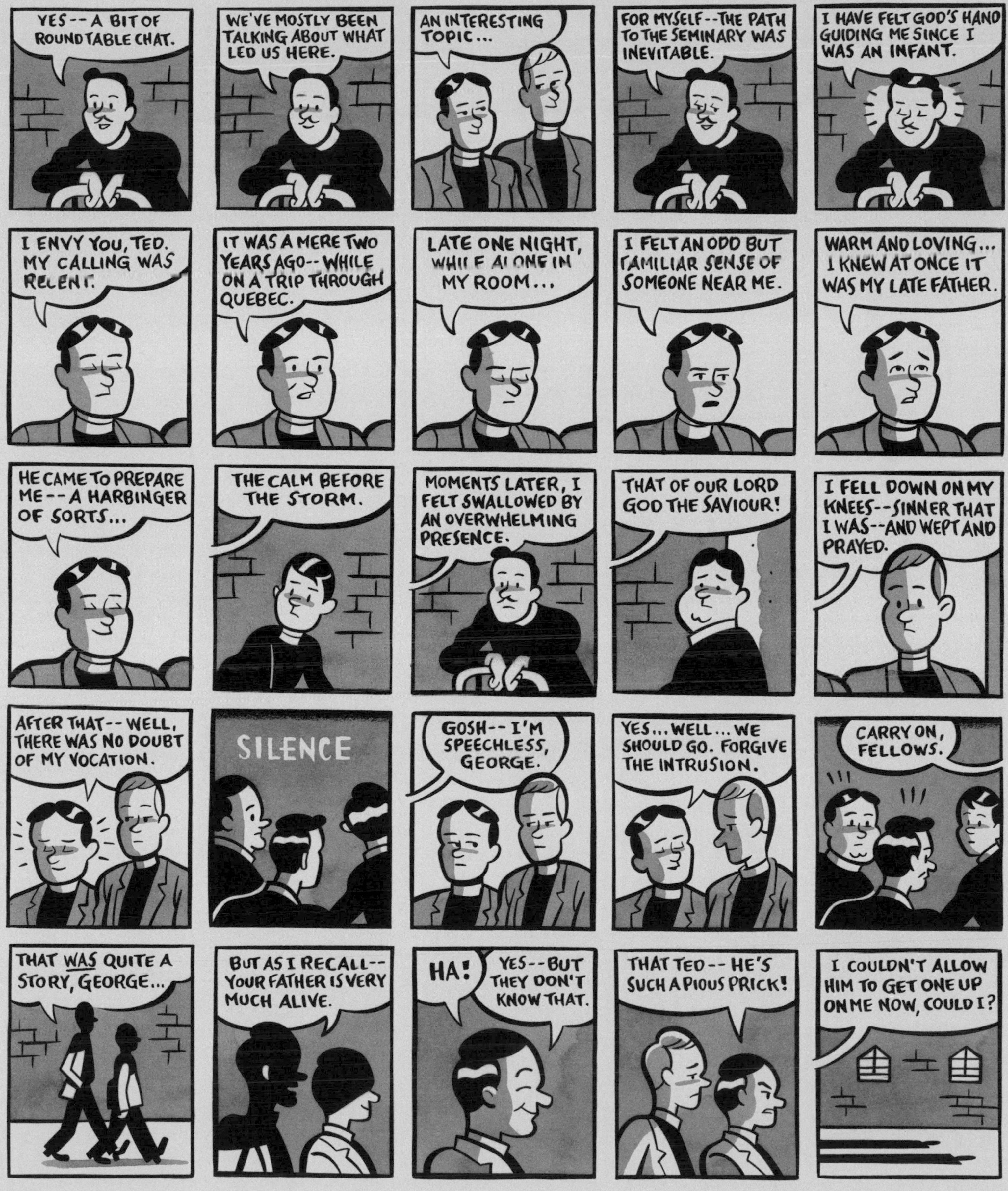
YES-- A BIT OF ROUNDTABLE CHAT.
WE'VE MOSTLY BEEN TALKING ABOUT WHAT LED US HERE.
AN INTERESTING TOPIC...
FOR MYSELF--THE PATH TO THE SEMINARY WAS INEVITABLE.
I HAVE FELT GOD'S HAND GUIDING ME SINCE I WAS AN INFANT.
I ENVY YOU, TED. MY CALLING WAS RECENT.
IT WAS A MERE TWO YEARS AGO-- WHILE ON A TRIP THROUGH QUEBEC.
LATE ONE NIGHT, WHILE ALONE IN MY ROOM...
I FELT AN ODD BUT FAMILIAR SENSE OF SOMEONE NEAR ME.
WARM AND LOVING... I KNEW AT ONCE IT WAS MY LATE FATHER.
HE CAME TO PREPARE ME-- A HARBINGER OF SORTS...
THE CALM BEFORE THE STORM.
MOMENTS LATER, I FELT SWALLOWED BY AN OVERWHELMING PRESENCE.
THAT OF OUR LORD GOD THE SAVIOUR!
I FELL DOWN ON MY KNEES--SINNER THAT I WAS--AND WEPT AND PRAYED.
AFTER THAT-- WELL, THERE WAS NO DOUBT OF MY VOCATION.
SILENCE
GOSH-- I'M SPEECHLESS, GEORGE.
YES... WELL... WE SHOULD GO. FORGIVE THE INTRUSION.
CARRY ON, FELLOWS.
THAT WAS QUITE A STORY, GEORGE...
BUT AS I RECALL-- YOUR FATHER IS VERY MUCH ALIVE.
HA!
YES--BUT THEY DON'T KNOW THAT.
THAT TED-- HE'S SUCH A PIOUS PRICK!
I COULDN'T ALLOW HIM TO GET ONE UP ON ME NOW, COULD I?

7:25 PM, OCTOBER 9, 1975

 HI! WOULD YOU TAKE US TO THE MELODY GRILL AT SWAN AND LAKESIDE?

I AM NEW DRIVER-- YOU DIRECT ME, MISS?

 GEORGE IS MAKING HIS WAY TO THE CORONET LECTURE HALL, WITH A STOP AT THE MELODY GRILL IN BETWEEN, A RITUAL HE HAS OBSERVED FOR THE LAST 22 YEARS.

SURE-- STAY ON KING UNTIL WEBER. TURN RIGHT AND THEN RIGHT AGAIN ON SWAN.

 IT IS JUST UNDER AN HOUR AND A HALF UNTIL GEORGE'S DEATH.

IF THEY'RE GOING TO HIRE FOREIGNERS, THEN YOU'D THINK...

UNCLE GEORGE! PLEASE!

 PERHAPS, AS YOUR NARRATOR, I'VE BEEN SOMEWHAT VAGUE ON CERTAIN POINTS UNTIL NOW, BUT ON THIS EVENT I HAVE MY FACTS STRAIGHT.

VERY WELL.

 Y'KNOW, I'VE ALWAYS FOUND THE CONTRAST INTERESTING BETWEEN THE INSIDE AND THE OUTSIDE OF A PERSON. THIS DUALITY MIGHT BE THE MOST PROFOUND EXPERIENCE IN HUMAN LIFE.

 JUST LOOK AT GEORGE-- HE'S STARTING UP ONE OF HIS YARNS. HE COULD NOT SEEM LESS INWARD.

UNCLE GEORGE, FINISH THAT STORY YOU WERE TELLING ABOUT FRITZ.

FRITZ! THAT DOPE!

 YET, AT THIS VERY MOMENT, HE IS LOOKING BACK TO THE DECK OF AN ICEBREAKER ON HIS MAIDEN VOYAGE INTO THE ARCTIC.

HE WAS ONE OF MY CREW ON THE TRIP TO BAFFIN ISLAND IN 1937.

THAT FOOL FELL THROUGH THE PACK ICE, SLEDGE AND ALL-- WE BARELY FISHED HIM OUT IN TIME.

 STANDING AT THE RAIL, LOOKING OUT ON THAT VAST GREEN SEA, HE'D SEEN HIS FIRST ICEBERG.

IT TOOK US TWO HOURS TO DRY HIM OUT, AND 10 MINUTES LATER HE FELL IN AGAIN.

 IT IS A MOMENT HE HAS OFTEN RETURNED TO.

WE WASTED SO MUCH TIME DRYING HIM OUT THAT WE HAD TO TURN BACK.

 THERE AT THE RAIL, AWASH IN CONFLICTING EMOTIONS.

I CERTAINLY NEVER HIRED HIM AGAIN, BUT CAPTAIN HIBBS DID THE NEXT YEAR.

 HE FELT AWE, OF COURSE, BUT ALSO TREPIDATION, FOR THE TASK AHEAD.

HIBBS TOLD ME FRITZ FELL THROUGH THE ICE TWICE ON THAT TRIP TOO.

HA, HA!

 IT WAS A FRIGHTENING VENTURE FOR A 35-YEAR-OLD MAN WHO HAD NEVER BEEN NORTH OF THE 60TH PARALLEL BEFORE.

THE SECOND TIME THEY NEVER FOUND HIM. LOST UNDER THE ICE.

OH, UNCLE GEORGE-- THAT'S NOT FUNNY. IT'S AWFUL!

 AS HE BREATHED IN THAT CRISP SEA AIR, HE ALSO FELT A REAL SENSE OF PROMISE-- A NEW LIFE OPENING UP.

YES, I S'POSE SO... BUT IT WAS VERY AMUSING THE WAY HIBBS TOLD IT.

 AND HERE, IN 1975, IS GEORGE NOW THINKING OF THE YEARS THAT FOLLOWED THAT VOYAGE?

HERE WE ARE.

 IS HE THINKING OF THE DECADES SPENT IN DUSTY OFFICES AND SOUR LECTURE HALLS?

 KEEP THE CHANGE.

AND. SORRY.

 IS HE THINKING OF DULL BUDGET MEETINGS AND COMPANY DINNERS?

O.K., UNCLE GEORGE, I'LL BE BACK TO GET YOU IN 45 MINUTES.

 IS HE WONDERING WHETHER THIS WAS THE LIFE OF PROMISE?

GET SOMETHING TO EAT!

YES, YES.

 THERE I CANNOT HELP YOU.

MELODY GRILL

BARGAIN

CARDS + GIFTS

ON THIS MATTER YOU ARE ON YOUR OWN.

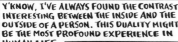

UNCLE GEORGE

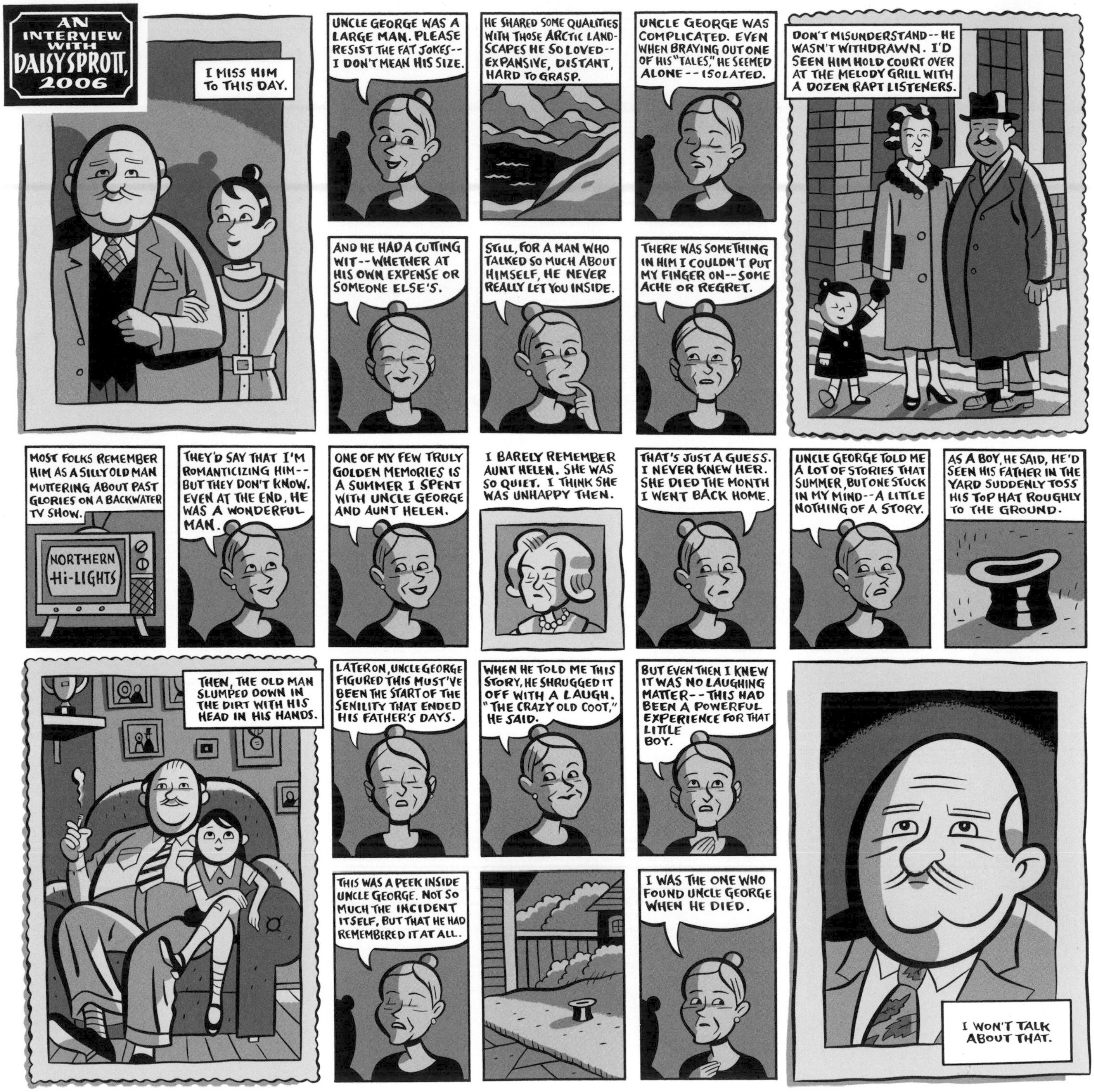
AN INTERVIEW WITH DAISY SPROTT, 2006
I MISS HIM TO THIS DAY.
UNCLE GEORGE WAS A LARGE MAN. PLEASE RESIST THE FAT JOKES-- I DON'T MEAN HIS SIZE.
HE SHARED SOME QUALITIES WITH THOSE ARCTIC LANDSCAPES HE SO LOVED-- EXPANSIVE, DISTANT, HARD TO GRASP.
UNCLE GEORGE WAS COMPLICATED. EVEN WHEN BRAYING OUT ONE OF HIS "TALES," HE SEEMED ALONE -- ISOLATED.
AND HE HAD A CUTTING WIT -- WHETHER AT HIS OWN EXPENSE OR SOMEONE ELSE'S.
STILL, FOR A MAN WHO TALKED SO MUCH ABOUT HIMSELF, HE NEVER REALLY LET YOU INSIDE.
THERE WAS SOMETHING IN HIM I COULDN'T PUT MY FINGER ON -- SOME ACHE OR REGRET.
DON'T MISUNDERSTAND -- HE WASN'T WITHDRAWN. I'D SEEN HIM HOLD COURT OVER AT THE MELODY GRILL WITH A DOZEN RAPT LISTENERS.
MOST FOLKS REMEMBER HIM AS A SILLY OLD MAN MUTTERING ABOUT PAST GLORIES ON A BACKWATER TV SHOW.
NORTHERN HI-LIGHTS
THEY'D SAY THAT I'M ROMANTICIZING HIM-- BUT THEY DON'T KNOW. EVEN AT THE END, HE WAS A WONDERFUL MAN.
ONE OF MY FEW TRULY GOLDEN MEMORIES IS A SUMMER I SPENT WITH UNCLE GEORGE AND AUNT HELEN.
I BARELY REMEMBER AUNT HELEN. SHE WAS SO QUIET. I THINK SHE WAS UNHAPPY THEN.
THAT'S JUST A GUESS. I NEVER KNEW HER. SHE DIED THE MONTH I WENT BACK HOME.
UNCLE GEORGE TOLD ME A LOT OF STORIES THAT SUMMER, BUT ONE STUCK IN MY MIND-- A LITTLE NOTHING OF A STORY.
AS A BOY, HE SAID, HE'D SEEN HIS FATHER IN THE YARD SUDDENLY TOSS HIS TOP HAT ROUGHLY TO THE GROUND.
THEN, THE OLD MAN SLUMPED DOWN IN THE DIRT WITH HIS HEAD IN HIS HANDS.
LATER ON, UNCLE GEORGE FIGURED THIS MUST'VE BEEN THE START OF THE SENILITY THAT ENDED HIS FATHER'S DAYS.
WHEN HE TOLD ME THIS STORY, HE SHRUGGED IT OFF WITH A LAUGH. "THE CRAZY OLD COOT," HE SAID.
BUT EVEN THEN I KNEW IT WAS NO LAUGHING MATTER-- THIS HAD BEEN A POWERFUL EXPERIENCE FOR THAT LITTLE BOY.
THIS WAS A PEEK INSIDE UNCLE GEORGE. NOT SO MUCH THE INCIDENT ITSELF, BUT THAT HE HAD REMEMBERED IT AT ALL.
I WAS THE ONE WHO FOUND UNCLE GEORGE WHEN HE DIED.
I WON'T TALK ABOUT THAT.

THE INSTITUTE of POLAR STUDIES

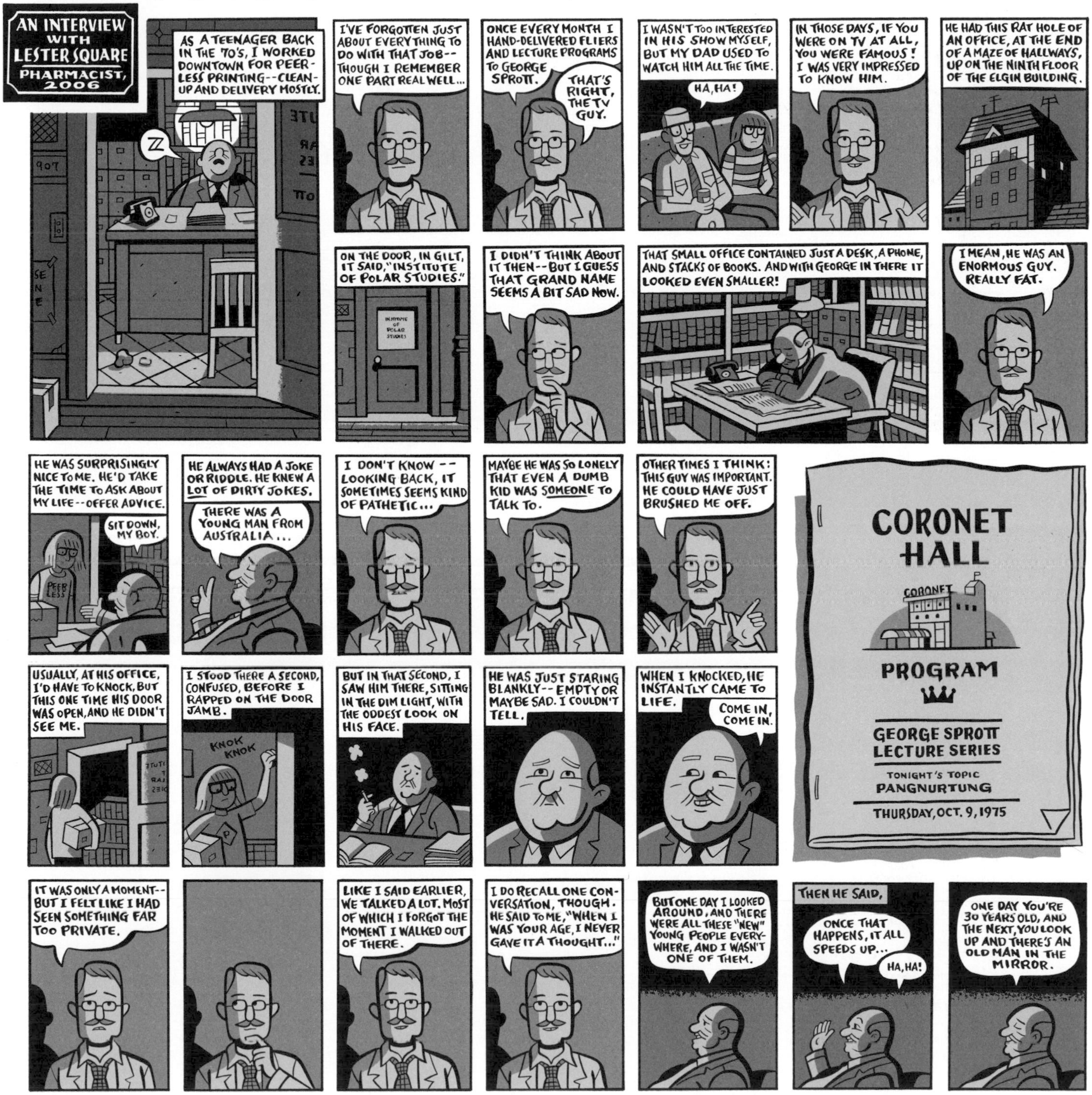
AN INTERVIEW WITH LESTER SQUARE
PHARMACIST, 2006
AS A TEENAGER BACK IN THE 70'S, I WORKED DOWNTOWN FOR PEERLESS PRINTING--CLEAN-UP AND DELIVERY MOSTLY.
ZZ
I'VE FORGOTTEN JUST ABOUT EVERYTHING TO DO WITH THAT JOB--THOUGH I REMEMBER ONE PART REAL WELL...
ONCE EVERY MONTH I HAND-DELIVERED FLIERS AND LECTURE PROGRAMS TO GEORGE SPROTT.
THAT'S RIGHT, THE TV GUY.
I WASN'T TOO INTERESTED IN HIS SHOW MYSELF, BUT MY DAD USED TO WATCH HIM ALL THE TIME.
HA, HA!
IN THOSE DAYS, IF YOU WERE ON TV AT ALL, YOU WERE FAMOUS! I WAS VERY IMPRESSED TO KNOW HIM.
HE HAD THIS RAT HOLE OF AN OFFICE, AT THE END OF A MAZE OF HALLWAYS, UP ON THE NINTH FLOOR OF THE ELGIN BUILDING.
ON THE DOOR, IN GILT, IT SAID, "INSTITUTE OF POLAR STUDIES."
I DIDN'T THINK ABOUT IT THEN--BUT I GUESS THAT GRAND NAME SEEMS A BIT SAD NOW.
THAT SMALL OFFICE CONTAINED JUST A DESK, A PHONE, AND STACKS OF BOOKS. AND WITH GEORGE IN THERE IT LOOKED EVEN SMALLER!
I MEAN, HE WAS AN ENORMOUS GUY. REALLY FAT.
HE WAS SURPRISINGLY NICE TO ME. HE'D TAKE THE TIME TO ASK ABOUT MY LIFE--OFFER ADVICE.
SIT DOWN, MY BOY.
PEERLESS
HE ALWAYS HAD A JOKE OR RIDDLE. HE KNEW A LOT OF DIRTY JOKES.
THERE WAS A YOUNG MAN FROM AUSTRALIA...
I DON'T KNOW--LOOKING BACK, IT SOMETIMES SEEMS KIND OF PATHETIC...
MAYBE HE WAS SO LONELY THAT EVEN A DUMB KID WAS SOMEONE TO TALK TO.
OTHER TIMES I THINK: THIS GUY WAS IMPORTANT. HE COULD HAVE JUST BRUSHED ME OFF.
CORONET HALL
CORONET
PROGRAM
GEORGE SPROTT LECTURE SERIES
TONIGHT'S TOPIC
PANGNURTUNG
THURSDAY, OCT. 9, 1975
USUALLY, AT HIS OFFICE, I'D HAVE TO KNOCK. BUT THIS ONE TIME HIS DOOR WAS OPEN, AND HE DIDN'T SEE ME.
I STOOD THERE A SECOND, CONFUSED, BEFORE I RAPPED ON THE DOOR JAMB.
KNOK KNOK
BUT IN THAT SECOND, I SAW HIM THERE, SITTING IN THE DIM LIGHT, WITH THE ODDEST LOOK ON HIS FACE.
HE WAS JUST STARING BLANKLY--EMPTY OR MAYBE SAD. I COULDN'T TELL.
WHEN I KNOCKED, HE INSTANTLY CAME TO LIFE.
COME IN, COME IN.
IT WAS ONLY A MOMENT--BUT I FELT LIKE I HAD SEEN SOMETHING FAR TOO PRIVATE.
LIKE I SAID EARLIER, WE TALKED A LOT. MOST OF WHICH I FORGOT THE MOMENT I WALKED OUT OF THERE.
I DO RECALL ONE CONVERSATION, THOUGH. HE SAID TO ME, "WHEN I WAS YOUR AGE, I NEVER GAVE IT A THOUGHT..."
BUT ONE DAY I LOOKED AROUND, AND THERE WERE ALL THESE "NEW" YOUNG PEOPLE EVERYWHERE, AND I WASN'T ONE OF THEM.
THEN HE SAID,
ONCE THAT HAPPENS, IT ALL SPEEDS UP...
HA, HA!
ONE DAY YOU'RE 30 YEARS OLD, AND THE NEXT, YOU LOOK UP AND THERE'S AN OLD MAN IN THE MIRROR.

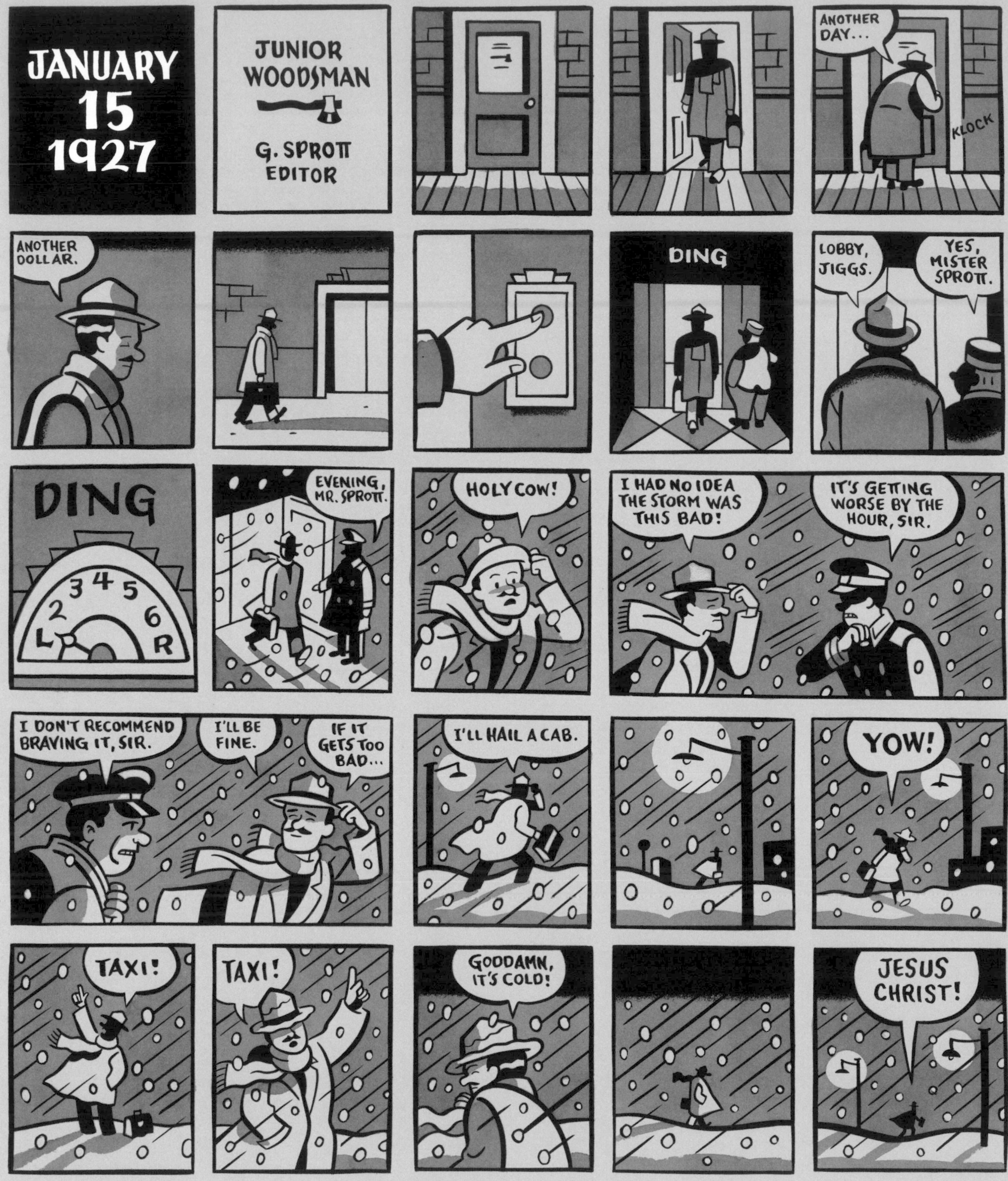

JANUARY 15 1927
JUNIOR WOODSMAN
G. SPROTT EDITOR
ANOTHER DAY...
KLOCK
ANOTHER DOLLAR.
DING
LOBBY, JIGGS.
YES, MISTER SPROTT.
DING
3 4 5
2 6
L R
EVENING, MR. SPROTT.
HOLY COW!
I HAD NO IDEA THE STORM WAS THIS BAD!
IT'S GETTING WORSE BY THE HOUR, SIR.
I DON'T RECOMMEND BRAVING IT, SIR.
I'LL BE FINE.
IF IT GETS TOO BAD...
I'LL HAIL A CAB.
YOW!
TAXI!
TAXI!
GODDAMN, IT'S COLD!
JESUS CHRIST!

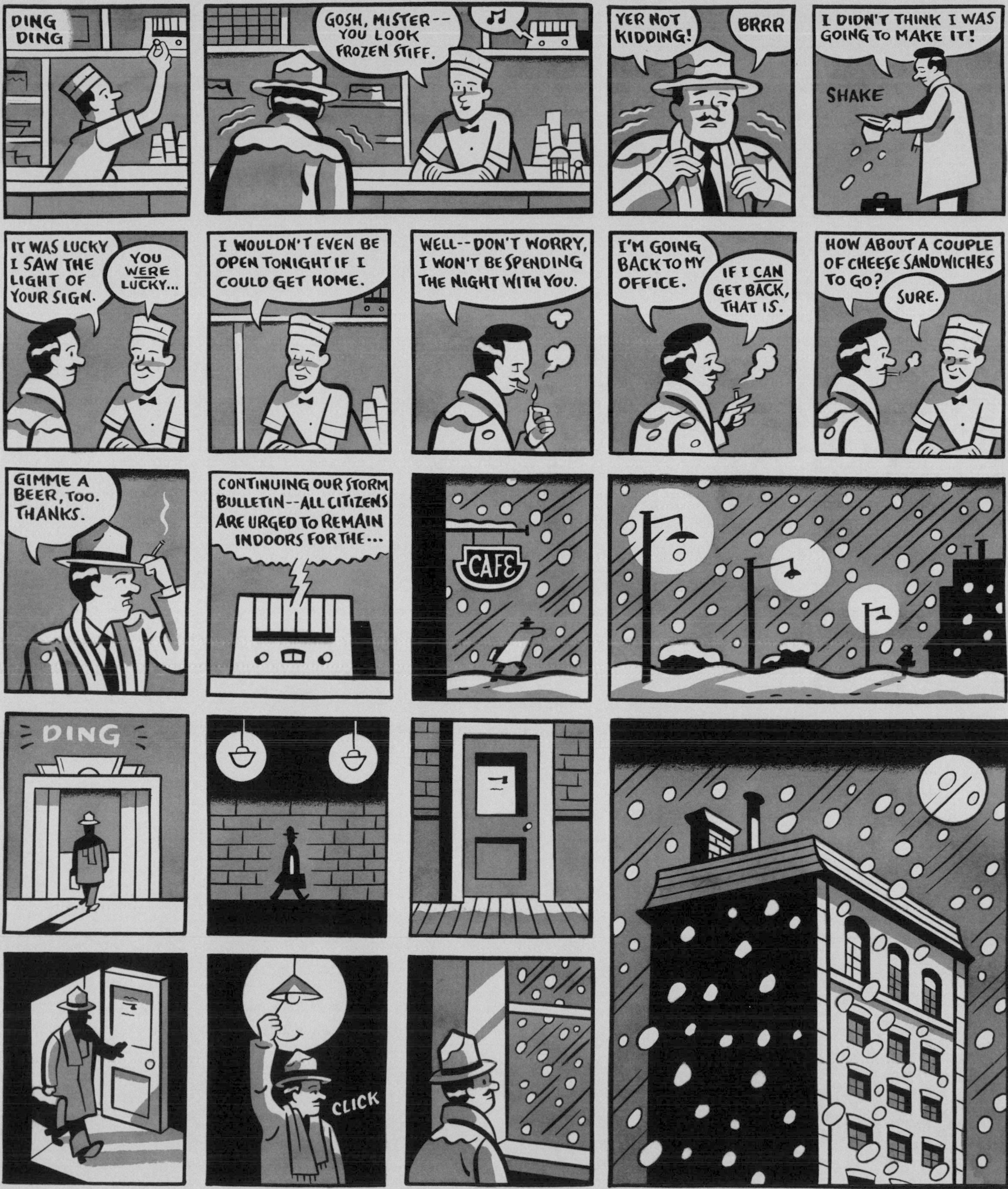
DING DING
GOSH, MISTER-- YOU LOOK FROZEN STIFF.
YER NOT KIDDING!
BRRR
I DIDN'T THINK I WAS GOING TO MAKE IT!
SHAKE
IT WAS LUCKY I SAW THE LIGHT OF YOUR SIGN.
YOU WERE LUCKY...
I WOULDN'T EVEN BE OPEN TONIGHT IF I COULD GET HOME.
WELL--DON'T WORRY, I WON'T BE SPENDING THE NIGHT WITH YOU.
I'M GOING BACK TO MY OFFICE.
IF I CAN GET BACK, THAT IS.
HOW ABOUT A COUPLE OF CHEESE SANDWICHES TO GO?
SURE.
GIMME A BEER, TOO. THANKS.
CONTINUING OUR STORM BULLETIN--ALL CITIZENS ARE URGED TO REMAIN INDOORS FOR THE...
CAFE
DING
CLICK

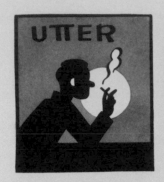
UTTER

SILENCE

The NORTH OWL

JUNIOR WOODSMAN

WHITE

WHITE OWL
LAGER BEER
DOMINION BREWERS LTD.

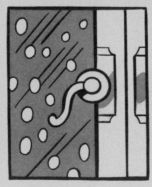

"ENJOY OUR HIGH-HAT SERVICE"

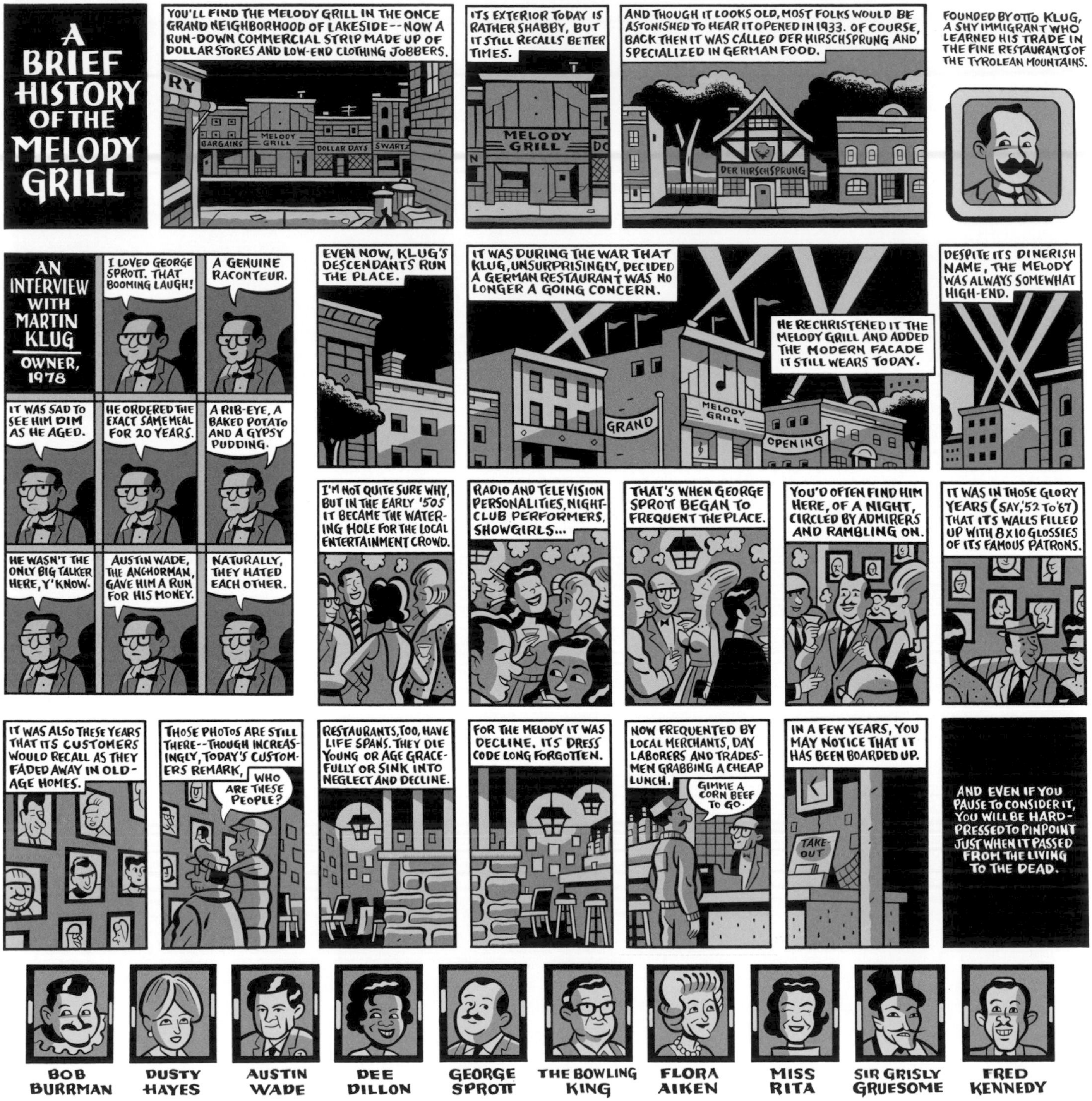

A BRIEF HISTORY OF THE MELODY GRILL
YOU'LL FIND THE MELODY GRILL IN THE ONCE GRAND NEIGHBORHOOD OF LAKESIDE--NOW A RUN-DOWN COMMERCIAL STRIP MADE UP OF DOLLAR STORES AND LOW-END CLOTHING JOBBERS.
BARGAINS
MELODY GRILL
DOLLAR DAYS
ITS EXTERIOR TODAY IS RATHER SHABBY, BUT IT STILL RECALLS BETTER TIMES.
MELODY GRILL
AND THOUGH IT LOOKS OLD, MOST FOLKS WOULD BE ASTONISHED TO HEAR IT OPENED IN 1933. OF COURSE, BACK THEN IT WAS CALLED DER HIRSCHSPRUNG AND SPECIALIZED IN GERMAN FOOD.
DER HIRSCHSPRUNG
FOUNDED BY OTTO KLUG, A SHY IMMIGRANT WHO LEARNED HIS TRADE IN THE FINE RESTAURANTS OF THE TYROLEAN MOUNTAINS.
AN INTERVIEW WITH MARTIN KLUG
OWNER, 1978
I LOVED GEORGE SPROTT. THAT BOOMING LAUGH!
A GENUINE RACONTEUR.
IT WAS SAD TO SEE HIM DIM AS HE AGED.
HE ORDERED THE EXACT SAME MEAL FOR 20 YEARS.
A RIB-EYE, A BAKED POTATO AND A GYPSY PUDDING.
HE WASN'T THE ONLY BIG TALKER HERE, Y'KNOW.
AUSTIN WADE, THE ANCHORMAN, GAVE HIM A RUN FOR HIS MONEY.
NATURALLY, THEY HATED EACH OTHER.
EVEN NOW, KLUG'S DESCENDANTS RUN THE PLACE.
IT WAS DURING THE WAR THAT KLUG, UNSURPRISINGLY, DECIDED A GERMAN RESTAURANT WAS NO LONGER A GOING CONCERN.
HE RECHRISTENED IT THE MELODY GRILL AND ADDED THE MODERN FACADE IT STILL WEARS TODAY.
GRAND
MELODY GRILL
OPENING
DESPITE ITS DINERISH NAME, THE MELODY WAS ALWAYS SOMEWHAT HIGH-END.
I'M NOT QUITE SURE WHY, BUT IN THE EARLY '50S IT BECAME THE WATERING HOLE FOR THE LOCAL ENTERTAINMENT CROWD.
RADIO AND TELEVISION PERSONALITIES, NIGHT-CLUB PERFORMERS, SHOWGIRLS...
THAT'S WHEN GEORGE SPROTT BEGAN TO FREQUENT THE PLACE.
YOU'D OFTEN FIND HIM HERE, OF A NIGHT, CIRCLED BY ADMIRERS AND RAMBLING ON.
IT WAS IN THOSE GLORY YEARS (SAY, '52 TO '67) THAT ITS WALLS FILLED UP WITH 8X10 GLOSSIES OF ITS FAMOUS PATRONS.
IT WAS ALSO THESE YEARS THAT ITS CUSTOMERS WOULD RECALL AS THEY FADED AWAY IN OLD-AGE HOMES.
THOSE PHOTOS ARE STILL THERE--THOUGH INCREASINGLY, TODAY'S CUSTOMERS REMARK,
WHO ARE THESE PEOPLE?
RESTAURANTS, TOO, HAVE LIFE SPANS. THEY DIE YOUNG OR AGE GRACEFULLY OR SINK INTO NEGLECT AND DECLINE.
FOR THE MELODY IT WAS DECLINE. ITS DRESS CODE LONG FORGOTTEN.
NOW FREQUENTED BY LOCAL MERCHANTS, DAY LABORERS AND TRADESMEN GRABBING A CHEAP LUNCH.
GIMME A CORN BEEF TO GO.
IN A FEW YEARS, YOU MAY NOTICE THAT IT HAS BEEN BOARDED UP.
TAKE-OUT
AND EVEN IF YOU PAUSE TO CONSIDER IT, YOU WILL BE HARD-PRESSED TO PINPOINT JUST WHEN IT PASSED FROM THE LIVING TO THE DEAD.
BOB BURRMAN
DUSTY HAYES
AUSTIN WADE
DEE DILLON
GEORGE SPROTT
THE BOWLING KING
FLORA AIKEN
MISS RITA
SIR GRISLY GRUESOME
FRED KENNEDY

MELODY
GRILL

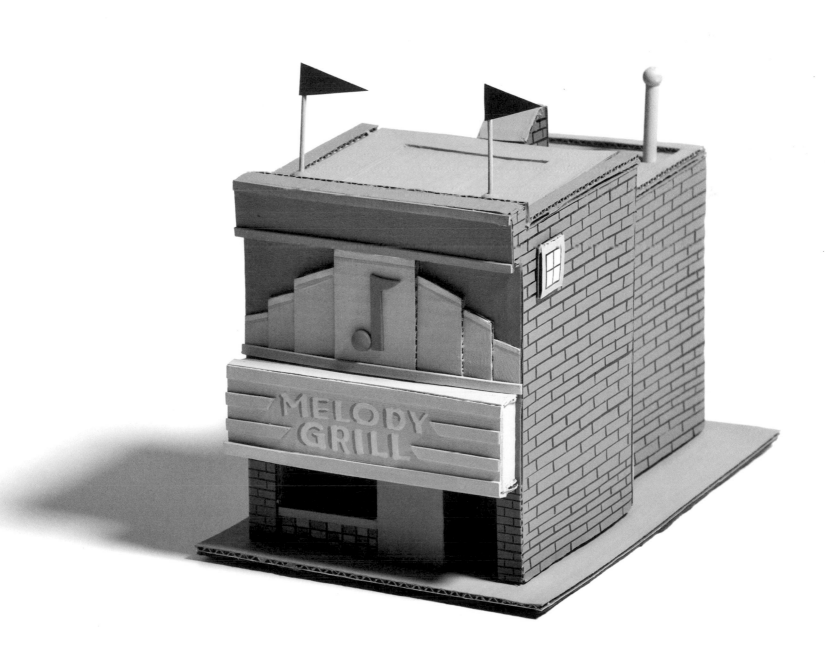

THE WHITE DREAM

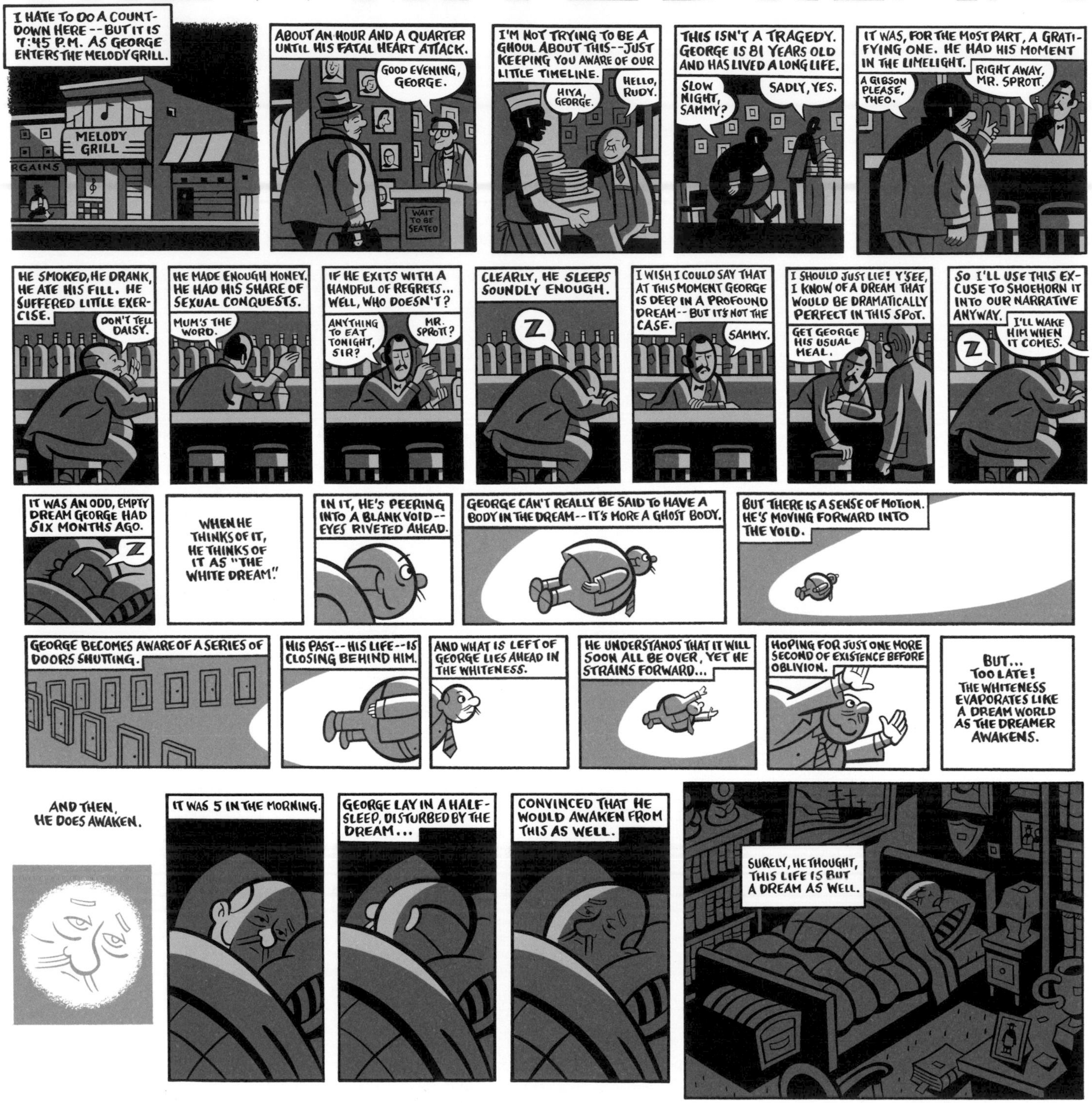

I HATE TO DO A COUNT-DOWN HERE--BUT IT IS 7:45 P.M. AS GEORGE ENTERS THE MELODY GRILL.
MELODY GRILL
RGAINS
ABOUT AN HOUR AND A QUARTER UNTIL HIS FATAL HEART ATTACK.
GOOD EVENING, GEORGE.
WAIT TO BE SEATED
I'M NOT TRYING TO BE A GHOUL ABOUT THIS--JUST KEEPING YOU AWARE OF OUR LITTLE TIMELINE.
HIYA, GEORGE.
HELLO, RUDY.
THIS ISN'T A TRAGEDY. GEORGE IS 81 YEARS OLD AND HAS LIVED A LONG LIFE.
SLOW NIGHT, SAMMY?
SADLY, YES.
IT WAS, FOR THE MOST PART, A GRATI-FYING ONE. HE HAD HIS MOMENT IN THE LIMELIGHT.
A GIBSON PLEASE, THEO.
RIGHT AWAY, MR. SPROTT.
HE SMOKED, HE DRANK, HE ATE HIS FILL. HE SUFFERED LITTLE EXER-CISE.
DON'T TELL DAISY.
HE MADE ENOUGH MONEY. HE HAD HIS SHARE OF SEXUAL CONQUESTS.
MUM'S THE WORD.
IF HE EXITS WITH A HANDFUL OF REGRETS... WELL, WHO DOESN'T?
ANYTHING TO EAT TONIGHT, SIR?
MR. SPROTT?
CLEARLY, HE SLEEPS SOUNDLY ENOUGH.
Z
I WISH I COULD SAY THAT AT THIS MOMENT GEORGE IS DEEP IN A PROFOUND DREAM--BUT IT'S NOT THE CASE.
SAMMY.
I SHOULD JUST LIE! Y'SEE, I KNOW OF A DREAM THAT WOULD BE DRAMATICALLY PERFECT IN THIS SPOT.
GET GEORGE HIS USUAL MEAL.
SO I'LL USE THIS EX-CUSE TO SHOEHORN IT INTO OUR NARRATIVE ANYWAY.
Z
I'LL WAKE HIM WHEN IT COMES.
IT WAS AN ODD, EMPTY DREAM GEORGE HAD SIX MONTHS AGO.
Z
WHEN HE THINKS OF IT, HE THINKS OF IT AS "THE WHITE DREAM."
IN IT, HE'S PEERING INTO A BLANK VOID--EYES RIVETED AHEAD.
GEORGE CAN'T REALLY BE SAID TO HAVE A BODY IN THE DREAM--IT'S MORE A GHOST BODY.
BUT THERE IS A SENSE OF MOTION. HE'S MOVING FORWARD INTO THE VOID.
GEORGE BECOMES AWARE OF A SERIES OF DOORS SHUTTING.
HIS PAST--HIS LIFE--IS CLOSING BEHIND HIM.
AND WHAT IS LEFT OF GEORGE LIES AHEAD IN THE WHITENESS.
HE UNDERSTANDS THAT IT WILL SOON ALL BE OVER, YET HE STRAINS FORWARD...
HOPING FOR JUST ONE MORE SECOND OF EXISTENCE BEFORE OBLIVION.
BUT... TOO LATE! THE WHITENESS EVAPORATES LIKE A DREAM WORLD AS THE DREAMER AWAKENS.
AND THEN, HE DOES AWAKEN.
IT WAS 5 IN THE MORNING.
GEORGE LAY IN A HALF-SLEEP, DISTURBED BY THE DREAM...
CONVINCED THAT HE WOULD AWAKEN FROM THIS AS WELL.
SURELY, HE THOUGHT, THIS LIFE IS BUT A DREAM AS WELL.

CKCK VIEWER'S GUIDE

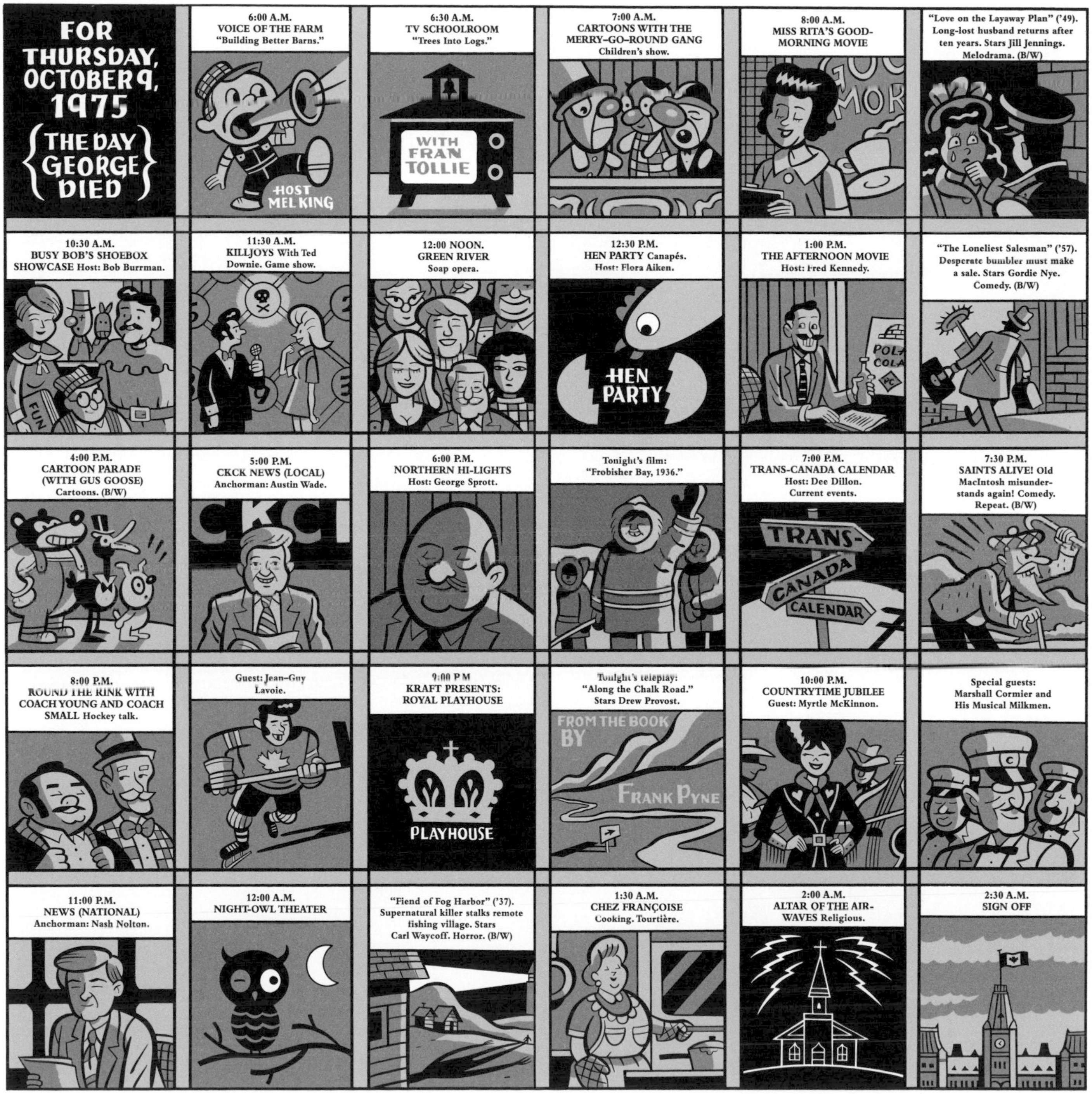
FOR THURSDAY, OCTOBER 9, 1975
{THE DAY GEORGE DIED}
6:00 A.M.
VOICE OF THE FARM
"Building Better Barns."
HOST MEL KING
6:30 A.M.
TV SCHOOLROOM
"Trees Into Logs."
WITH FRAN TOLLIE
7:00 A.M.
CARTOONS WITH THE MERRY-GO-ROUND GANG
Children's show.
8:00 A.M.
MISS RITA'S GOOD-MORNING MOVIE
"Love on the Layaway Plan" ('49). Long-lost husband returns after ten years. Stars Jill Jennings. Melodrama. (B/W)
10:30 A.M.
BUSY BOB'S SHOEBOX SHOWCASE Host: Bob Burrman.
FUN
11:30 A.M.
KILLJOYS With Ted Downie. Game show.
12:00 NOON.
GREEN RIVER
Soap opera.
12:30 P.M.
HEN PARTY Canapés.
Host: Flora Aiken.
HEN PARTY
1:00 P.M.
THE AFTERNOON MOVIE
Host: Fred Kennedy.
"The Loneliest Salesman" ('57). Desperate bumbler must make a sale. Stars Gordie Nye. Comedy. (B/W)
4:00 P.M.
CARTOON PARADE (WITH GUS GOOSE)
Cartoons. (B/W)
5:00 P.M.
CKCK NEWS (LOCAL)
Anchorman: Austin Wade.
6:00 P.M.
NORTHERN HI-LIGHTS
Host: George Sprott.
Tonight's film:
"Frobisher Bay, 1936."
7:00 P.M.
TRANS-CANADA CALENDAR
Host: Dee Dillon.
Current events.
TRANS-
CANADA
CALENDAR
7:30 P.M.
SAINTS ALIVE! Old MacIntosh misunderstands again! Comedy. Repeat. (B/W)
8:00 P.M.
ROUND THE RINK WITH COACH YOUNG AND COACH SMALL Hockey talk.
Guest: Jean-Guy Lavoie.
9:00 P.M.
KRAFT PRESENTS: ROYAL PLAYHOUSE
PLAYHOUSE
Tonight's teleplay:
"Along the Chalk Road."
Stars Drew Provost.
FROM THE BOOK BY
FRANK PYNE
10:00 P.M.
COUNTRYTIME JUBILEE
Guest: Myrtle McKinnon.
Special guests:
Marshall Cormier and His Musical Milkmen.
11:00 P.M.
NEWS (NATIONAL)
Anchorman: Nash Nolton.
12:00 A.M.
NIGHT-OWL THEATER
"Fiend of Fog Harbor" ('37). Supernatural killer stalks remote fishing village. Stars Carl Waycoff. Horror. (B/W)
1:30 A.M.
CHEZ FRANÇOISE
Cooking. Tourtière.
2:00 A.M.
ALTAR OF THE AIR-WAVES Religious.
2:30 A.M.
SIGN OFF

THE DAUGHTER

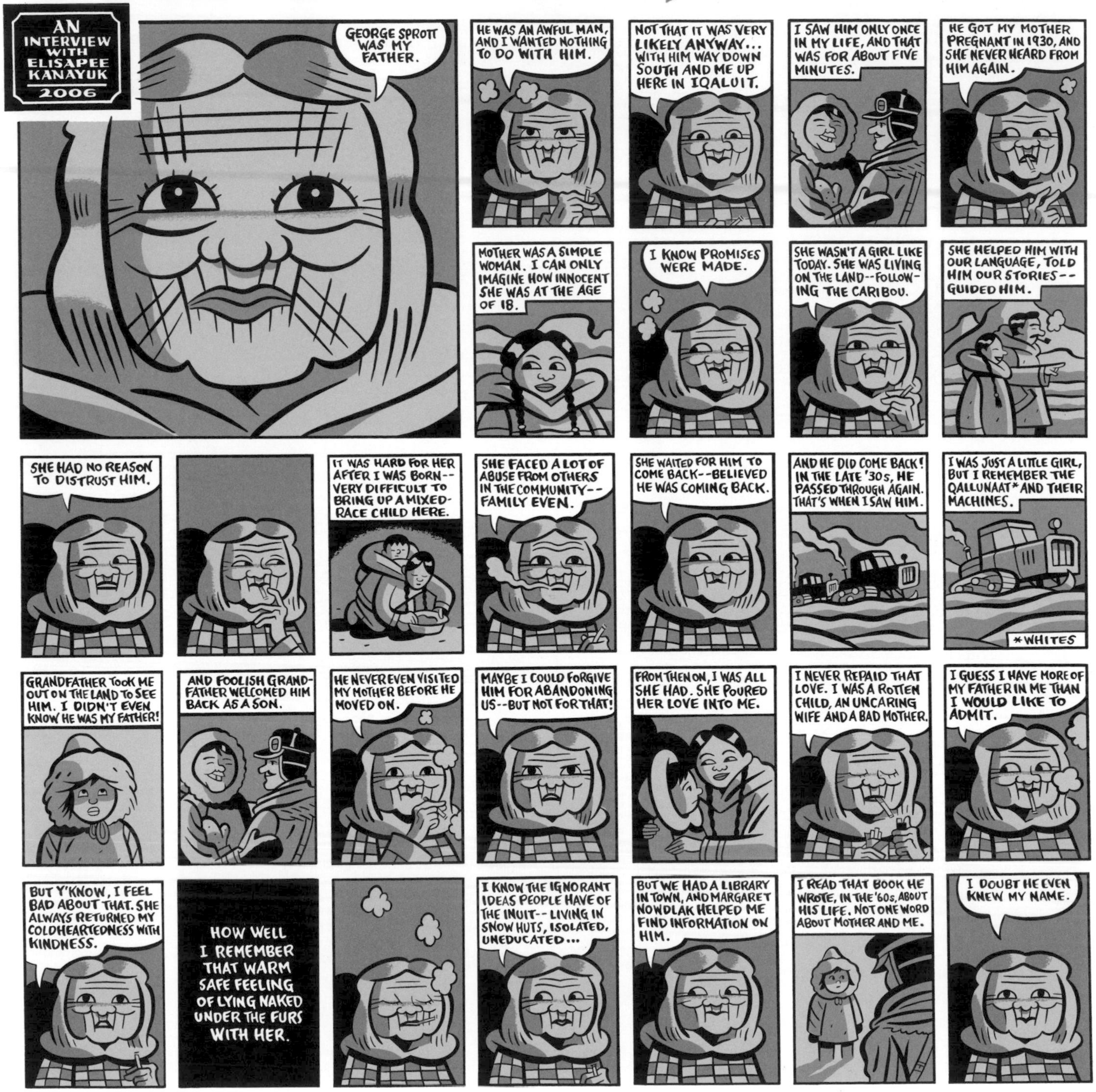
AN INTERVIEW WITH ELISAPEE KANAYUK 2006
GEORGE SPROTT WAS MY FATHER.
HE WAS AN AWFUL MAN, AND I WANTED NOTHING TO DO WITH HIM.
NOT THAT IT WAS VERY LIKELY ANYWAY... WITH HIM WAY DOWN SOUTH AND ME UP HERE IN IQALUIT.
I SAW HIM ONLY ONCE IN MY LIFE, AND THAT WAS FOR ABOUT FIVE MINUTES.
HE GOT MY MOTHER PREGNANT IN 1930, AND SHE NEVER HEARD FROM HIM AGAIN.
MOTHER WAS A SIMPLE WOMAN. I CAN ONLY IMAGINE HOW INNOCENT SHE WAS AT THE AGE OF 18.
I KNOW PROMISES WERE MADE.
SHE WASN'T A GIRL LIKE TODAY. SHE WAS LIVING ON THE LAND--FOLLOWING THE CARIBOU.
SHE HELPED HIM WITH OUR LANGUAGE, TOLD HIM OUR STORIES--GUIDED HIM.
SHE HAD NO REASON TO DISTRUST HIM.
IT WAS HARD FOR HER AFTER I WAS BORN--VERY DIFFICULT TO BRING UP A MIXED-RACE CHILD HERE.
SHE FACED A LOT OF ABUSE FROM OTHERS IN THE COMMUNITY--FAMILY EVEN.
SHE WAITED FOR HIM TO COME BACK--BELIEVED HE WAS COMING BACK.
AND HE DID COME BACK! IN THE LATE '30s, HE PASSED THROUGH AGAIN. THAT'S WHEN I SAW HIM.
I WAS JUST A LITTLE GIRL, BUT I REMEMBER THE QALLUNAAT* AND THEIR MACHINES.
*WHITES
GRANDFATHER TOOK ME OUT ON THE LAND TO SEE HIM. I DIDN'T EVEN KNOW HE WAS MY FATHER!
AND FOOLISH GRANDFATHER WELCOMED HIM BACK AS A SON.
HE NEVER EVEN VISITED MY MOTHER BEFORE HE MOVED ON.
MAYBE I COULD FORGIVE HIM FOR ABANDONING US--BUT NOT FOR THAT!
FROM THEN ON, I WAS ALL SHE HAD. SHE POURED HER LOVE INTO ME.
I NEVER REPAID THAT LOVE. I WAS A ROTTEN CHILD, AN UNCARING WIFE AND A BAD MOTHER.
I GUESS I HAVE MORE OF MY FATHER IN ME THAN I WOULD LIKE TO ADMIT.
BUT Y'KNOW, I FEEL BAD ABOUT THAT. SHE ALWAYS RETURNED MY COLDHEARTEDNESS WITH KINDNESS.
HOW WELL I REMEMBER THAT WARM SAFE FEELING OF LYING NAKED UNDER THE FURS WITH HER.
I KNOW THE IGNORANT IDEAS PEOPLE HAVE OF THE INUIT--LIVING IN SNOW HUTS, ISOLATED, UNEDUCATED...
BUT WE HAD A LIBRARY IN TOWN, AND MARGARET NOWDLAK HELPED ME FIND INFORMATION ON HIM.
I READ THAT BOOK HE WROTE, IN THE '60s, ABOUT HIS LIFE. NOT ONE WORD ABOUT MOTHER AND ME.
I DOUBT HE EVEN KNEW MY NAME.

A FEW WORDS FROM THE MAN HIMSELF

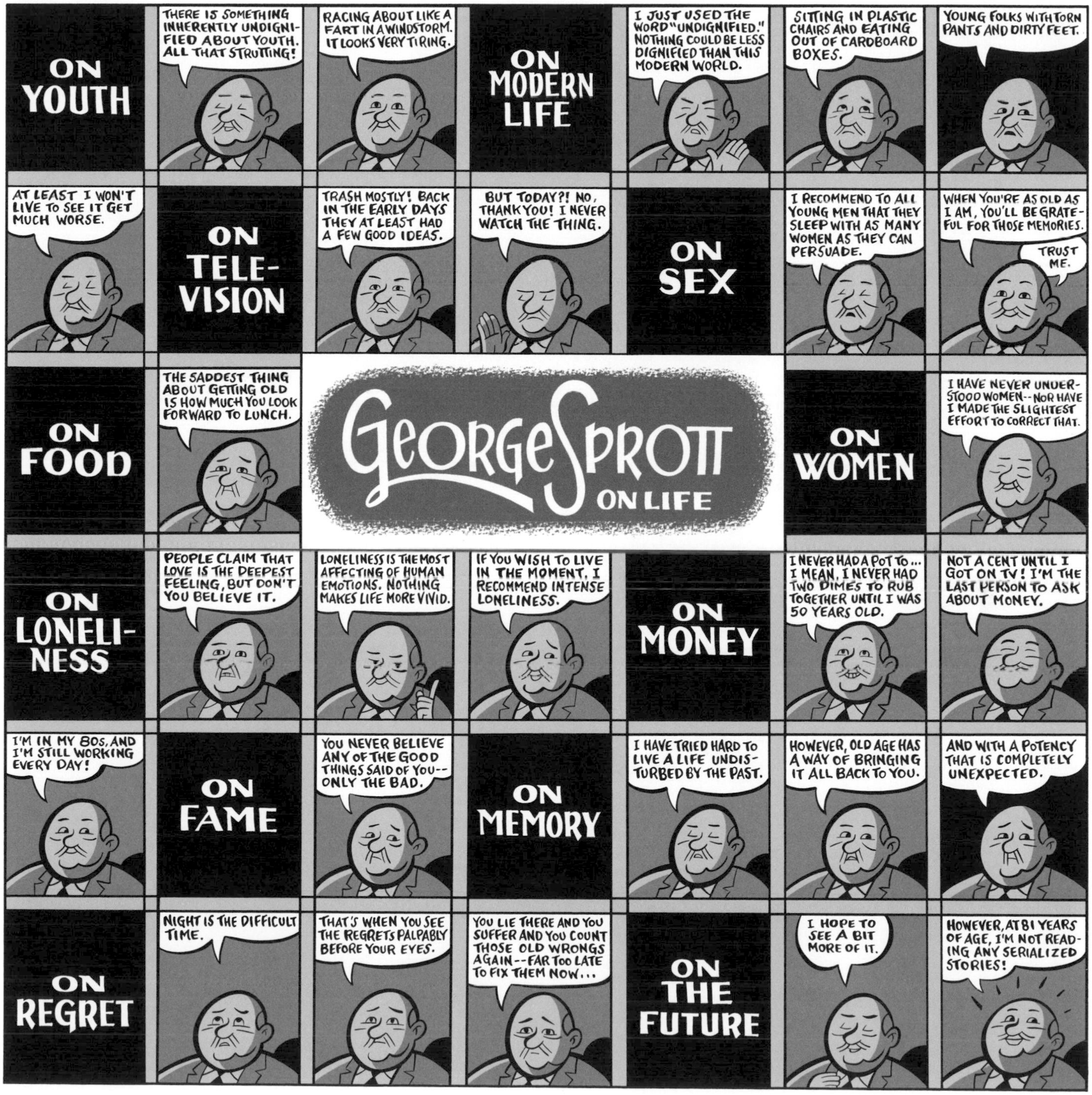

ON YOUTH
THERE IS SOMETHING INHERENTLY UNDIGNIFIED ABOUT YOUTH. ALL THAT STRUTTING!
RACING ABOUT LIKE A FART IN A WINDSTORM. IT LOOKS VERY TIRING.
ON MODERN LIFE
I JUST USED THE WORD "UNDIGNIFIED." NOTHING COULD BE LESS DIGNIFIED THAN THIS MODERN WORLD.
SITTING IN PLASTIC CHAIRS AND EATING OUT OF CARDBOARD BOXES.
YOUNG FOLKS WITH TORN PANTS AND DIRTY FEET.
AT LEAST I WON'T LIVE TO SEE IT GET MUCH WORSE.
ON TELE-VISION
TRASH MOSTLY! BACK IN THE EARLY DAYS THEY AT LEAST HAD A FEW GOOD IDEAS.
BUT TODAY?! NO, THANK YOU! I NEVER WATCH THE THING.
ON SEX
I RECOMMEND TO ALL YOUNG MEN THAT THEY SLEEP WITH AS MANY WOMEN AS THEY CAN PERSUADE.
WHEN YOU'RE AS OLD AS I AM, YOU'LL BE GRATEFUL FOR THOSE MEMORIES.
TRUST ME.
ON FOOD
THE SADDEST THING ABOUT GETTING OLD IS HOW MUCH YOU LOOK FORWARD TO LUNCH.
GEORGE SPROTT ON LIFE
ON WOMEN
I HAVE NEVER UNDERSTOOD WOMEN-- NOR HAVE I MADE THE SLIGHTEST EFFORT TO CORRECT THAT.
ON LONELI-NESS
PEOPLE CLAIM THAT LOVE IS THE DEEPEST FEELING, BUT DON'T YOU BELIEVE IT.
LONELINESS IS THE MOST AFFECTING OF HUMAN EMOTIONS. NOTHING MAKES LIFE MORE VIVID.
IF YOU WISH TO LIVE IN THE MOMENT, I RECOMMEND INTENSE LONELINESS.
ON MONEY
I NEVER HAD A POT TO... I MEAN, I NEVER HAD TWO DIMES TO RUB TOGETHER UNTIL I WAS 50 YEARS OLD.
NOT A CENT UNTIL I GOT ON TV! I'M THE LAST PERSON TO ASK ABOUT MONEY.
I'M IN MY 80s, AND I'M STILL WORKING EVERY DAY!
ON FAME
YOU NEVER BELIEVE ANY OF THE GOOD THINGS SAID OF YOU-- ONLY THE BAD.
ON MEMORY
I HAVE TRIED HARD TO LIVE A LIFE UNDISTURBED BY THE PAST.
HOWEVER, OLD AGE HAS A WAY OF BRINGING IT ALL BACK TO YOU.
AND WITH A POTENCY THAT IS COMPLETELY UNEXPECTED.
ON REGRET
NIGHT IS THE DIFFICULT TIME.
THAT'S WHEN YOU SEE THE REGRETS PALPABLY BEFORE YOUR EYES.
YOU LIE THERE AND YOU SUFFER AND YOU COUNT THOSE OLD WRONGS AGAIN--FAR TOO LATE TO FIX THEM NOW...
ON THE FUTURE
I HOPE TO SEE A BIT MORE OF IT.
HOWEVER, AT 81 YEARS OF AGE, I'M NOT READING ANY SERIALIZED STORIES!

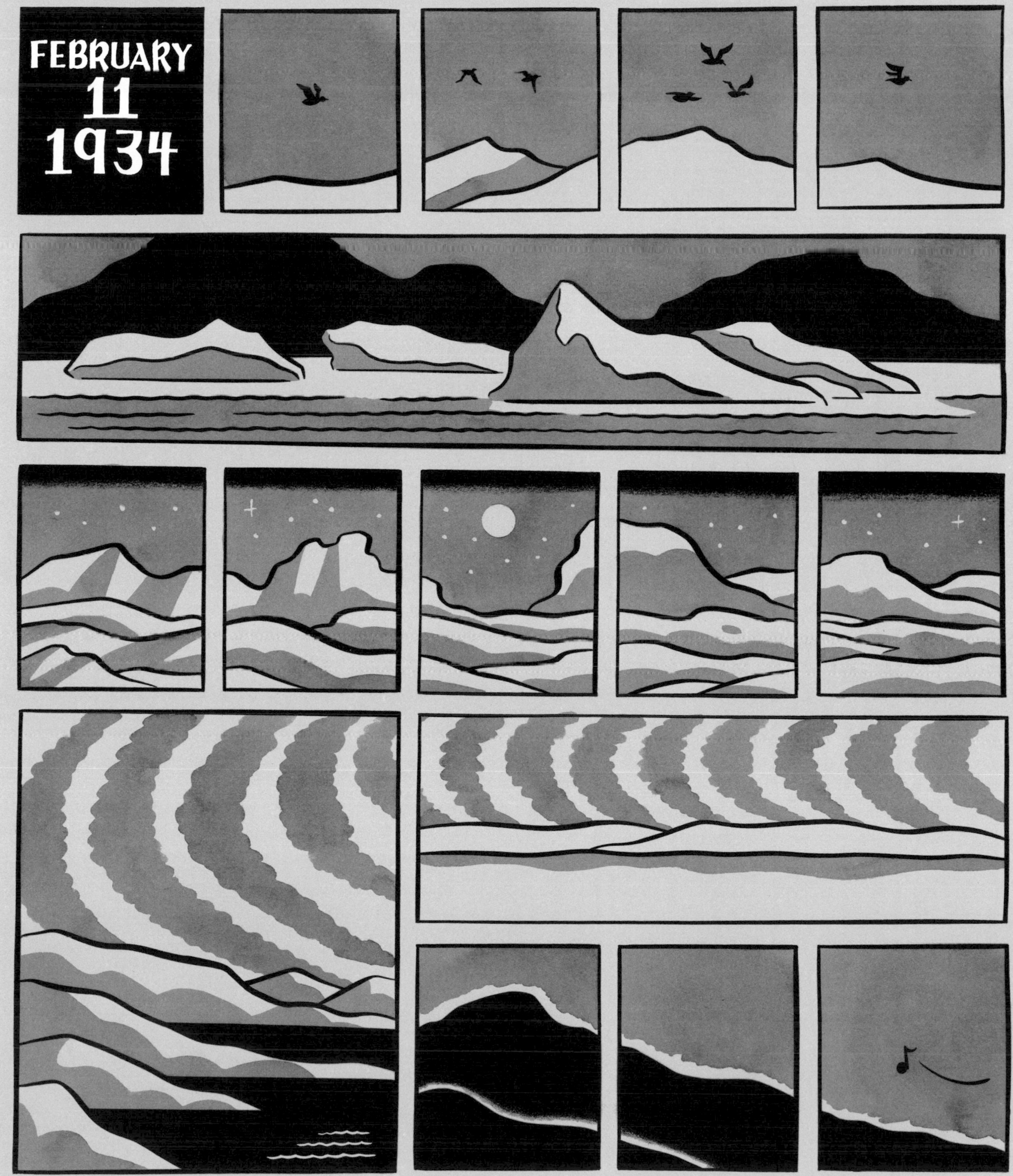
FEBRUARY
11
1934

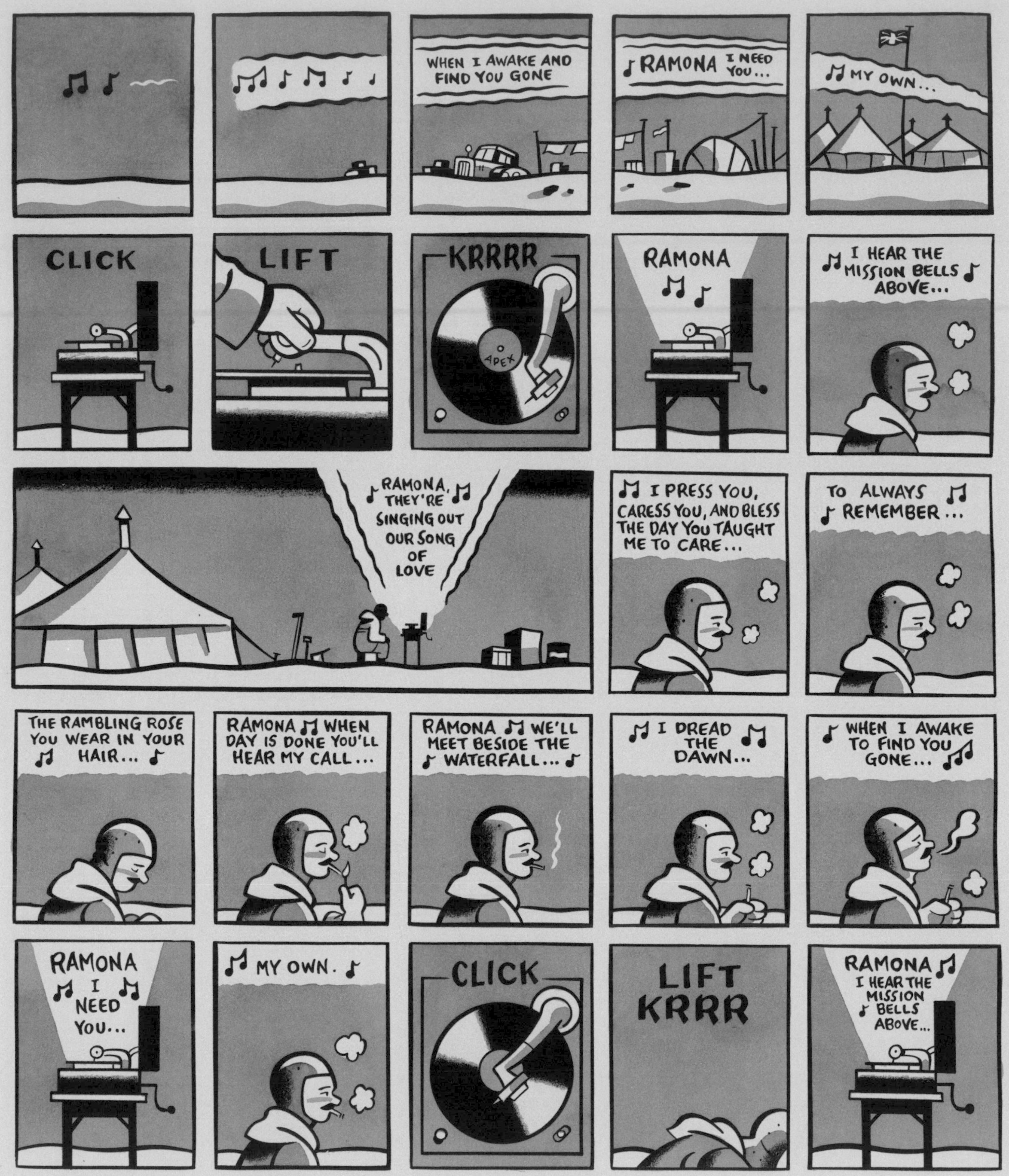

WHEN I AWAKE AND FIND YOU GONE
RAMONA I NEED YOU...
MY OWN...
CLICK
LIFT
KRRRR
APEX
RAMONA
I HEAR THE MISSION BELLS ABOVE...
RAMONA, THEY'RE SINGING OUT OUR SONG OF LOVE
I PRESS YOU, CARESS YOU, AND BLESS THE DAY YOU TAUGHT ME TO CARE...
TO ALWAYS REMEMBER...
THE RAMBLING ROSE YOU WEAR IN YOUR HAIR...
RAMONA WHEN DAY IS DONE YOU'LL HEAR MY CALL...
RAMONA WE'LL MEET BESIDE THE WATERFALL...
I DREAD THE DAWN...
WHEN I AWAKE TO FIND YOU GONE...
RAMONA I NEED YOU...
MY OWN.
CLICK
LIFT
KRRR
RAMONA I HEAR THE MISSION BELLS ABOVE...

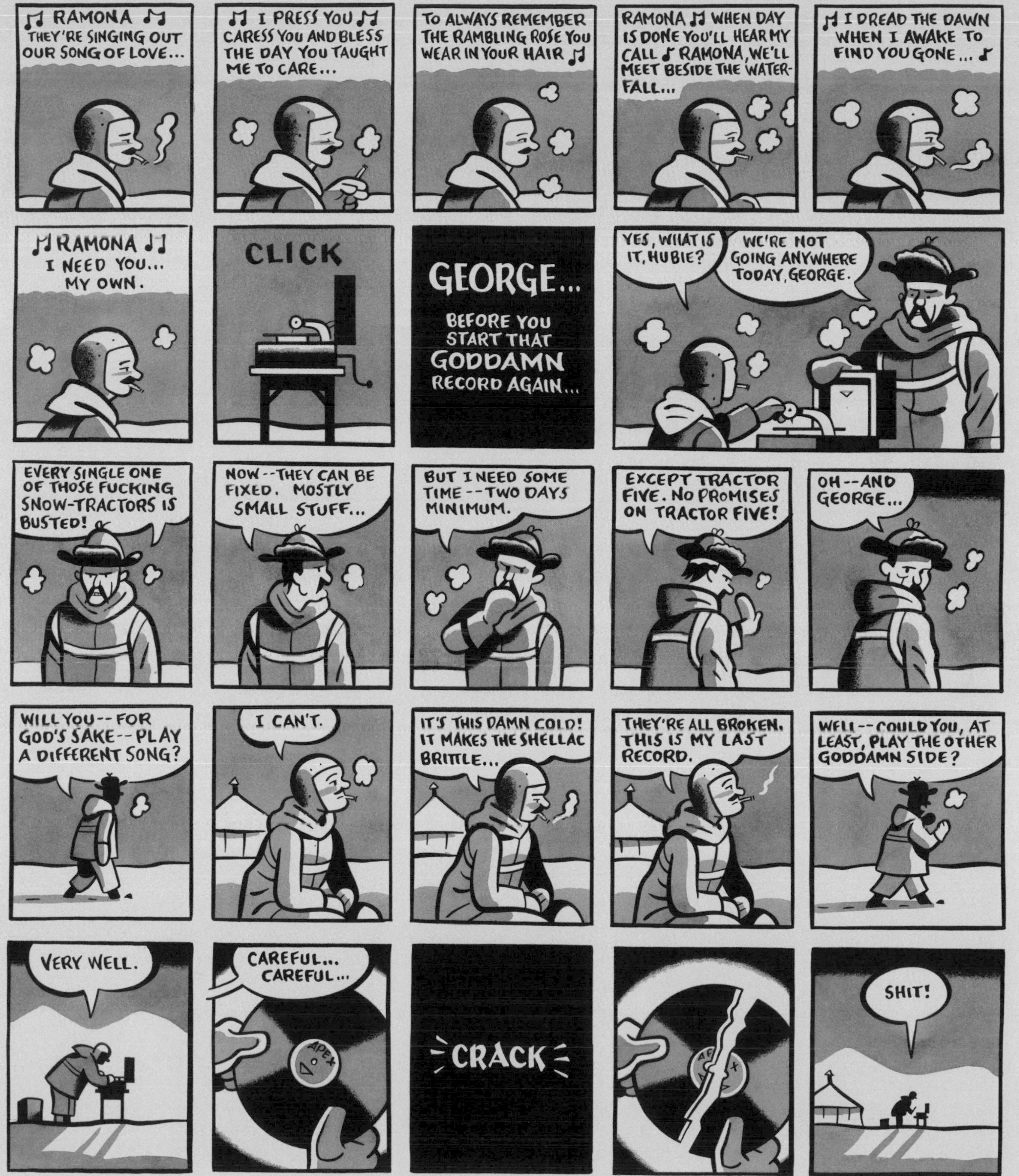
♫ RAMONA ♫ THEY'RE SINGING OUT OUR SONG OF LOVE...
♫ I PRESS YOU ♫ CARESS YOU AND BLESS THE DAY YOU TAUGHT ME TO CARE...
TO ALWAYS REMEMBER THE RAMBLING ROSE YOU WEAR IN YOUR HAIR ♫
RAMONA ♫ WHEN DAY IS DONE YOU'LL HEAR MY CALL ♪ RAMONA, WE'LL MEET BESIDE THE WATER-FALL...
♫ I DREAD THE DAWN WHEN I AWAKE TO FIND YOU GONE... ♪
♫ RAMONA ♫ I NEED YOU... MY OWN.
CLICK
GEORGE... BEFORE YOU START THAT GODDAMN RECORD AGAIN...
YES, WHAT IS IT, HUBIE?
WE'RE NOT GOING ANYWHERE TODAY, GEORGE.
EVERY SINGLE ONE OF THOSE FUCKING SNOW-TRACTORS IS BUSTED!
NOW--THEY CAN BE FIXED. MOSTLY SMALL STUFF...
BUT I NEED SOME TIME--TWO DAYS MINIMUM.
EXCEPT TRACTOR FIVE. NO PROMISES ON TRACTOR FIVE!
OH--AND GEORGE...
WILL YOU--FOR GOD'S SAKE--PLAY A DIFFERENT SONG?
I CAN'T.
IT'S THIS DAMN COLD! IT MAKES THE SHELLAC BRITTLE...
THEY'RE ALL BROKEN. THIS IS MY LAST RECORD.
WELL--COULD YOU, AT LEAST, PLAY THE OTHER GODDAMN SIDE?
VERY WELL.
CAREFUL... CAREFUL...
APEX
CRACK
SHIT!

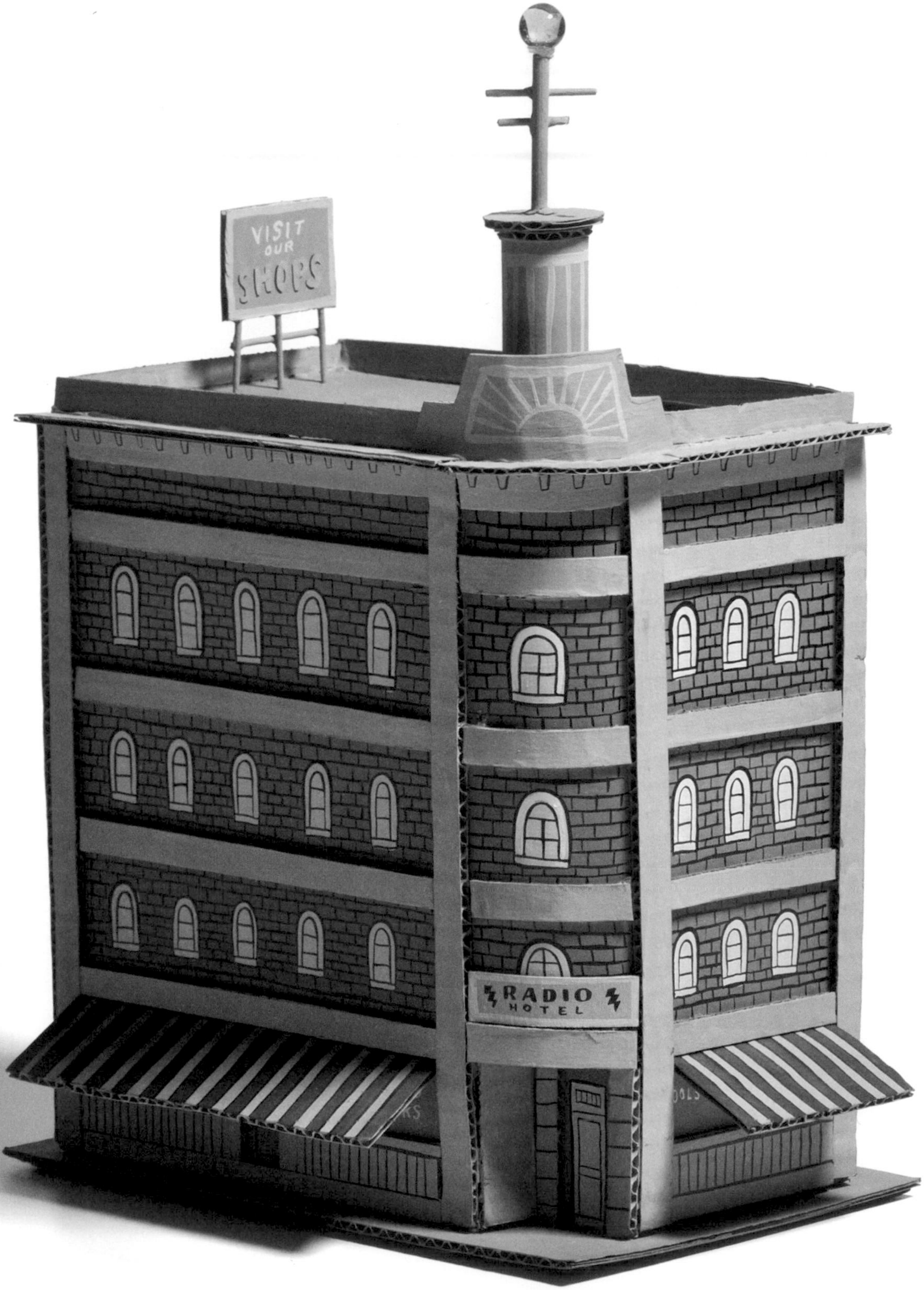
VISIT OUR SHOPS
RADIO HOTEL

5th FLOOR, END of THE HALL

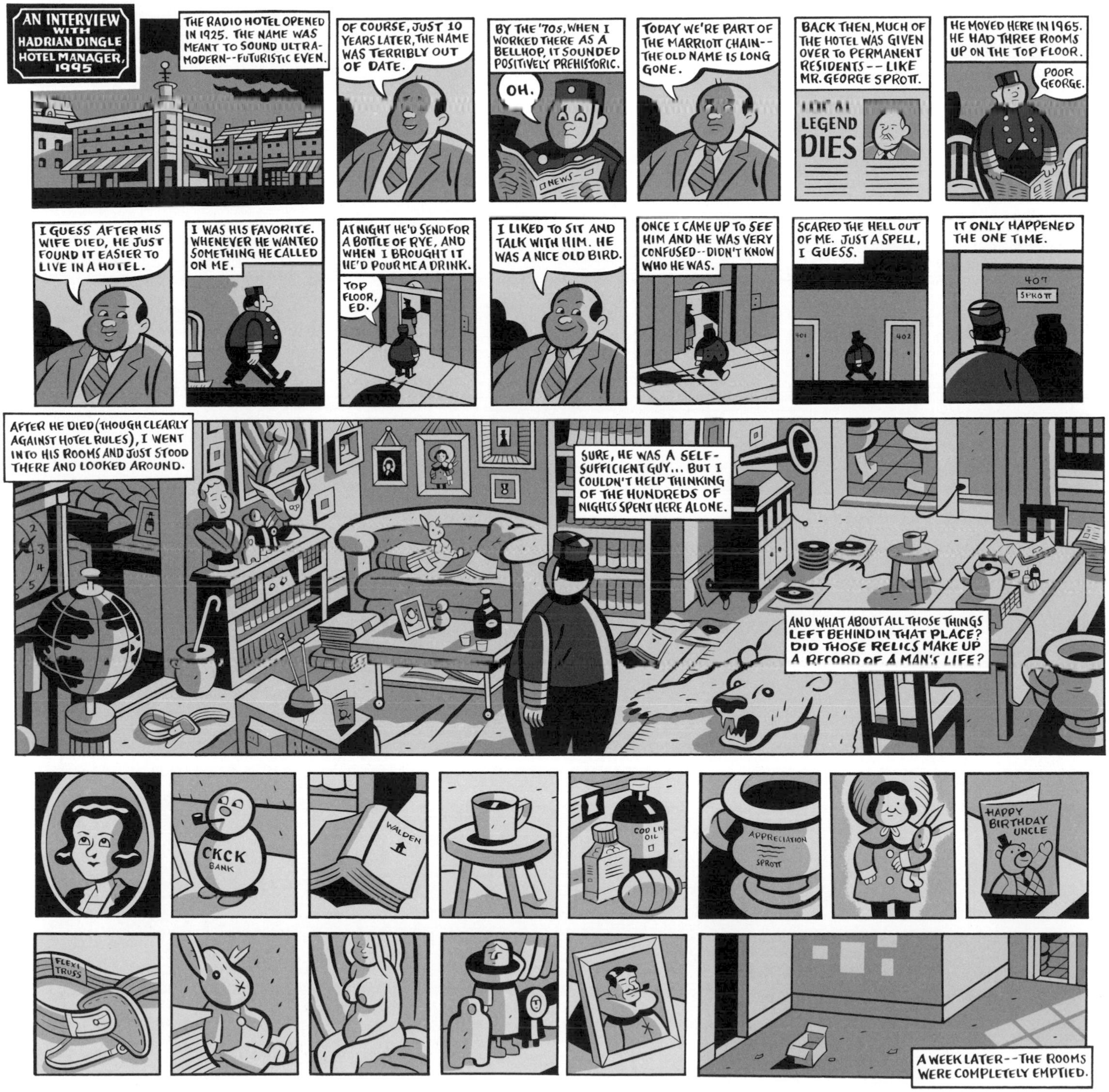

AN INTERVIEW WITH HADRIAN DINGLE
HOTEL MANAGER, 1995
THE RADIO HOTEL OPENED IN 1925. THE NAME WAS MEANT TO SOUND ULTRA-MODERN--FUTURISTIC EVEN.
OF COURSE, JUST 10 YEARS LATER, THE NAME WAS TERRIBLY OUT OF DATE.
BY THE '70S, WHEN I WORKED THERE AS A BELLHOP, IT SOUNDED POSITIVELY PREHISTORIC.
OH.
NEWS
TODAY WE'RE PART OF THE MARRIOTT CHAIN--THE OLD NAME IS LONG GONE.
BACK THEN, MUCH OF THE HOTEL WAS GIVEN OVER TO PERMANENT RESIDENTS--LIKE MR. GEORGE SPROTT.
LEGEND DIES
HE MOVED HERE IN 1965. HE HAD THREE ROOMS UP ON THE TOP FLOOR.
POOR GEORGE.
I GUESS AFTER HIS WIFE DIED, HE JUST FOUND IT EASIER TO LIVE IN A HOTEL.
I WAS HIS FAVORITE. WHENEVER HE WANTED SOMETHING HE CALLED ON ME.
AT NIGHT HE'D SEND FOR A BOTTLE OF RYE, AND WHEN I BROUGHT IT HE'D POUR ME A DRINK.
TOP FLOOR, ED.
I LIKED TO SIT AND TALK WITH HIM. HE WAS A NICE OLD BIRD.
ONCE I CAME UP TO SEE HIM AND HE WAS VERY CONFUSED--DIDN'T KNOW WHO HE WAS.
SCARED THE HELL OUT OF ME. JUST A SPELL, I GUESS.
401
402
IT ONLY HAPPENED THE ONE TIME.
407
SPROTT
AFTER HE DIED (THOUGH CLEARLY AGAINST HOTEL RULES), I WENT INTO HIS ROOMS AND JUST STOOD THERE AND LOOKED AROUND.
SURE, HE WAS A SELF-SUFFICIENT GUY... BUT I COULDN'T HELP THINKING OF THE HUNDREDS OF NIGHTS SPENT HERE ALONE.
AND WHAT ABOUT ALL THOSE THINGS LEFT BEHIND IN THAT PLACE? DID THOSE RELICS MAKE UP A RECORD OF A MAN'S LIFE?
CKCK BANK
WALDEN
OIL
APPRECIATION
SPROTT
HAPPY BIRTHDAY UNCLE
FLEXI TRUSS
A WEEK LATER--THE ROOMS WERE COMPLETELY EMPTIED.

A FUNNY DREAM

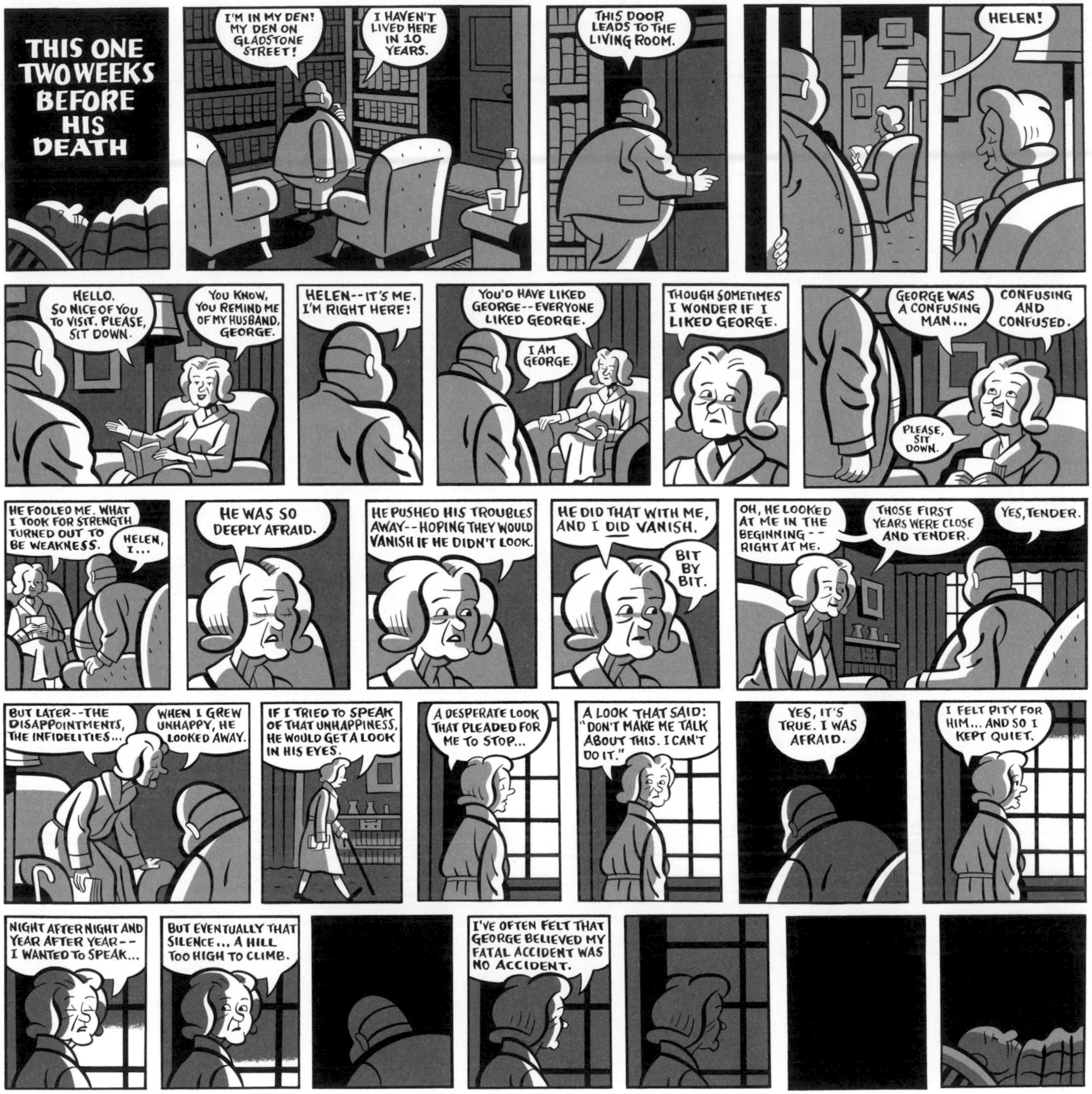
THIS ONE TWO WEEKS BEFORE HIS DEATH
I'M IN MY DEN! MY DEN ON GLADSTONE STREET!
I HAVEN'T LIVED HERE IN 10 YEARS.
THIS DOOR LEADS TO THE LIVING ROOM.
HELEN!
HELLO. SO NICE OF YOU TO VISIT. PLEASE, SIT DOWN.
YOU KNOW, YOU REMIND ME OF MY HUSBAND, GEORGE.
HELEN--IT'S ME. I'M RIGHT HERE!
YOU'D HAVE LIKED GEORGE--EVERYONE LIKED GEORGE.
I AM GEORGE.
THOUGH SOMETIMES I WONDER IF I LIKED GEORGE.
GEORGE WAS A CONFUSING MAN...
CONFUSING AND CONFUSED.
PLEASE, SIT DOWN.
HE FOOLED ME. WHAT I TOOK FOR STRENGTH TURNED OUT TO BE WEAKNESS.
HELEN, I...
HE WAS SO DEEPLY AFRAID.
HE PUSHED HIS TROUBLES AWAY--HOPING THEY WOULD VANISH IF HE DIDN'T LOOK.
HE DID THAT WITH ME, AND I DID VANISH.
BIT BY BIT.
OH, HE LOOKED AT ME IN THE BEGINNING--RIGHT AT ME.
THOSE FIRST YEARS WERE CLOSE AND TENDER.
YES, TENDER.
BUT LATER--THE DISAPPOINTMENTS, THE INFIDELITIES...
WHEN I GREW UNHAPPY, HE LOOKED AWAY.
IF I TRIED TO SPEAK OF THAT UNHAPPINESS, HE WOULD GET A LOOK IN HIS EYES.
A DESPERATE LOOK THAT PLEADED FOR ME TO STOP...
A LOOK THAT SAID: "DON'T MAKE ME TALK ABOUT THIS. I CAN'T DO IT."
YES, IT'S TRUE. I WAS AFRAID.
I FELT PITY FOR HIM... AND SO I KEPT QUIET.
NIGHT AFTER NIGHT AND YEAR AFTER YEAR--I WANTED TO SPEAK...
BUT EVENTUALLY THAT SILENCE... A HILL TOO HIGH TO CLIMB.
I'VE OFTEN FELT THAT GEORGE BELIEVED MY FATAL ACCIDENT WAS NO ACCIDENT.

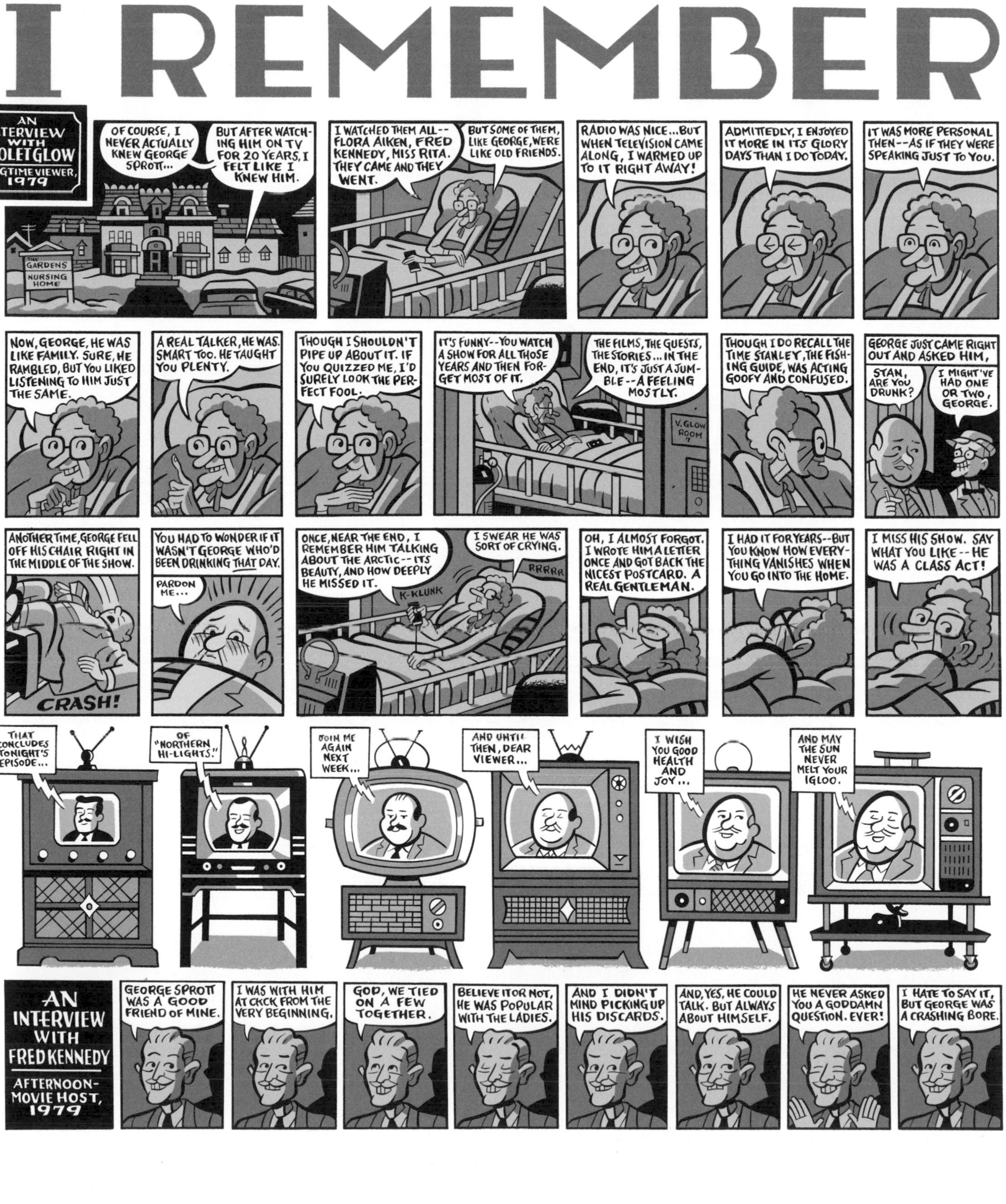
I REMEMBER
AN INTERVIEW WITH VIOLET GLOW
LONGTIME VIEWER, 1979
OF COURSE, I NEVER ACTUALLY KNEW GEORGE SPROTT...
BUT AFTER WATCHING HIM ON TV FOR 20 YEARS, I FELT LIKE I KNEW HIM.
THE GARDENS NURSING HOME
I WATCHED THEM ALL-- FLORA AIKEN, FRED KENNEDY, MISS RITA. THEY CAME AND THEY WENT.
BUT SOME OF THEM, LIKE GEORGE, WERE LIKE OLD FRIENDS.
RADIO WAS NICE...BUT WHEN TELEVISION CAME ALONG, I WARMED UP TO IT RIGHT AWAY!
ADMITTEDLY, I ENJOYED IT MORE IN ITS GLORY DAYS THAN I DO TODAY.
IT WAS MORE PERSONAL THEN--AS IF THEY WERE SPEAKING JUST TO YOU.
NOW, GEORGE, HE WAS LIKE FAMILY. SURE, HE RAMBLED, BUT YOU LIKED LISTENING TO HIM JUST THE SAME.
A REAL TALKER, HE WAS. SMART TOO. HE TAUGHT YOU PLENTY.
THOUGH I SHOULDN'T PIPE UP ABOUT IT. IF YOU QUIZZED ME, I'D SURELY LOOK THE PERFECT FOOL.
IT'S FUNNY--YOU WATCH A SHOW FOR ALL THOSE YEARS AND THEN FORGET MOST OF IT.
THE FILMS, THE GUESTS, THE STORIES... IN THE END, IT'S JUST A JUMBLE--A FEELING MOSTLY.
V. GLOW ROOM
THOUGH I DO RECALL THE TIME STANLEY, THE FISHING GUIDE, WAS ACTING GOOFY AND CONFUSED.
GEORGE JUST CAME RIGHT OUT AND ASKED HIM,
STAN, ARE YOU DRUNK?
I MIGHT'VE HAD ONE OR TWO, GEORGE.
ANOTHER TIME, GEORGE FELL OFF HIS CHAIR RIGHT IN THE MIDDLE OF THE SHOW.
CRASH!
YOU HAD TO WONDER IF IT WASN'T GEORGE WHO'D BEEN DRINKING THAT DAY.
PARDON ME...
ONCE, NEAR THE END, I REMEMBER HIM TALKING ABOUT THE ARCTIC--ITS BEAUTY, AND HOW DEEPLY HE MISSED IT.
I SWEAR HE WAS SORT OF CRYING.
RRRRR
K-KLUNK
OH, I ALMOST FORGOT. I WROTE HIM A LETTER ONCE AND GOT BACK THE NICEST POSTCARD. A REAL GENTLEMAN.
I HAD IT FOR YEARS--BUT YOU KNOW HOW EVERYTHING VANISHES WHEN YOU GO INTO THE HOME.
I MISS HIS SHOW. SAY WHAT YOU LIKE--HE WAS A CLASS ACT!
THAT CONCLUDES TONIGHT'S EPISODE...
OF "NORTHERN HI-LIGHTS."
JOIN ME AGAIN NEXT WEEK...
AND UNTIL THEN, DEAR VIEWER...
I WISH YOU GOOD HEALTH AND JOY...
AND MAY THE SUN NEVER MELT YOUR IGLOO.
AN INTERVIEW WITH FRED KENNEDY
AFTERNOON-MOVIE HOST, 1979
GEORGE SPROTT WAS A GOOD FRIEND OF MINE.
I WAS WITH HIM AT CKCK FROM THE VERY BEGINNING.
GOD, WE TIED ON A FEW TOGETHER.
BELIEVE IT OR NOT, HE WAS POPULAR WITH THE LADIES.
AND I DIDN'T MIND PICKING UP HIS DISCARDS.
AND, YES, HE COULD TALK. BUT ALWAYS ABOUT HIMSELF.
HE NEVER ASKED YOU A GODDAMN QUESTION. EVER!
I HATE TO SAY IT, BUT GEORGE WAS A CRASHING BORE.

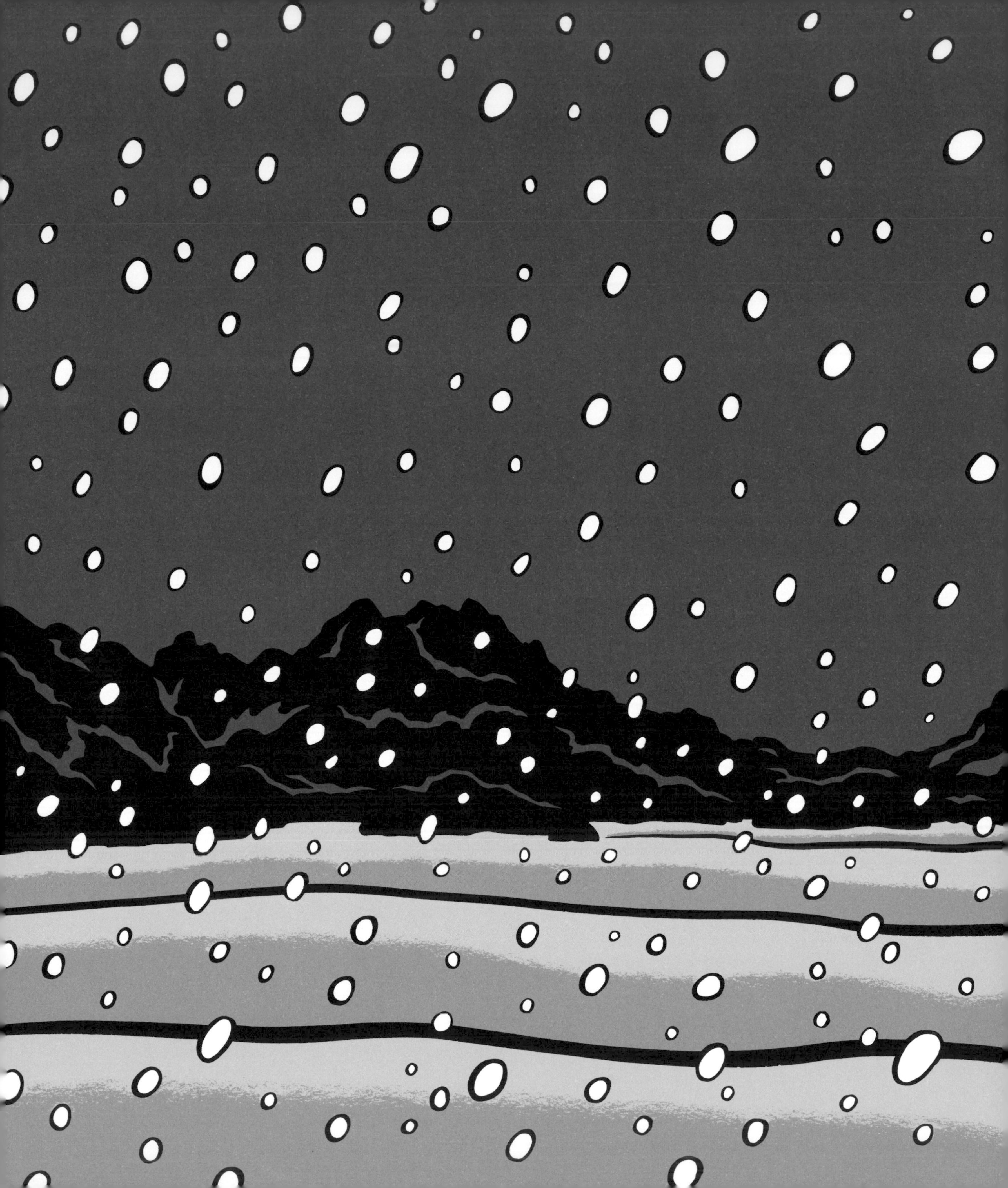

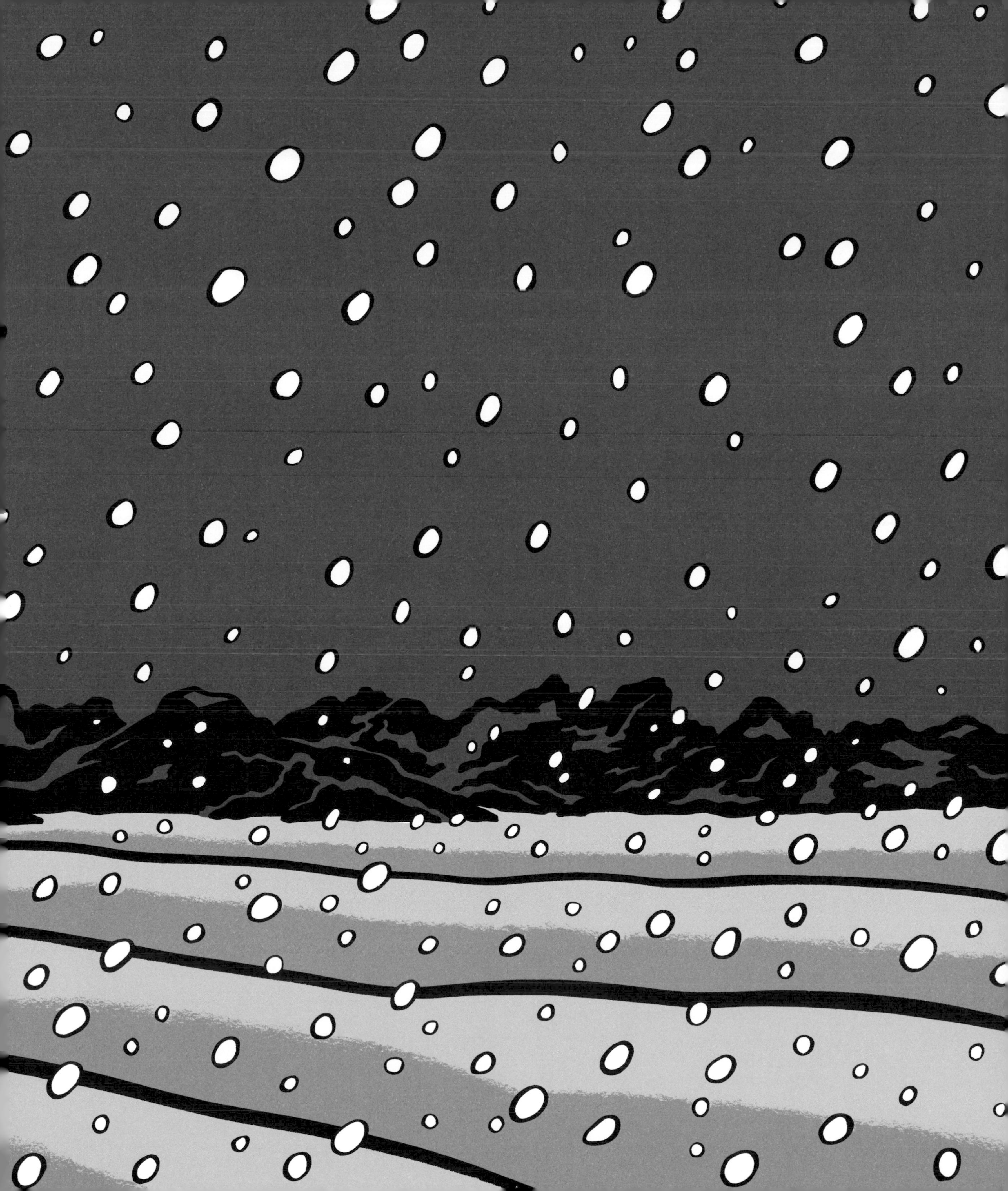

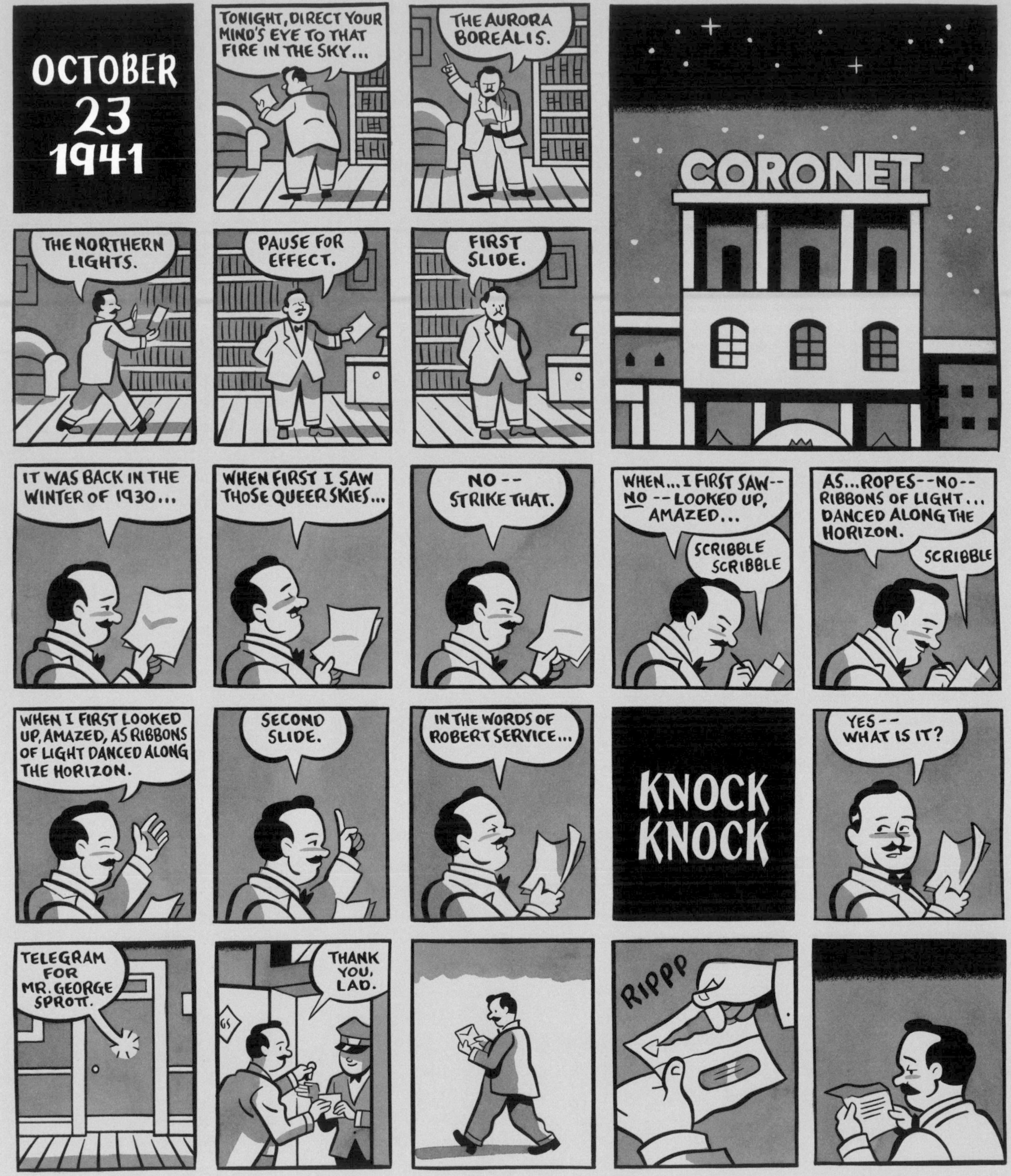
OCTOBER
23
1941
TONIGHT, DIRECT YOUR MIND'S EYE TO THAT FIRE IN THE SKY...
THE AURORA BOREALIS.
CORONET
THE NORTHERN LIGHTS.
PAUSE FOR EFFECT.
FIRST SLIDE.
IT WAS BACK IN THE WINTER OF 1930...
WHEN FIRST I SAW THOSE QUEER SKIES...
NO -- STRIKE THAT.
WHEN... I FIRST SAW-- NO -- LOOKED UP, AMAZED...
SCRIBBLE SCRIBBLE
AS... ROPES--NO-- RIBBONS OF LIGHT... DANCED ALONG THE HORIZON.
SCRIBBLE
WHEN I FIRST LOOKED UP, AMAZED, AS RIBBONS OF LIGHT DANCED ALONG THE HORIZON.
SECOND SLIDE.
IN THE WORDS OF ROBERT SERVICE...
KNOCK KNOCK
YES -- WHAT IS IT?
TELEGRAM FOR MR. GEORGE SPROTT.
GS
THANK YOU, LAD.
RIPPP

CANADIAN NATIONAL
TELEGRAM
5377
A7
TO: MR. G. SPROTT
DOMINION
FROM: 45 LAKE ST.
GALT, ONTARIO
IT IS WITH DEEP REGRET THAT I INFORM YOU OF YOUR FATHER'S DEATH.
HE PASSED LAST NIGHT AT 10:45 P.M., WITHOUT SUFFERING, WHILE IN A PROFOUND SLEEP.
HIS WIFE OF SOME 50 YEARS WAS BY HIS BEDSIDE.
YOU MAY TAKE SOME SOLACE FROM THE TRANQUILITY OF HIS EXIT FROM THIS WORLD.
YOUR MOTHER, THOUGH GRIEF STRICKEN, IS BEARING UP WELL.
PLEASE TELEGRAPH YOUR ARRIVAL TIME.
MY REGRETS,
DR. L.A. GARRISON
DEEP REGRET
R'S DEATH.
LAST NIGHT
PFT
5 P.M., WI
ND SLEEP.
SOLACE FR
THIS WORLD
GH GRIEF
TRANQUILIT

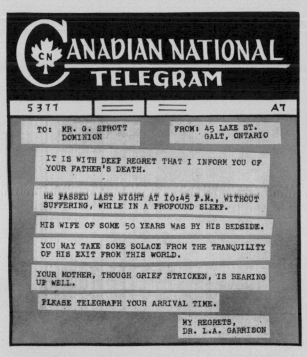

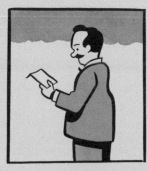

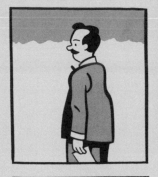

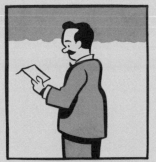

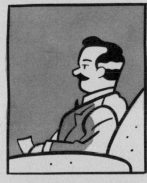

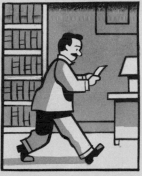

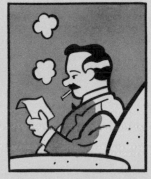

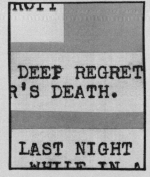

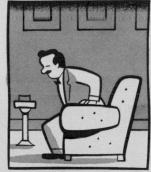

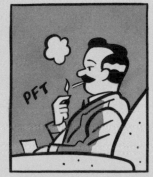

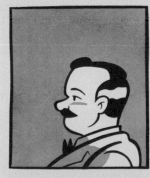

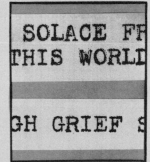

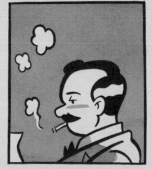

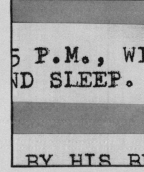

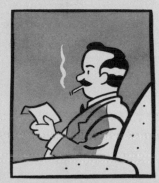

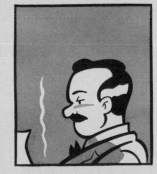

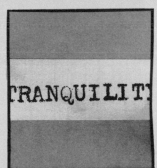

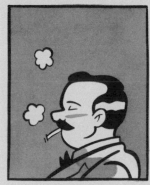

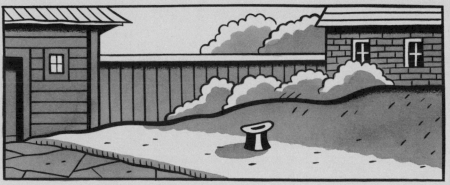

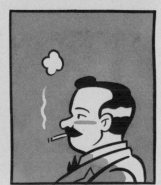

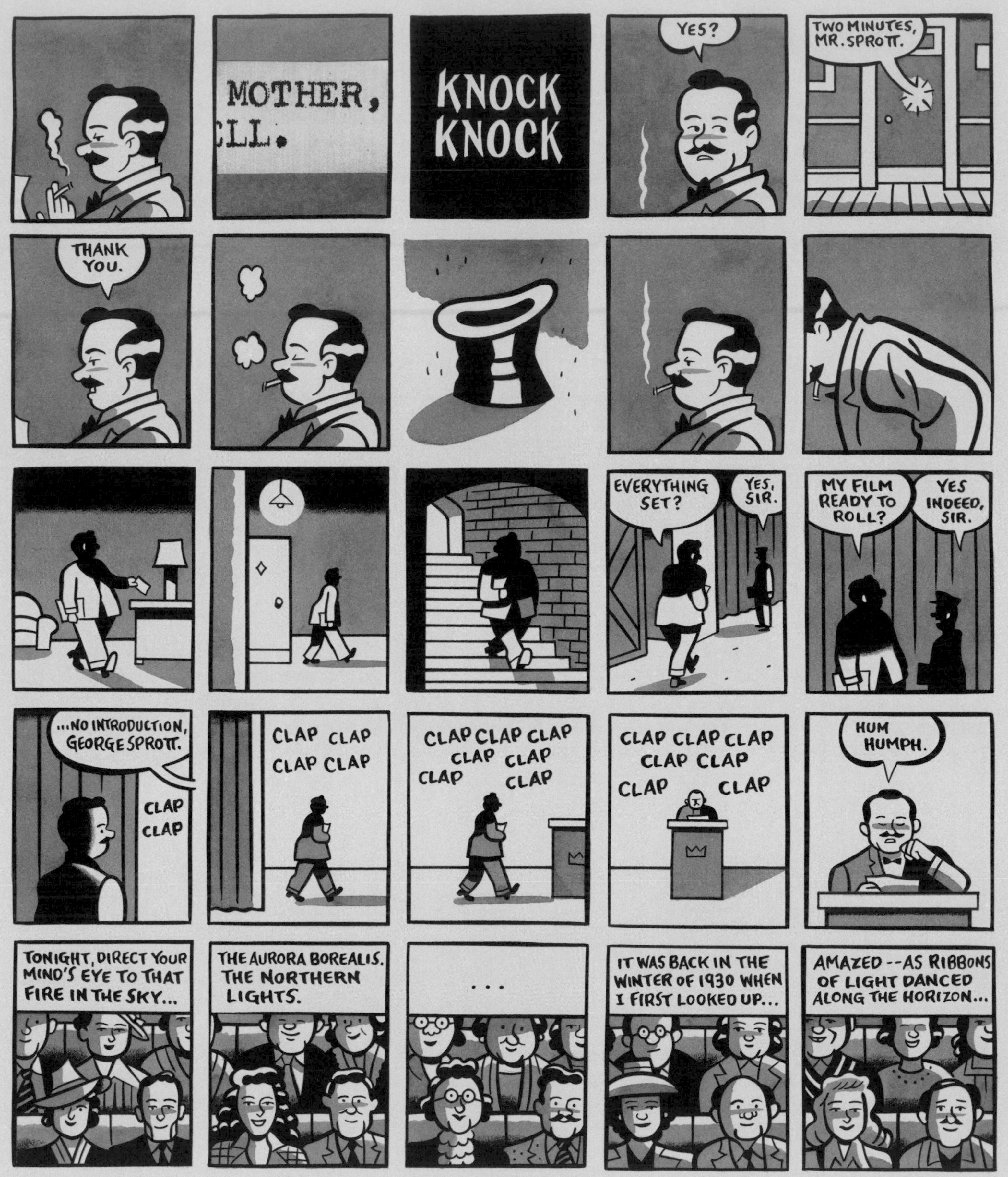
MOTHER,
LL.
KNOCK KNOCK
YES?
TWO MINUTES, MR. SPROTT.
THANK YOU.
EVERYTHING SET?
YES, SIR.
MY FILM READY TO ROLL?
YES INDEED, SIR.
...NO INTRODUCTION, GEORGE SPROTT.
CLAP CLAP
CLAP CLAP CLAP CLAP
CLAP CLAP CLAP CLAP CLAP CLAP CLAP
CLAP CLAP CLAP CLAP CLAP CLAP CLAP
HUM HUMPH.
TONIGHT, DIRECT YOUR MIND'S EYE TO THAT FIRE IN THE SKY...
THE AURORA BOREALIS. THE NORTHERN LIGHTS.
...
IT WAS BACK IN THE WINTER OF 1930 WHEN I FIRST LOOKED UP...
AMAZED--AS RIBBONS OF LIGHT DANCED ALONG THE HORIZON...

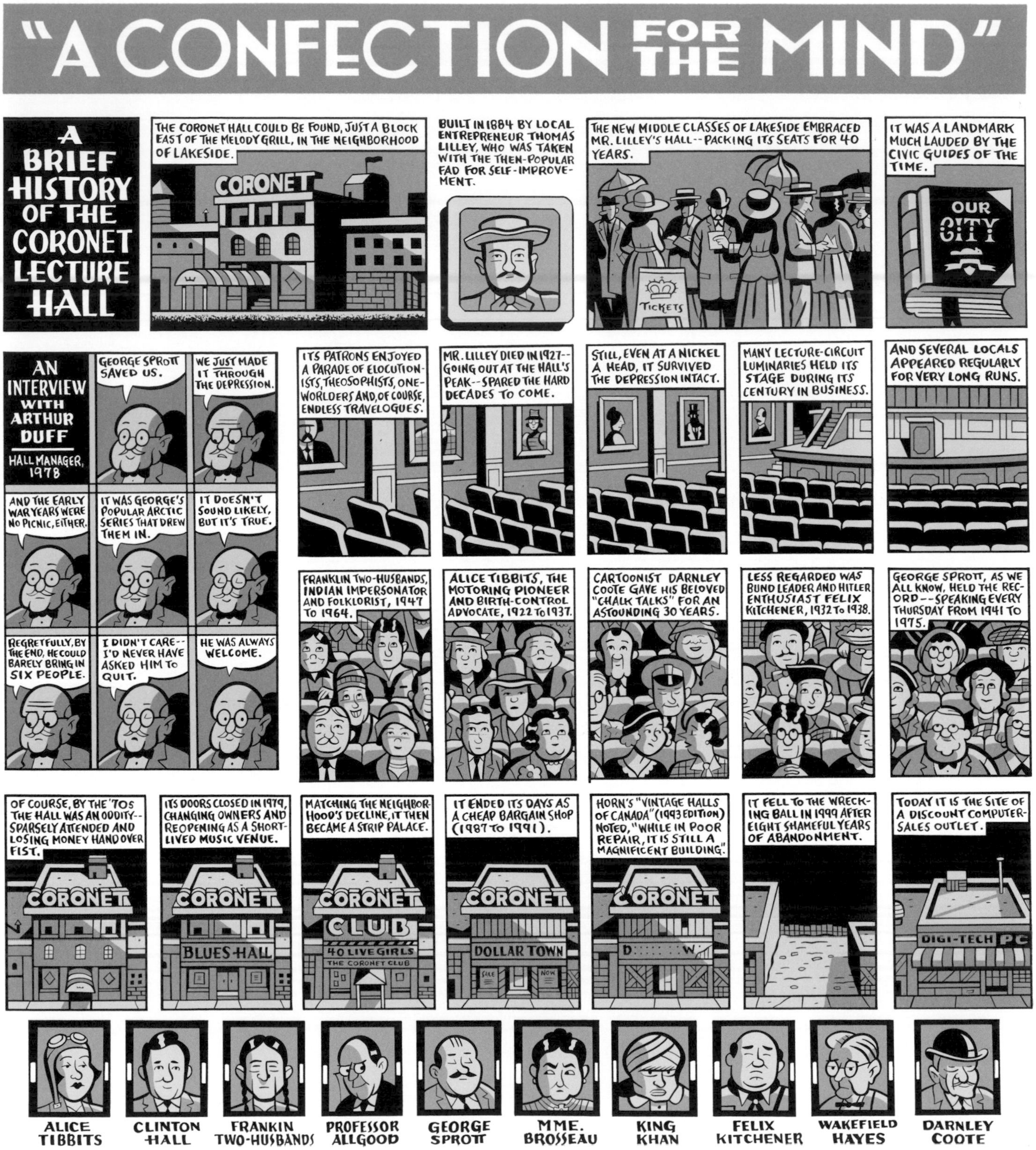
"A CONFECTION FOR THE MIND"
A BRIEF HISTORY OF THE CORONET LECTURE HALL
THE CORONET HALL COULD BE FOUND, JUST A BLOCK EAST OF THE MELODY GRILL, IN THE NEIGHBORHOOD OF LAKESIDE.
CORONET
BUILT IN 1884 BY LOCAL ENTREPRENEUR THOMAS LILLEY, WHO WAS TAKEN WITH THE THEN-POPULAR FAD FOR SELF-IMPROVEMENT.
THE NEW MIDDLE CLASSES OF LAKESIDE EMBRACED MR. LILLEY'S HALL--PACKING ITS SEATS FOR 40 YEARS.
TICKETS
IT WAS A LANDMARK MUCH LAUDED BY THE CIVIC GUIDES OF THE TIME.
OUR CITY
AN INTERVIEW WITH ARTHUR DUFF
HALL MANAGER, 1978
GEORGE SPROTT SAVED US.
WE JUST MADE IT THROUGH THE DEPRESSION.
AND THE EARLY WAR YEARS WERE NO PICNIC, EITHER.
IT WAS GEORGE'S POPULAR ARCTIC SERIES THAT DREW THEM IN.
IT DOESN'T SOUND LIKELY, BUT IT'S TRUE.
REGRETFULLY, BY THE END, HE COULD BARELY BRING IN SIX PEOPLE.
I DIDN'T CARE--I'D NEVER HAVE ASKED HIM TO QUIT.
HE WAS ALWAYS WELCOME.
ITS PATRONS ENJOYED A PARADE OF ELOCUTIONISTS, THEOSOPHISTS, ONE-WORLDERS AND, OF COURSE, ENDLESS TRAVELOGUES.
MR. LILLEY DIED IN 1927--GOING OUT AT THE HALL'S PEAK--SPARED THE HARD DECADES TO COME.
STILL, EVEN AT A NICKEL A HEAD, IT SURVIVED THE DEPRESSION INTACT.
MANY LECTURE-CIRCUIT LUMINARIES HELD ITS STAGE DURING ITS CENTURY IN BUSINESS.
AND SEVERAL LOCALS APPEARED REGULARLY FOR VERY LONG RUNS.
FRANKLIN TWO-HUSBANDS, INDIAN IMPERSONATOR AND FOLKLORIST, 1947 TO 1964.
ALICE TIBBITS, THE MOTORING PIONEER AND BIRTH-CONTROL ADVOCATE, 1922 TO 1937.
CARTOONIST DARNLEY COOTE GAVE HIS BELOVED "CHALK TALKS" FOR AN ASTOUNDING 30 YEARS.
LESS REGARDED WAS BUND LEADER AND HITLER ENTHUSIAST FELIX KITCHENER, 1932 TO 1938.
GEORGE SPROTT, AS WE ALL KNOW, HELD THE RECORD--SPEAKING EVERY THURSDAY FROM 1941 TO 1975.
OF COURSE, BY THE '70S THE HALL WAS AN ODDITY--SPARSELY ATTENDED AND LOSING MONEY HAND OVER FIST.
CORONET
ITS DOORS CLOSED IN 1979, CHANGING OWNERS AND REOPENING AS A SHORT-LIVED MUSIC VENUE.
CORONET
BLUES HALL
MATCHING THE NEIGHBORHOOD'S DECLINE, IT THEN BECAME A STRIP PALACE.
CORONET CLUB
40 LIVE GIRLS
THE CORONET CLUB
IT ENDED ITS DAYS AS A CHEAP BARGAIN SHOP (1987 TO 1991).
CORONET
DOLLAR TOWN
SALE
NOW
HORN'S "VINTAGE HALLS OF CANADA" (1993 EDITION) NOTED, "WHILE IN POOR REPAIR, IT IS STILL A MAGNIFICENT BUILDING."
CORONET
IT FELL TO THE WRECKING BALL IN 1999 AFTER EIGHT SHAMEFUL YEARS OF ABANDONMENT.
TODAY IT IS THE SITE OF A DISCOUNT COMPUTER-SALES OUTLET.
DIGI-TECH PC
ALICE TIBBITS
CLINTON HALL
FRANKIN TWO-HUSBANDS
PROFESSOR ALLGOOD
GEORGE SPROTT
MME. BROSSEAU
KING KHAN
FELIX KITCHENER
WAKEFIELD HAYES
DARNLEY COOTE

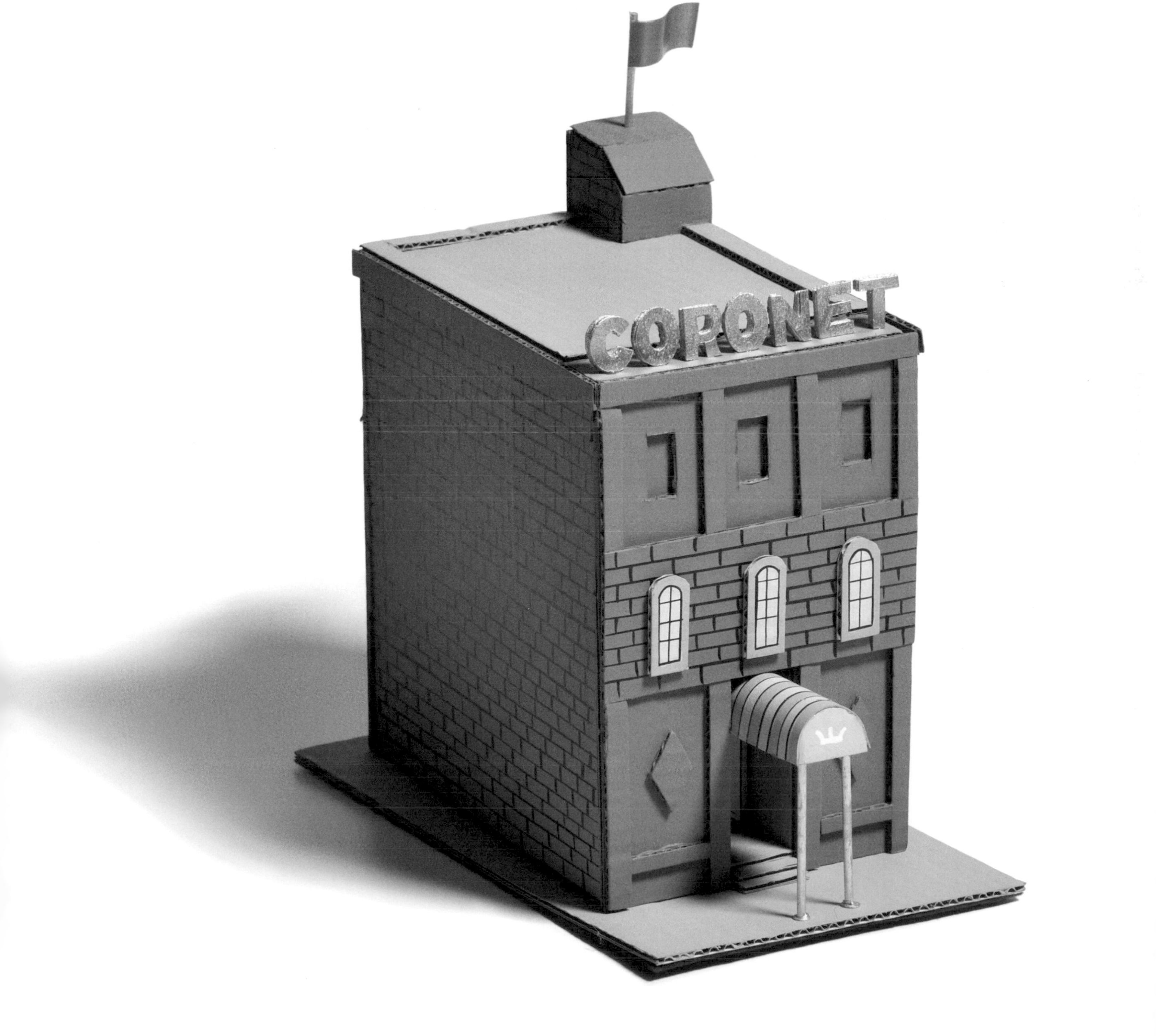
CORONET

8:25 PM, OCTOBER 9, 1975

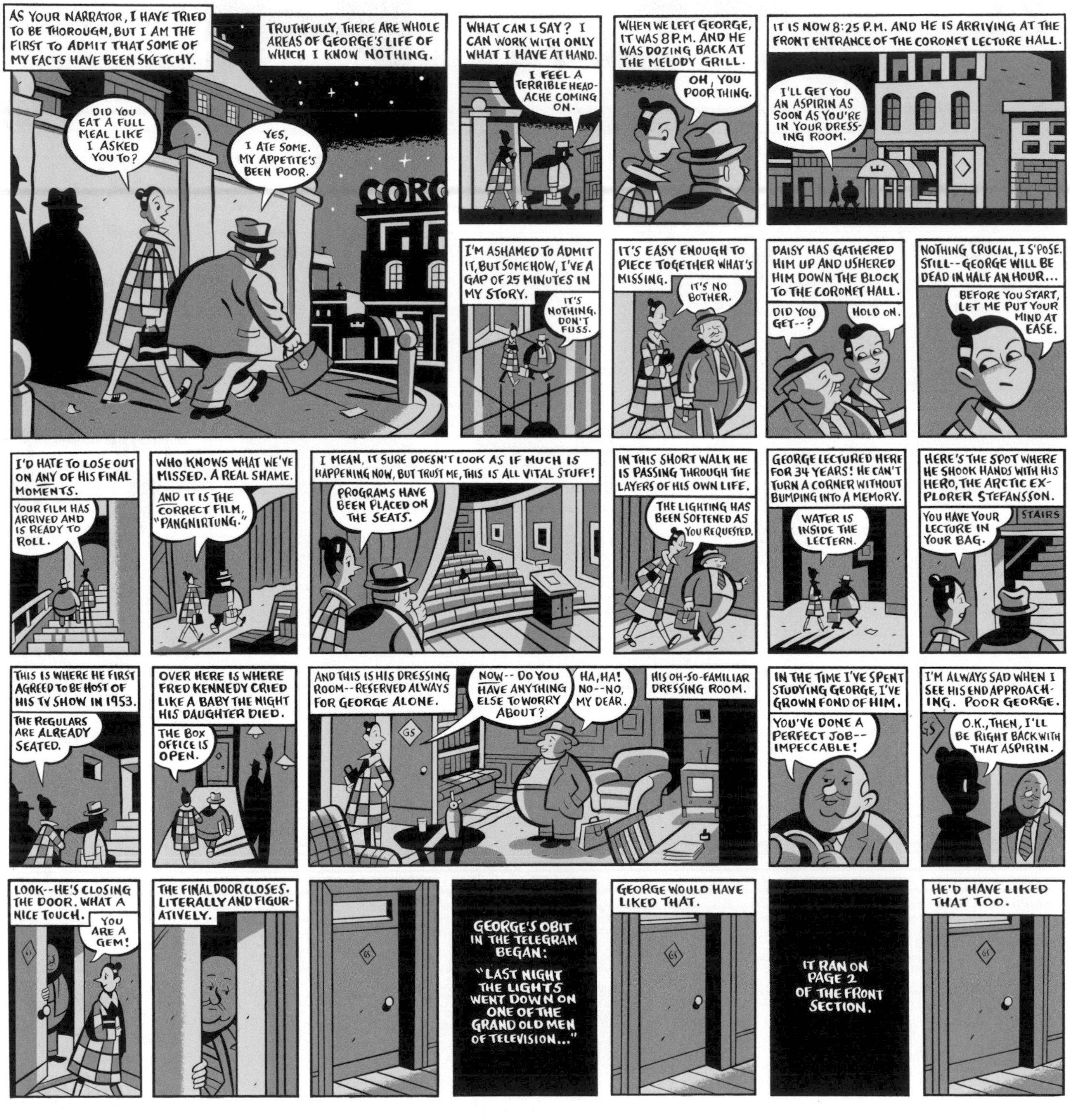

AS YOUR NARRATOR, I HAVE TRIED TO BE THOROUGH, BUT I AM THE FIRST TO ADMIT THAT SOME OF MY FACTS HAVE BEEN SKETCHY.
TRUTHFULLY, THERE ARE WHOLE AREAS OF GEORGE'S LIFE OF WHICH I KNOW NOTHING.
DID YOU EAT A FULL MEAL LIKE I ASKED YOU TO?
YES, I ATE SOME. MY APPETITE'S BEEN POOR.
CORO
WHAT CAN I SAY? I CAN WORK WITH ONLY WHAT I HAVE AT HAND.
I FEEL A TERRIBLE HEAD-ACHE COMING ON.
WHEN WE LEFT GEORGE, IT WAS 8 P.M. AND HE WAS DOZING BACK AT THE MELODY GRILL.
OH, YOU POOR THING.
IT IS NOW 8:25 P.M. AND HE IS ARRIVING AT THE FRONT ENTRANCE OF THE CORONET LECTURE HALL.
I'LL GET YOU AN ASPIRIN AS SOON AS YOU'RE IN YOUR DRESS-ING ROOM.
I'M ASHAMED TO ADMIT IT, BUT SOMEHOW, I'VE A GAP OF 25 MINUTES IN MY STORY.
IT'S NOTHING. DON'T FUSS.
IT'S EASY ENOUGH TO PIECE TOGETHER WHAT'S MISSING.
IT'S NO BOTHER.
DAISY HAS GATHERED HIM UP AND USHERED HIM DOWN THE BLOCK TO THE CORONET HALL.
DID YOU GET--?
HOLD ON.
NOTHING CRUCIAL, I S'POSE. STILL--GEORGE WILL BE DEAD IN HALF AN HOUR...
BEFORE YOU START, LET ME PUT YOUR MIND AT EASE.
I'D HATE TO LOSE OUT ON ANY OF HIS FINAL MOMENTS.
YOUR FILM HAS ARRIVED AND IS READY TO ROLL.
WHO KNOWS WHAT WE'VE MISSED. A REAL SHAME.
AND IT IS THE CORRECT FILM, "PANGNIRTUNG."
I MEAN, IT SURE DOESN'T LOOK AS IF MUCH IS HAPPENING NOW, BUT TRUST ME, THIS IS ALL VITAL STUFF!
PROGRAMS HAVE BEEN PLACED ON THE SEATS.
IN THIS SHORT WALK HE IS PASSING THROUGH THE LAYERS OF HIS OWN LIFE.
THE LIGHTING HAS BEEN SOFTENED AS YOU REQUESTED.
GEORGE LECTURED HERE FOR 34 YEARS! HE CAN'T TURN A CORNER WITHOUT BUMPING INTO A MEMORY.
WATER IS INSIDE THE LECTERN.
HERE'S THE SPOT WHERE HE SHOOK HANDS WITH HIS HERO, THE ARCTIC EX-PLORER STEFANSSON.
YOU HAVE YOUR LECTURE IN YOUR BAG.
STAIRS
THIS IS WHERE HE FIRST AGREED TO BE HOST OF HIS TV SHOW IN 1953.
THE REGULARS ARE ALREADY SEATED.
OVER HERE IS WHERE FRED KENNEDY CRIED LIKE A BABY THE NIGHT HIS DAUGHTER DIED.
THE BOX OFFICE IS OPEN.
AND THIS IS HIS DRESSING ROOM--RESERVED ALWAYS FOR GEORGE ALONE.
NOW--DO YOU HAVE ANYTHING ELSE TO WORRY ABOUT?
HA, HA! NO--NO, MY DEAR.
HIS OH-SO-FAMILIAR DRESSING ROOM.
GS
IN THE TIME I'VE SPENT STUDYING GEORGE, I'VE GROWN FOND OF HIM.
YOU'VE DONE A PERFECT JOB--IMPECCABLE!
I'M ALWAYS SAD WHEN I SEE HIS END APPROACH-ING. POOR GEORGE.
O.K., THEN, I'LL BE RIGHT BACK WITH THAT ASPIRIN.
GS
LOOK--HE'S CLOSING THE DOOR. WHAT A NICE TOUCH.
YOU ARE A GEM!
THE FINAL DOOR CLOSES. LITERALLY AND FIGUR-ATIVELY.
GEORGE'S OBIT IN THE TELEGRAM BEGAN:
"LAST NIGHT THE LIGHTS WENT DOWN ON ONE OF THE GRAND OLD MEN OF TELEVISION..."
GEORGE WOULD HAVE LIKED THAT.
IT RAN ON PAGE 2 OF THE FRONT SECTION.
HE'D HAVE LIKED THAT TOO.

EVERY THURSDAY

AN INTERVIEW WITH ROSE HUMBLY LECTURE ATTENDEE, 2003
I ATTENDED EVERY GEORGE SPROTT LECTURE FROM 1956 TO 1975.
I WASN'T THE ONLY ONE EITHER. THERE WERE FIVE OF US WHO CAME EVERY WEEK.
ALL SEATS 5¢ DAILY
OPEN
CENTURY THEATER
I'M SURE GEORGE MUST HAVE RECOGNIZED OUR FACES-- THOUGH HE NEVER SPOKE TO ANY OF US PERSONALLY.
IN LATER YEARS WE WERE THE ONLY FACES IN THE HALL.
IT ISN'T THAT I FOUND GEORGE SO RIVETING-- I ATTENDED EVERY LECTURE AT CORONET HALL.
AS DID THE OTHERS. MOST HALLS HAVE THEIR REGULARS--THOSE WHO WILL LISTEN TO ANYONE.
FOR ME, IT WAS JUST A PLEASANT HABIT I FELL INTO.
I NEVER MARRIED, AND I DIDN'T CARE MUCH FOR MOVIES OR TELEVISION.
GOING THERE GAVE ME THE FEELING OF BEING IN THE THICK OF THINGS.
ESPECIALLY IN THE EARLY YEARS, WHEN IT WAS WELL-ATTENDED.
LATER ON, IT WAS A RESTFUL PLACE, AWAY FROM THE WORLD.
Y'KNOW, IN ALL THOSE YEARS, WE REGULARS NEVER SPOKE TO ONE ANOTHER.
I KNEW EACH OF THEM ONLY BY A PRIVATE NICKNAME.
THERE WAS THE BIRD LADY...
THE LUMBERJACK...
MR. MUSTACHIO...
THE ADMIRAL.
LORD KNOWS WHAT THEY CALLED ME!
COME TO THINK OF IT, PERHAPS THEY SPOKE TO ONE ANOTHER WHEN I WASN'T AROUND... IT'S POSSIBLE.
I IMAGINE GEORGE THOUGHT WE WERE THERE JUST FOR HIM--HIS BIGGEST ADMIRERS.
THAT'S FINE. I HOPE THAT MADE HIM HAPPY.
Y'KNOW, I NEVER ACTUALLY SAW GEORGE'S TELEVISION PROGRAM.
NOT EVEN ONCE.
Z
WHEN THEY TORE THE CORONET DOWN, I MADE AN ARRANGEMENT TO ACQUIRE THE HUGE LETTERS THAT SAT UP ON THE ROOF OF THE BUILDING.
CORONET
I HAVE A LARGE HOME, AND I'D PLANNED TO SET THEM UP IN THE BASEMENT.
UNFORTUNATELY, AN ODD THING OCCURRED BEFORE I COULD PICK THEM UP.
SOMEONE BROKE INTO THE WAREHOUSE AND STOLE THE T AND ONE OF THE O'S.
WHO WOULD DO SUCH A THING? NOW THEY ONLY SPELL "CRONE"!
GOOD GRACIOUS! WHAT WILL I DO WITH THAT?!

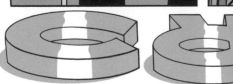

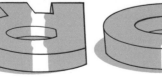

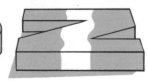

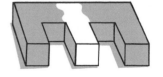

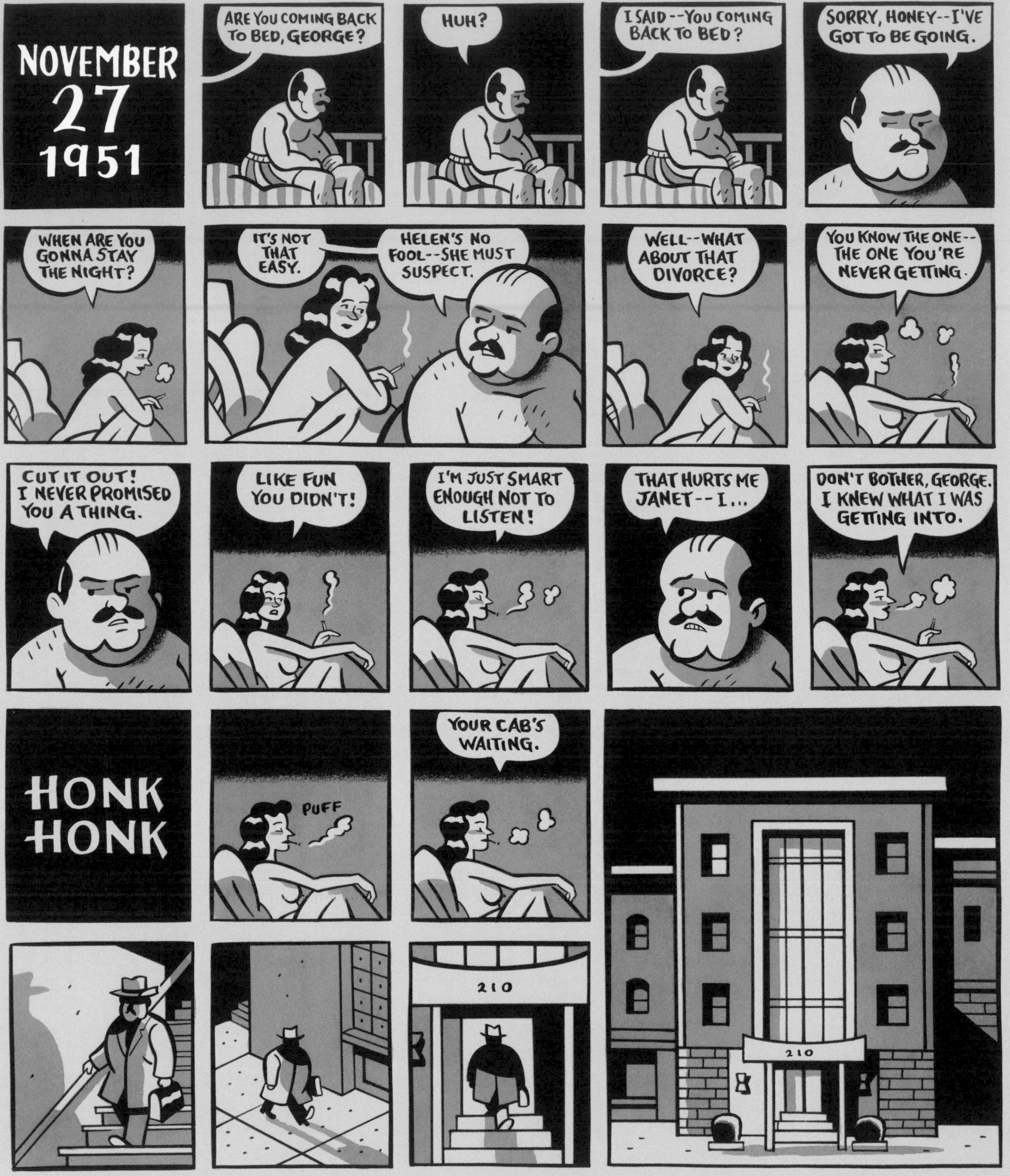
NOVEMBER 27 1951
ARE YOU COMING BACK TO BED, GEORGE?
HUH?
I SAID--YOU COMING BACK TO BED?
SORRY, HONEY--I'VE GOT TO BE GOING.
WHEN ARE YOU GONNA STAY THE NIGHT?
IT'S NOT THAT EASY.
HELEN'S NO FOOL--SHE MUST SUSPECT.
WELL--WHAT ABOUT THAT DIVORCE?
YOU KNOW THE ONE--THE ONE YOU'RE NEVER GETTING.
CUT IT OUT! I NEVER PROMISED YOU A THING.
LIKE FUN YOU DIDN'T!
I'M JUST SMART ENOUGH NOT TO LISTEN!
THAT HURTS ME JANET--I...
DON'T BOTHER, GEORGE. I KNEW WHAT I WAS GETTING INTO.
HONK HONK
PUFF
YOUR CAB'S WAITING.
210
210

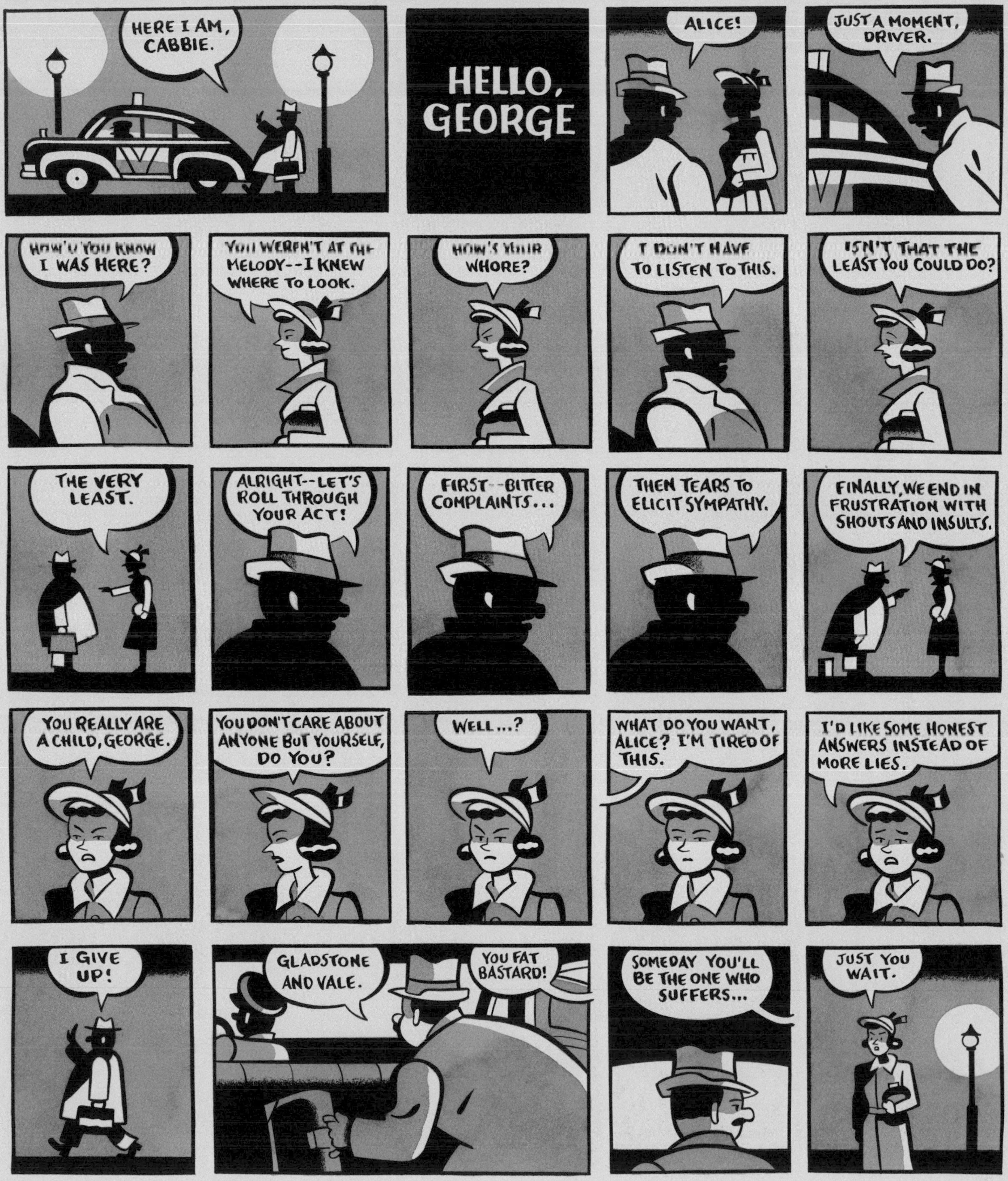
HERE I AM, CABBIE.
HELLO, GEORGE
ALICE!
JUST A MOMENT, DRIVER.
HOW'D YOU KNOW I WAS HERE?
YOU WEREN'T AT THE MELODY--I KNEW WHERE TO LOOK.
HOW'S YOUR WHORE?
I DON'T HAVE TO LISTEN TO THIS.
ISN'T THAT THE LEAST YOU COULD DO?
THE VERY LEAST.
ALRIGHT--LET'S ROLL THROUGH YOUR ACT!
FIRST--BITTER COMPLAINTS...
THEN TEARS TO ELICIT SYMPATHY.
FINALLY, WE END IN FRUSTRATION WITH SHOUTS AND INSULTS.
YOU REALLY ARE A CHILD, GEORGE.
YOU DON'T CARE ABOUT ANYONE BUT YOURSELF, DO YOU?
WELL...?
WHAT DO YOU WANT, ALICE? I'M TIRED OF THIS.
I'D LIKE SOME HONEST ANSWERS INSTEAD OF MORE LIES.
I GIVE UP!
GLADSTONE AND VALE.
YOU FAT BASTARD!
SOMEDAY YOU'LL BE THE ONE WHO SUFFERS...
JUST YOU WAIT.

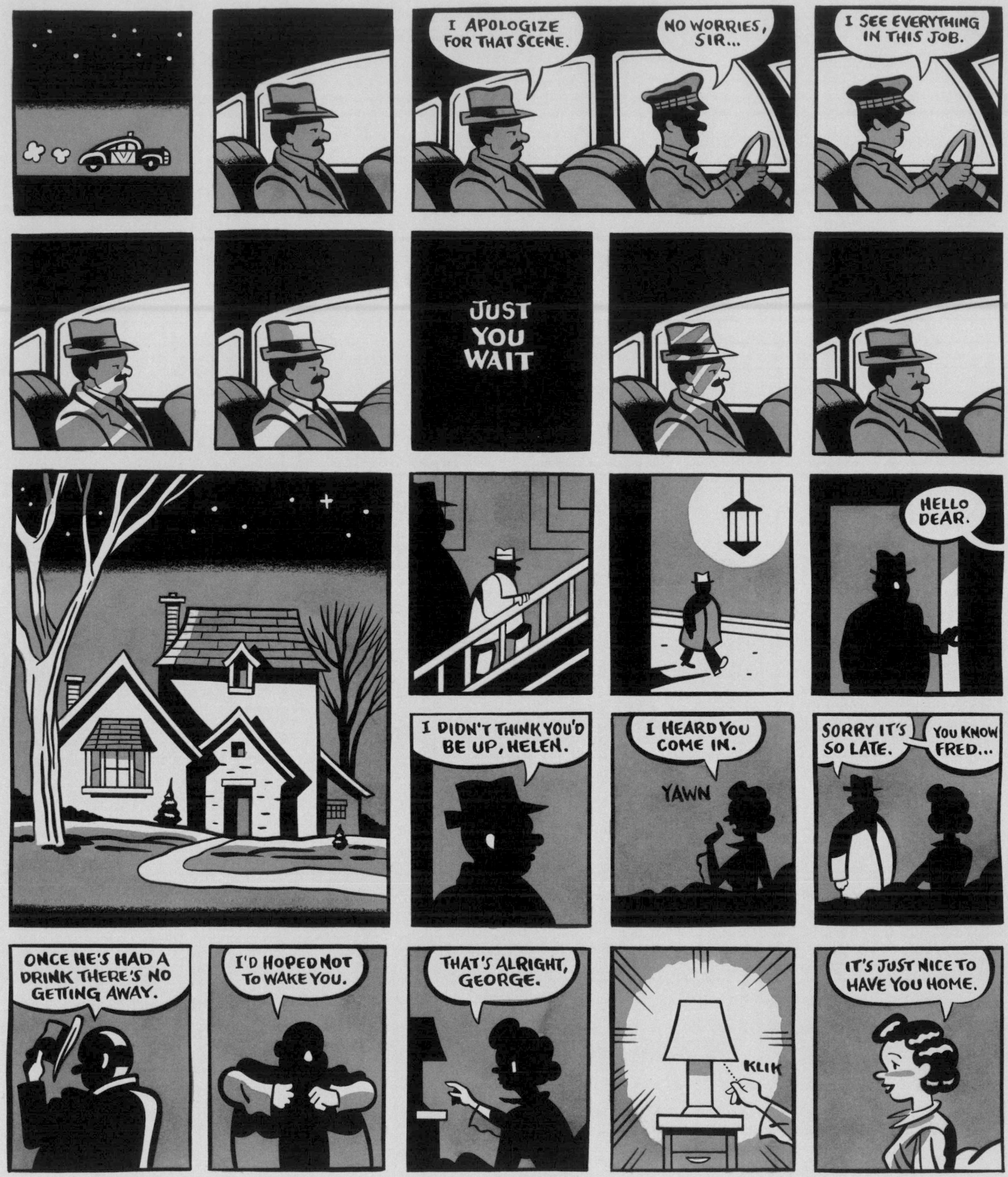

I APOLOGIZE FOR THAT SCENE.
NO WORRIES, SIR...
I SEE EVERYTHING IN THIS JOB.
JUST YOU WAIT
HELLO DEAR.
I DIDN'T THINK YOU'D BE UP, HELEN.
I HEARD YOU COME IN.
YAWN
SORRY IT'S SO LATE.
YOU KNOW FRED...
ONCE HE'S HAD A DRINK THERE'S NO GETTING AWAY.
I'D HOPED NOT TO WAKE YOU.
THAT'S ALRIGHT, GEORGE.
KLIK
IT'S JUST NICE TO HAVE YOU HOME.

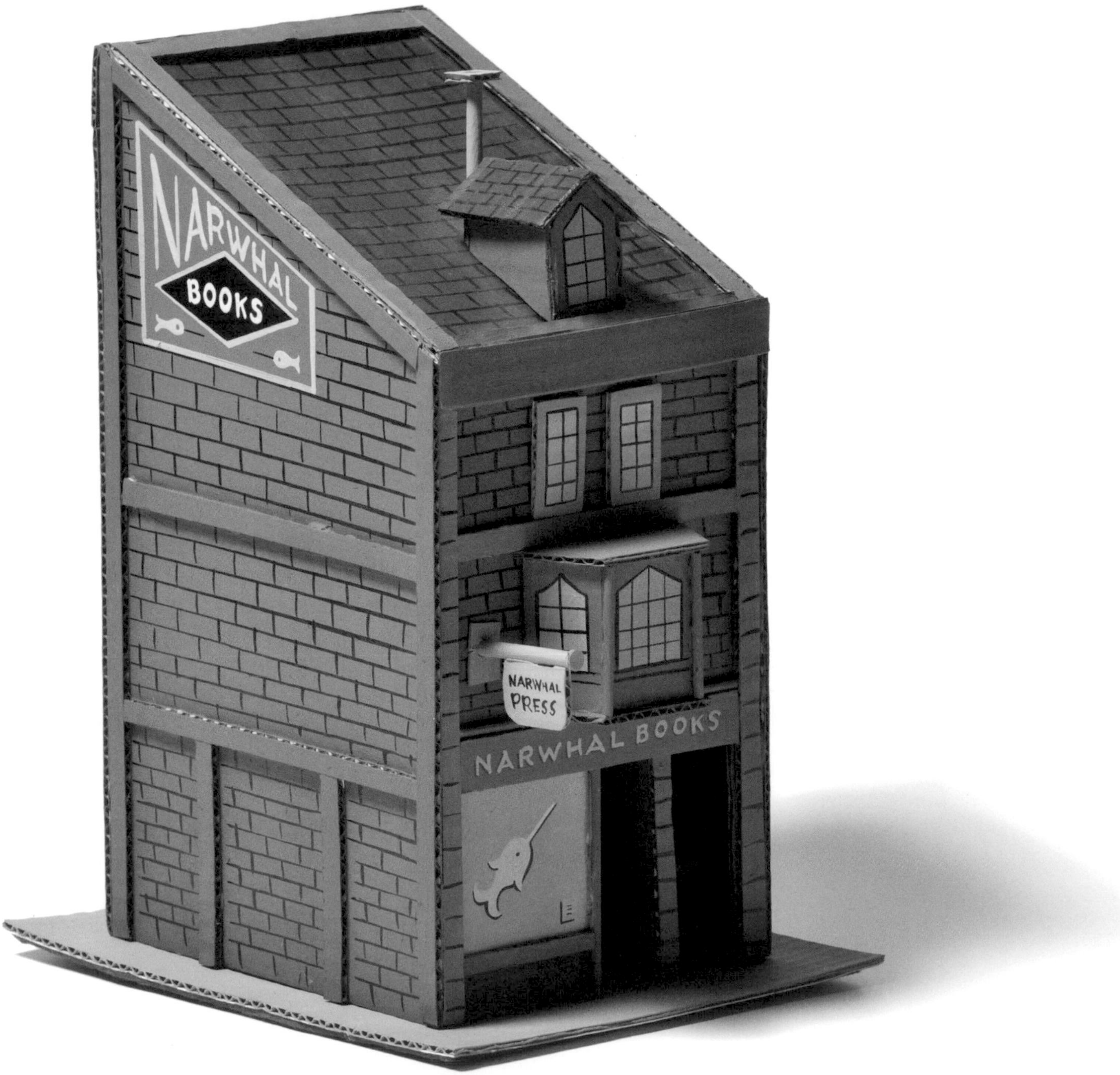
NARWHAL
BOOKS
NARWHAL
PRESS
NARWHAL BOOKS

THE NARWHAL PRESS

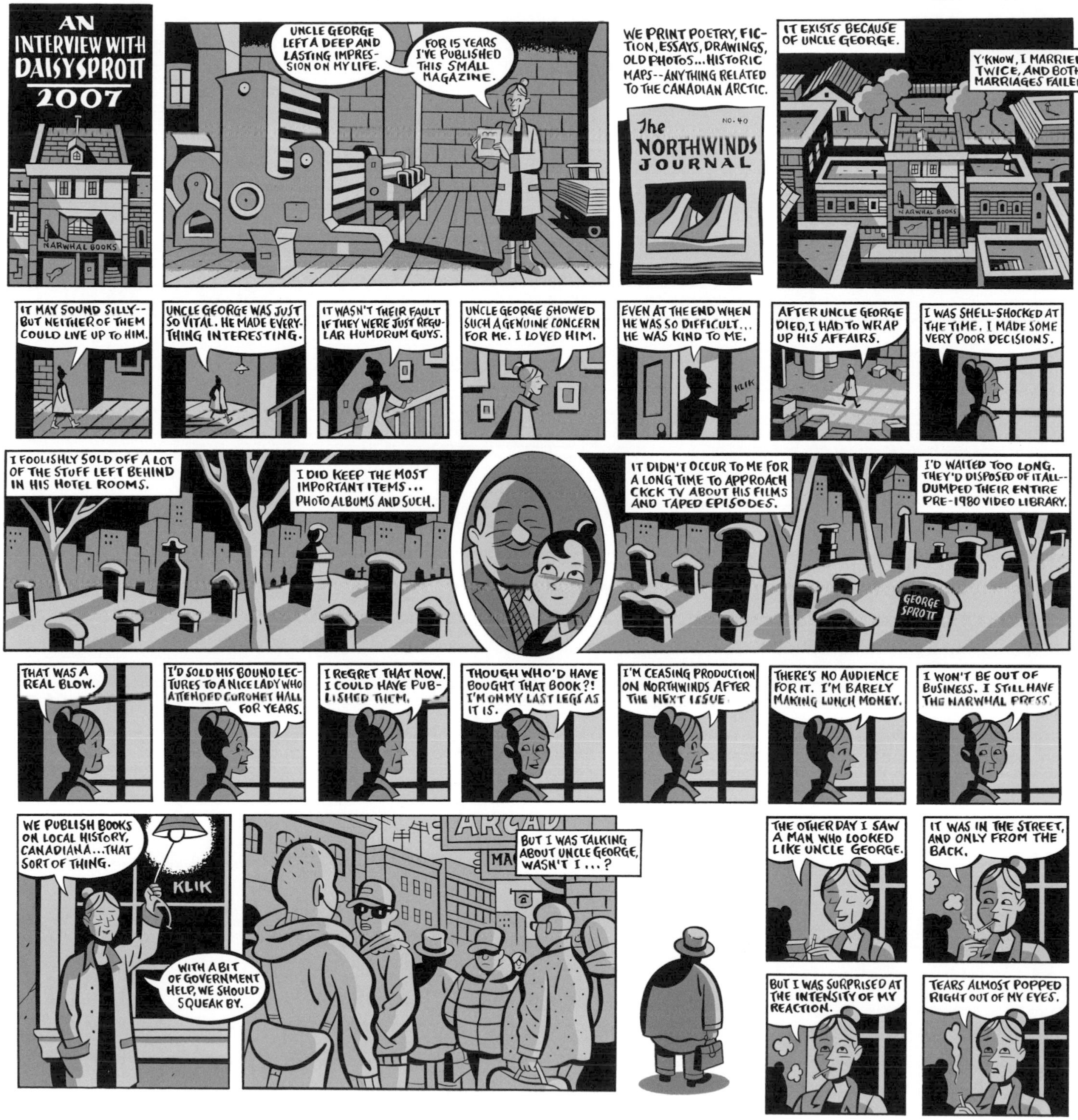
AN INTERVIEW WITH DAISY SPROTT
2007
NARWHAL BOOKS
UNCLE GEORGE LEFT A DEEP AND LASTING IMPRESSION ON MY LIFE.
FOR 15 YEARS I'VE PUBLISHED THIS SMALL MAGAZINE.
WE PRINT POETRY, FICTION, ESSAYS, DRAWINGS, OLD PHOTOS... HISTORIC MAPS--ANYTHING RELATED TO THE CANADIAN ARCTIC.
The NORTHWINDS JOURNAL
NO. 40
IT EXISTS BECAUSE OF UNCLE GEORGE.
Y'KNOW, I MARRIED TWICE, AND BOTH MARRIAGES FAILED.
NARWHAL BOOKS
IT MAY SOUND SILLY--BUT NEITHER OF THEM COULD LIVE UP TO HIM.
UNCLE GEORGE WAS JUST SO VITAL. HE MADE EVERYTHING INTERESTING.
IT WASN'T THEIR FAULT IF THEY WERE JUST REGULAR HUMDRUM GUYS.
UNCLE GEORGE SHOWED SUCH A GENUINE CONCERN FOR ME. I LOVED HIM.
EVEN AT THE END WHEN HE WAS SO DIFFICULT... HE WAS KIND TO ME.
KLIK
AFTER UNCLE GEORGE DIED, I HAD TO WRAP UP HIS AFFAIRS.
I WAS SHELL-SHOCKED AT THE TIME. I MADE SOME VERY POOR DECISIONS.
I FOOLISHLY SOLD OFF A LOT OF THE STUFF LEFT BEHIND IN HIS HOTEL ROOMS.
I DID KEEP THE MOST IMPORTANT ITEMS... PHOTO ALBUMS AND SUCH.
IT DIDN'T OCCUR TO ME FOR A LONG TIME TO APPROACH CKCK TV ABOUT HIS FILMS AND TAPED EPISODES.
I'D WAITED TOO LONG. THEY'D DISPOSED OF IT ALL--DUMPED THEIR ENTIRE PRE-1980 VIDEO LIBRARY.
GEORGE SPROTT
THAT WAS A REAL BLOW.
I'D SOLD HIS BOUND LECTURES TO A NICE LADY WHO ATTENDED CORONET HALL FOR YEARS.
I REGRET THAT NOW. I COULD HAVE PUBLISHED THEM.
THOUGH WHO'D HAVE BOUGHT THAT BOOK?! I'M ON MY LAST LEGS AS IT IS.
I'M CEASING PRODUCTION ON NORTHWINDS AFTER THE NEXT ISSUE.
THERE'S NO AUDIENCE FOR IT. I'M BARELY MAKING LUNCH MONEY.
I WON'T BE OUT OF BUSINESS. I STILL HAVE THE NARWHAL PRESS.
WE PUBLISH BOOKS ON LOCAL HISTORY, CANADIANA... THAT SORT OF THING.
KLIK
WITH A BIT OF GOVERNMENT HELP, WE SHOULD SQUEAK BY.
ARCAD
MA
BUT I WAS TALKING ABOUT UNCLE GEORGE, WASN'T I...?
THE OTHER DAY I SAW A MAN WHO LOOKED LIKE UNCLE GEORGE.
IT WAS IN THE STREET, AND ONLY FROM THE BACK.
BUT I WAS SURPRISED AT THE INTENSITY OF MY REACTION.
TEARS ALMOST POPPED RIGHT OUT OF MY EYES.

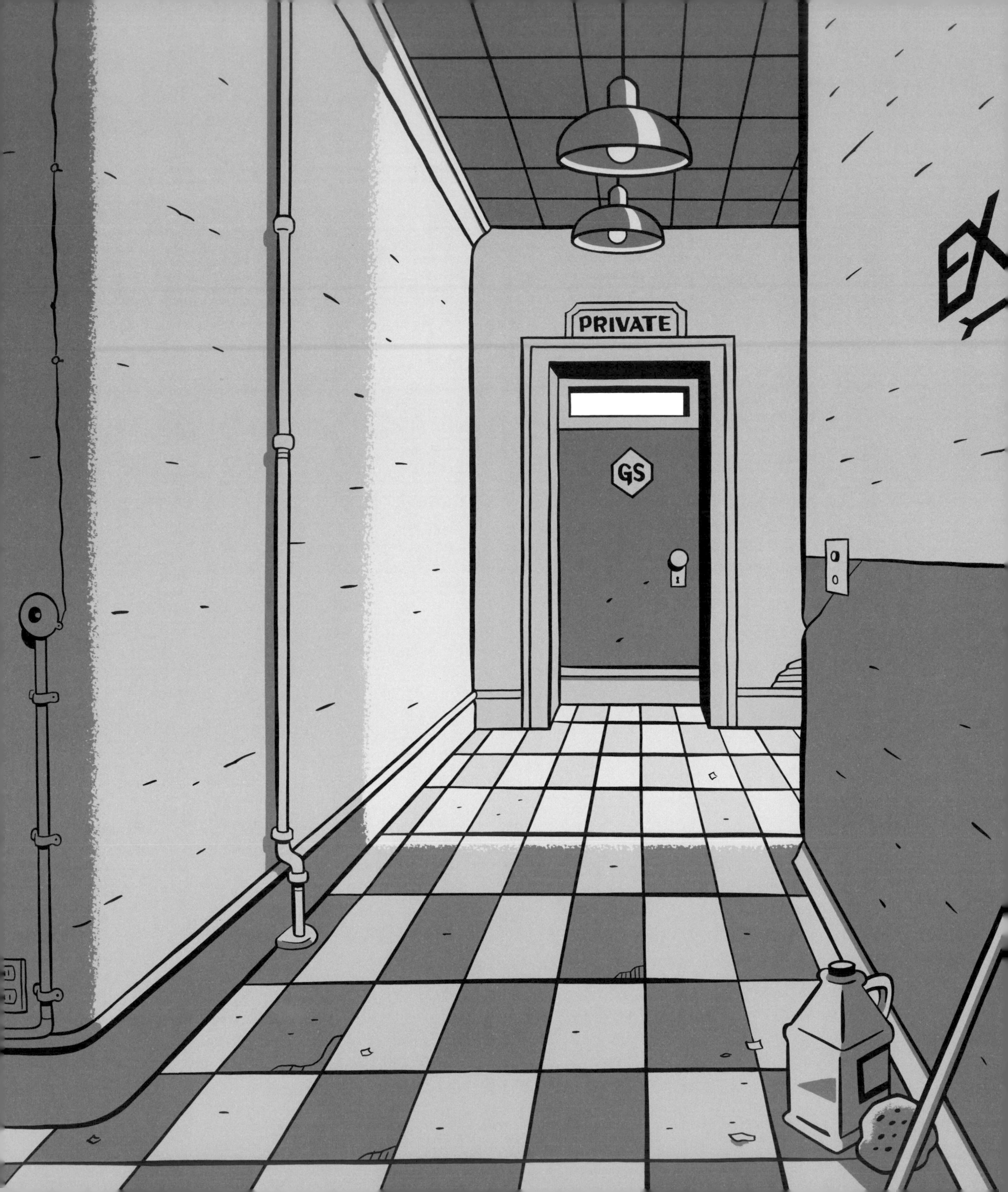
PRIVATE
GS

AND SO, HERE WE ARE

THE TIME HAS COME.

NINE O'CLOCK AND MERE MOMENTS UNTIL GEORGE'S DEATH.

DAISY IS OFF WANDERING ABOUT, TRACKING DOWN AN ASPIRIN.

SHE'LL BE GONE ONLY 10 MINUTES, BUT A LOT CAN HAPPEN IN 10 MINUTES.

POOR DAISY. SHE'LL NEVER SEE UNCLE GEORGE ALIVE AGAIN.

CONSIDERING MY TRACK RECORD, YOU MIGHT BE SURPRISED AT HOW WELL I KNOW THESE LAST MOMENTS.

BUT TRUST ME, I KNOW THEM INTIMATELY. SECOND BY SECOND.

IN FACT, IT IS RIGHT NOW, AS GEORGE MENTALLY REHEARSES HIS LECTURE, THAT IT STRIKES.

JUST 7 SECONDS AFTER 9 O'CLOCK, A PAIN BEGINS IN GEORGE'S CHEST.

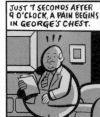

AND NOW THAT THE MOMENT HAS COME... I FIND THAT I CAN'T SHOW IT TO YOU. IT'S TOO AWFUL.

INSTEAD, LET'S JUMP A MINUTE AHEAD TO GEORGE, NOW CRUMPLED ON THE FLOOR...

STRUGGLING LIKE A TURTLE STUCK ON ITS BACK.

EVEN NOW, EVERYTHING IS DIMMING -- HE HAS BUT A FEW SECONDS OF COGNIZANCE LEFT.

IT IS IN THESE FINAL SECONDS THAT A GHOSTLY PROCESSION PASSES BEFORE HIM.

DISTANT OLIVE MOTT...

ABANDONED KULLU KANAYUK...

AND DISAPPOINTED HELEN SPROTT.

OH, WHAT A DIS-HEARTENING PARADE.

PERHAPS GEORGE WOULD HAVE BEEN HAPPIER TO SEE ALL THOSE OTHER, BRIEFLY KNOWN WOMEN PASS BY INSTEAD.

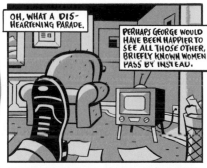

HIS MANY CONQUESTS-- WHO MAY HAVE JUDGED HIM LESS HARSHLY.

AT LEAST HE WAS SPARED A VISIT FROM HIS NE-GLECTED MOTHER AND HIS BASTARD CHILD.

AS THE GHOSTS DEPART, GEORGE IS OVERCOME BY A GREAT WAVE OF REGRET.

HE FEELS A SHOWER OF TEARS POUR DOWN HIS FACE.

THOUGH IN REALITY NOT A SINGLE TEARDROP HAS FALLEN FROM HIS EYES.

WHY AM I LOOKING UP AT THE CEILING? HE WONDERS.

GEORGE CONCLUDES HE MUST BE TAKING A NAP. HE IS VERY TIRED.

HE WHISPERS A FEW CONFUSED WORDS INTO THE EMPTY ROOM.

HELEN, MY FEET... I CAN'T FIND THE FLOOR...

AND AT 9:01 P.M. OF OCT. 9, 1975, GEORGE SPROTT PASSES FROM THIS LIFE.

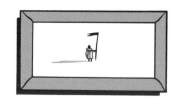

AT 9:03 P.M., DAISY RETURNS.

KNOK KNOK

IT'S JUST ME. I'M COMING IN.

I WILL SPARE YOU THIS SCENE AS WELL.

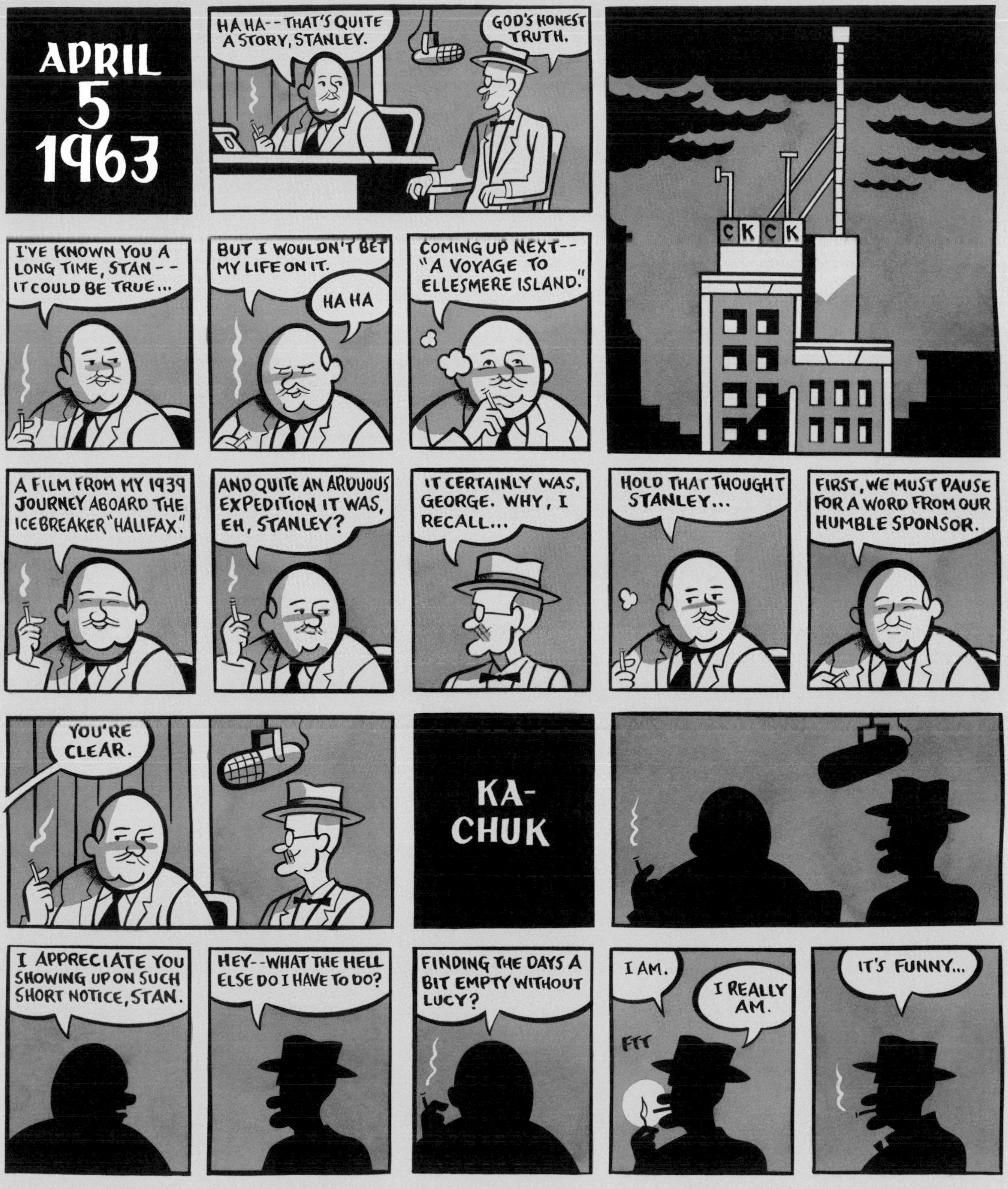
APRIL 5 1963
HA HA--THAT'S QUITE A STORY, STANLEY.
GOD'S HONEST TRUTH.
CKCK
I'VE KNOWN YOU A LONG TIME, STAN--IT COULD BE TRUE...
BUT I WOULDN'T BET MY LIFE ON IT.
HA HA
COMING UP NEXT--"A VOYAGE TO ELLESMERE ISLAND."
A FILM FROM MY 1939 JOURNEY ABOARD THE ICEBREAKER "HALIFAX."
AND QUITE AN ARDUOUS EXPEDITION IT WAS, EH, STANLEY?
IT CERTAINLY WAS, GEORGE. WHY, I RECALL...
HOLD THAT THOUGHT STANLEY...
FIRST, WE MUST PAUSE FOR A WORD FROM OUR HUMBLE SPONSOR.
YOU'RE CLEAR.
KA-CHUK
I APPRECIATE YOU SHOWING UP ON SUCH SHORT NOTICE, STAN.
HEY--WHAT THE HELL ELSE DO I HAVE TO DO?
FINDING THE DAYS A BIT EMPTY WITHOUT LUCY?
I AM.
I REALLY AM.
FTT
IT'S FUNNY...

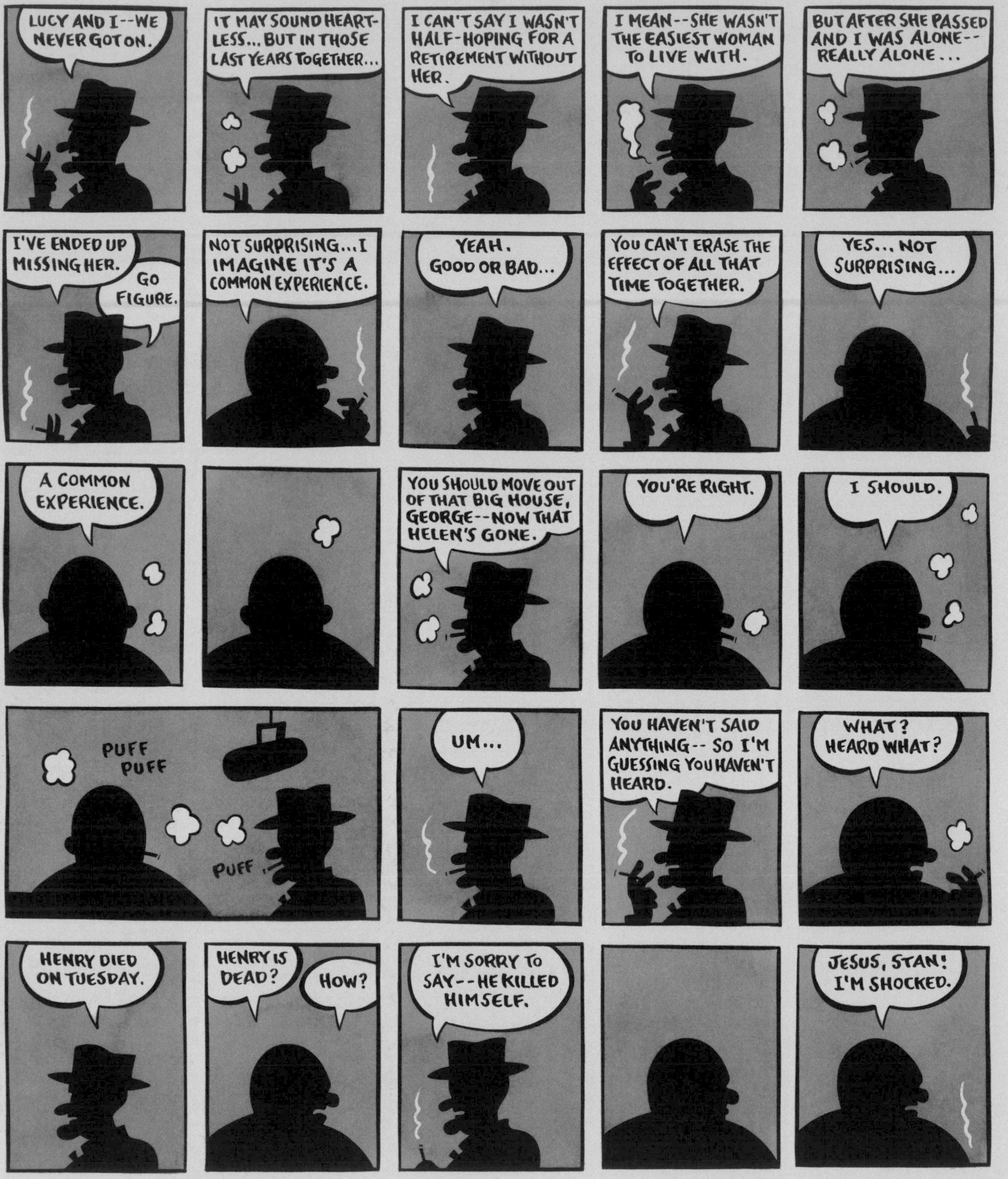
LUCY AND I--WE NEVER GOT ON.
IT MAY SOUND HEARTLESS... BUT IN THOSE LAST YEARS TOGETHER...
I CAN'T SAY I WASN'T HALF-HOPING FOR A RETIREMENT WITHOUT HER.
I MEAN--SHE WASN'T THE EASIEST WOMAN TO LIVE WITH.
BUT AFTER SHE PASSED AND I WAS ALONE--REALLY ALONE...
I'VE ENDED UP MISSING HER.
GO FIGURE.
NOT SURPRISING... I IMAGINE IT'S A COMMON EXPERIENCE.
YEAH. GOOD OR BAD...
YOU CAN'T ERASE THE EFFECT OF ALL THAT TIME TOGETHER.
YES... NOT SURPRISING...
A COMMON EXPERIENCE.
YOU SHOULD MOVE OUT OF THAT BIG HOUSE, GEORGE--NOW THAT HELEN'S GONE.
YOU'RE RIGHT.
I SHOULD.
PUFF PUFF
PUFF
UM...
YOU HAVEN'T SAID ANYTHING-- SO I'M GUESSING YOU HAVEN'T HEARD.
WHAT? HEARD WHAT?
HENRY DIED ON TUESDAY.
HENRY IS DEAD?
HOW?
I'M SORRY TO SAY--HE KILLED HIMSELF.
JESUS, STAN! I'M SHOCKED.

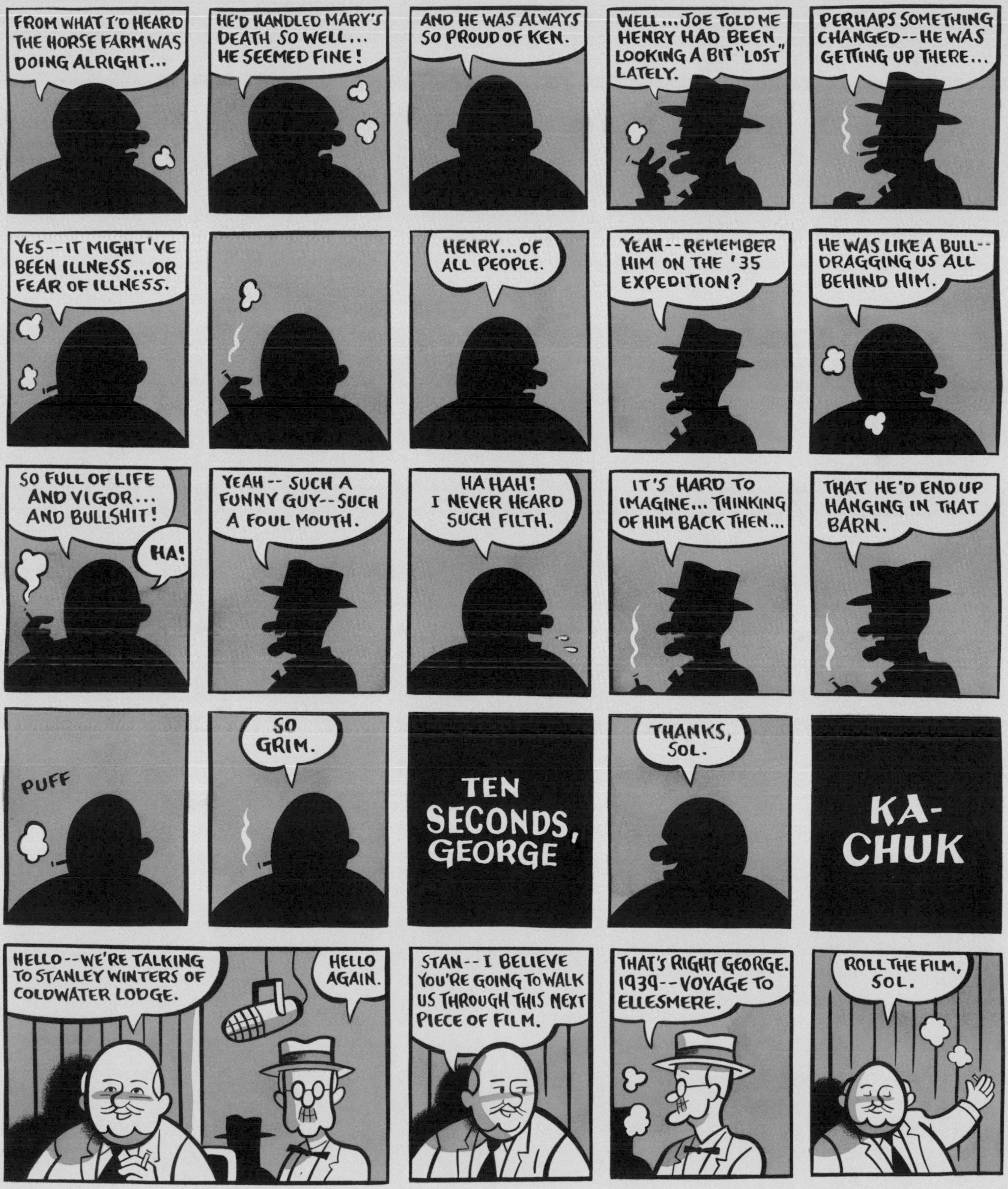
FROM WHAT I'D HEARD THE HORSE FARM WAS DOING ALRIGHT...
HE'D HANDLED MARY'S DEATH SO WELL... HE SEEMED FINE!
AND HE WAS ALWAYS SO PROUD OF KEN.
WELL... JOE TOLD ME HENRY HAD BEEN LOOKING A BIT "LOST" LATELY.
PERHAPS SOMETHING CHANGED--HE WAS GETTING UP THERE...
YES--IT MIGHT'VE BEEN ILLNESS...OR FEAR OF ILLNESS.
HENRY...OF ALL PEOPLE.
YEAH--REMEMBER HIM ON THE '35 EXPEDITION?
HE WAS LIKE A BULL--DRAGGING US ALL BEHIND HIM.
SO FULL OF LIFE AND VIGOR... AND BULLSHIT!
HA!
YEAH--SUCH A FUNNY GUY--SUCH A FOUL MOUTH.
HA HAH! I NEVER HEARD SUCH FILTH.
IT'S HARD TO IMAGINE... THINKING OF HIM BACK THEN...
THAT HE'D END UP HANGING IN THAT BARN.
PUFF
SO GRIM.
TEN SECONDS, GEORGE
THANKS, SOL.
KA-CHUK
HELLO--WE'RE TALKING TO STANLEY WINTERS OF COLDWATER LODGE.
HELLO AGAIN.
STAN--I BELIEVE YOU'RE GOING TO WALK US THROUGH THIS NEXT PIECE OF FILM.
THAT'S RIGHT GEORGE. 1939--VOYAGE TO ELLESMERE.
ROLL THE FILM, SOL.

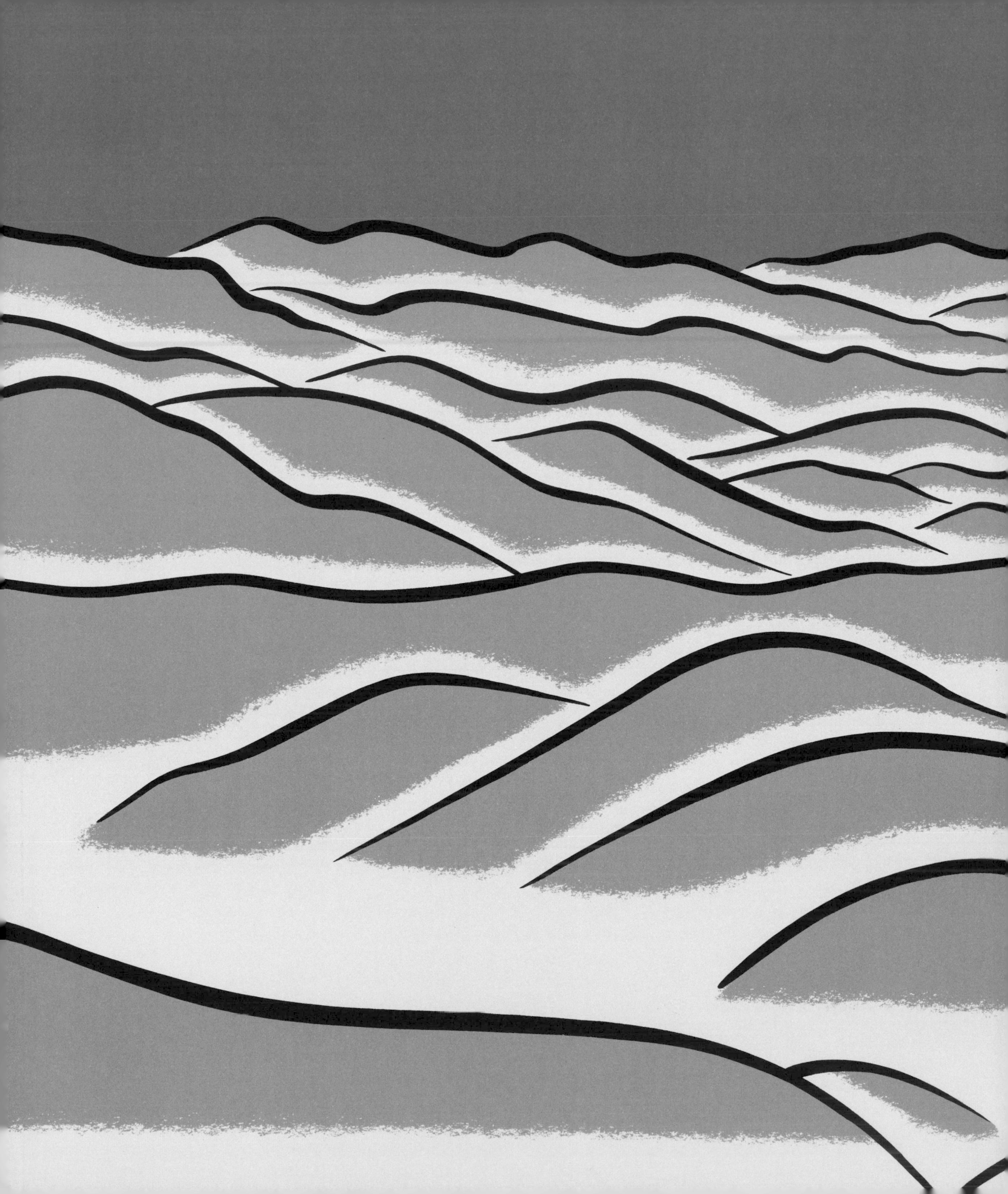

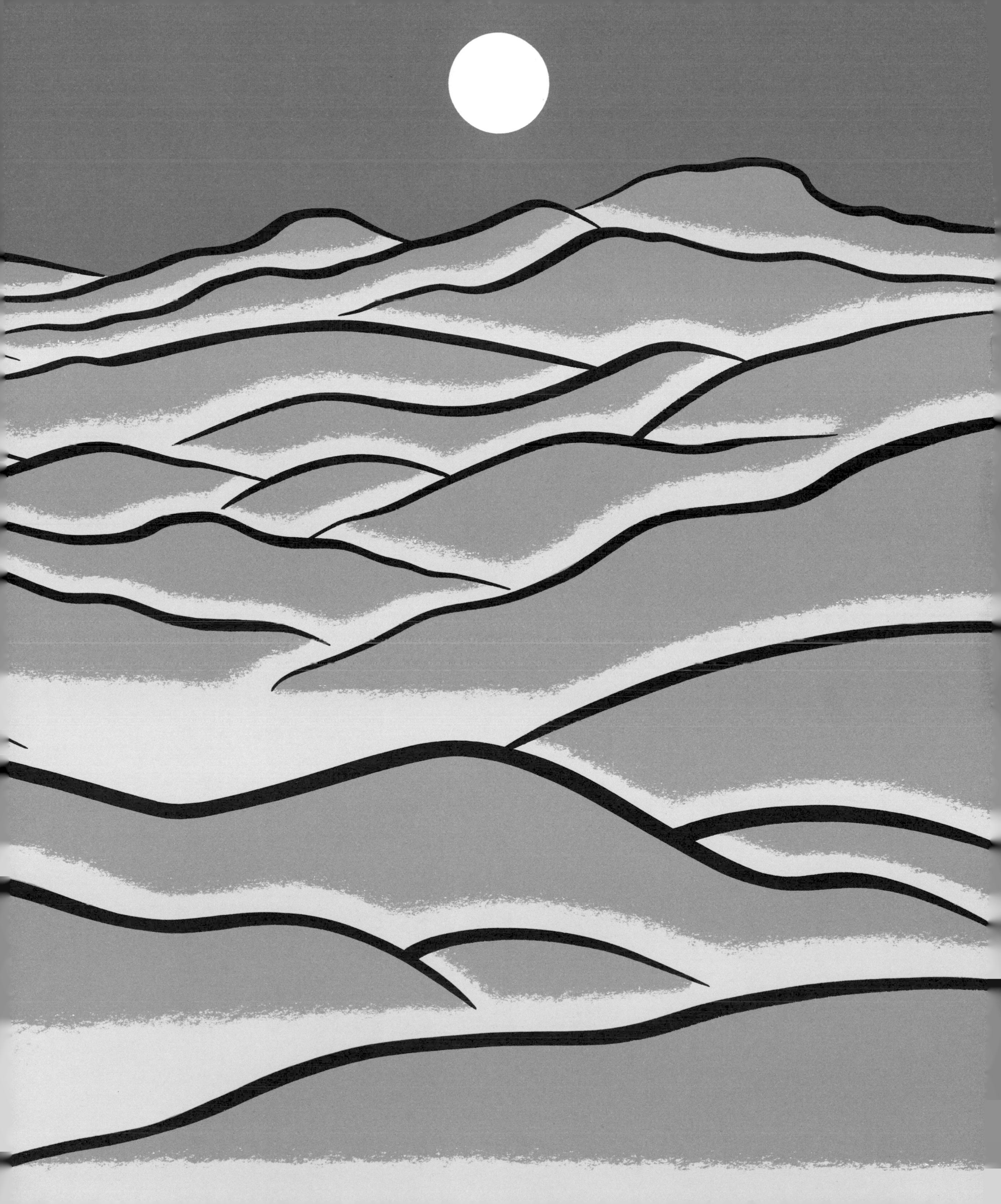

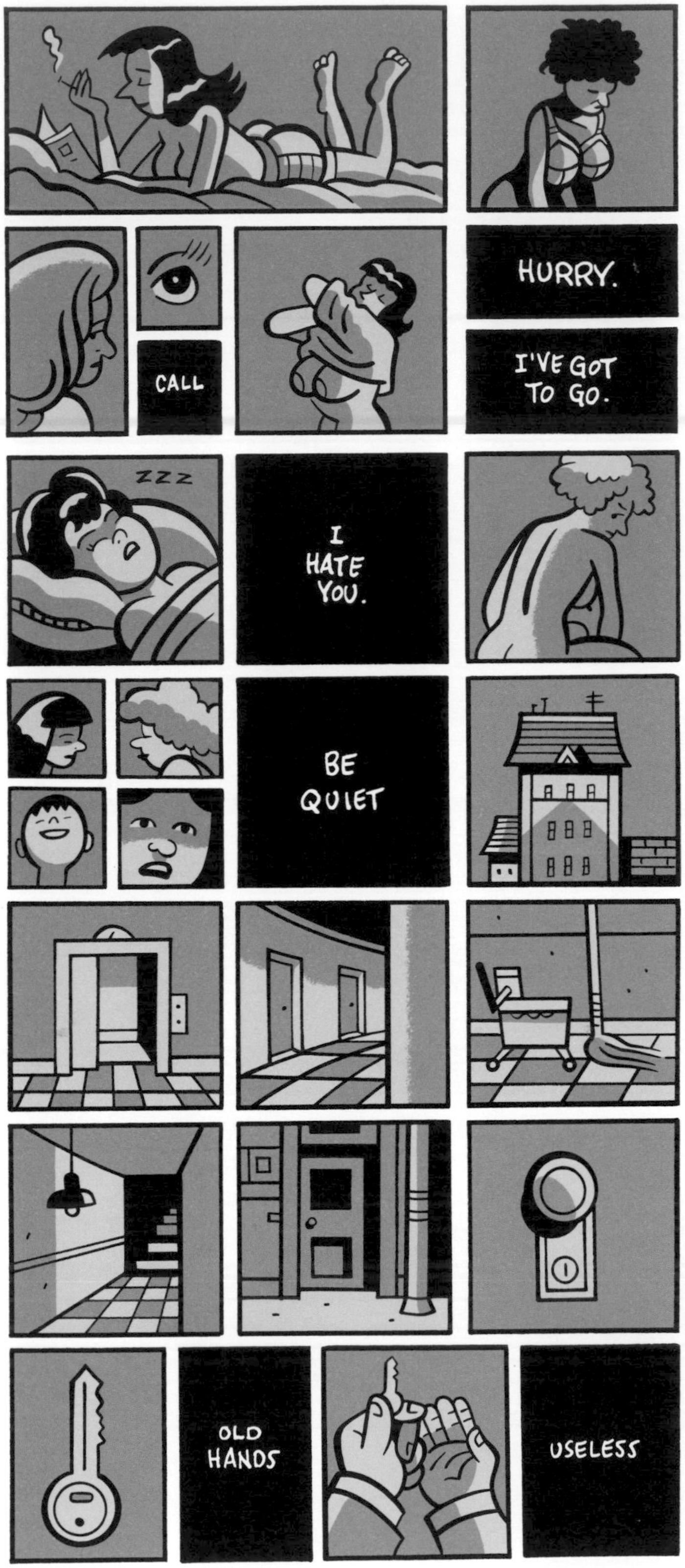
CALL
HURRY.
I'VE GOT TO GO.
ZZZ
I HATE YOU.
BE QUIET
OLD HANDS
USELESS

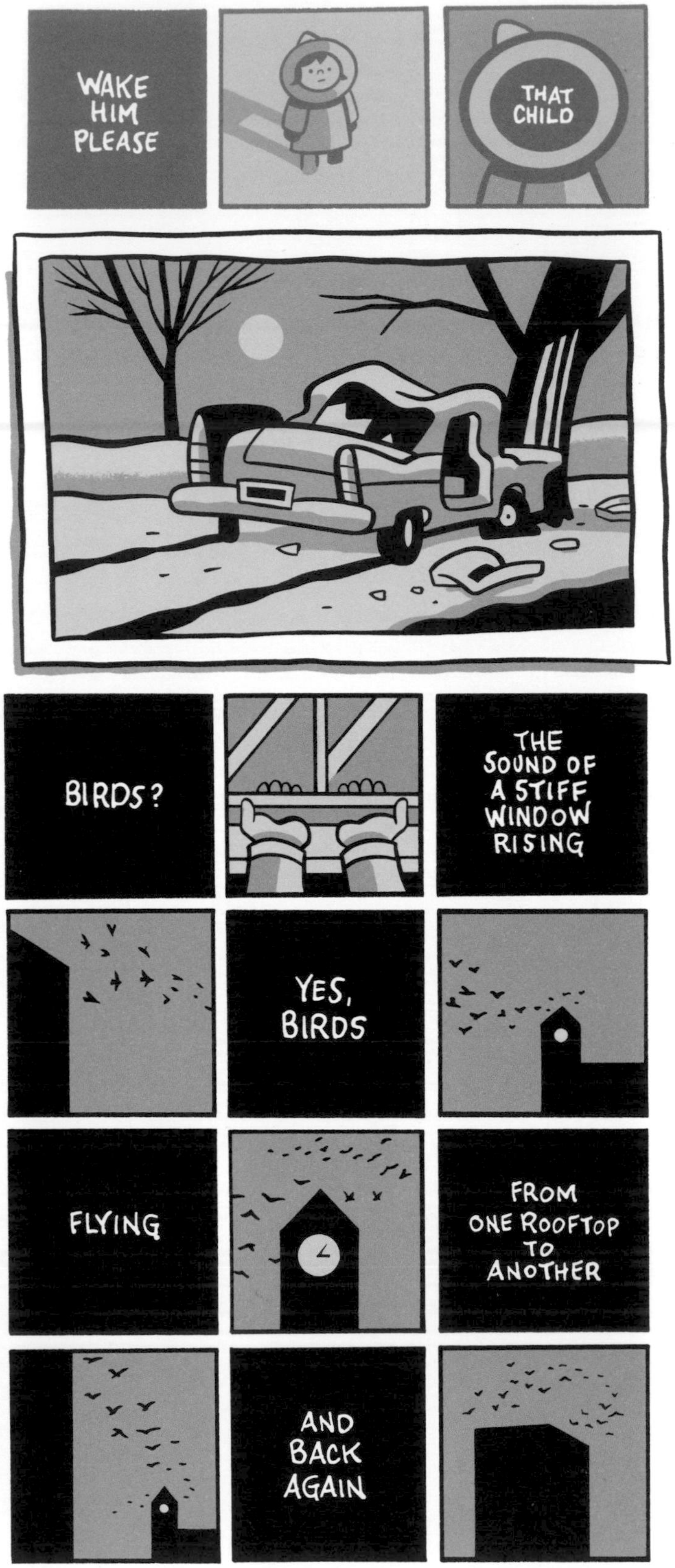
WAKE HIM PLEASE
THAT CHILD
BIRDS?
THE SOUND OF A STIFF WINDOW RISING
YES, BIRDS
FLYING
FROM ONE ROOFTOP TO ANOTHER
AND BACK AGAIN

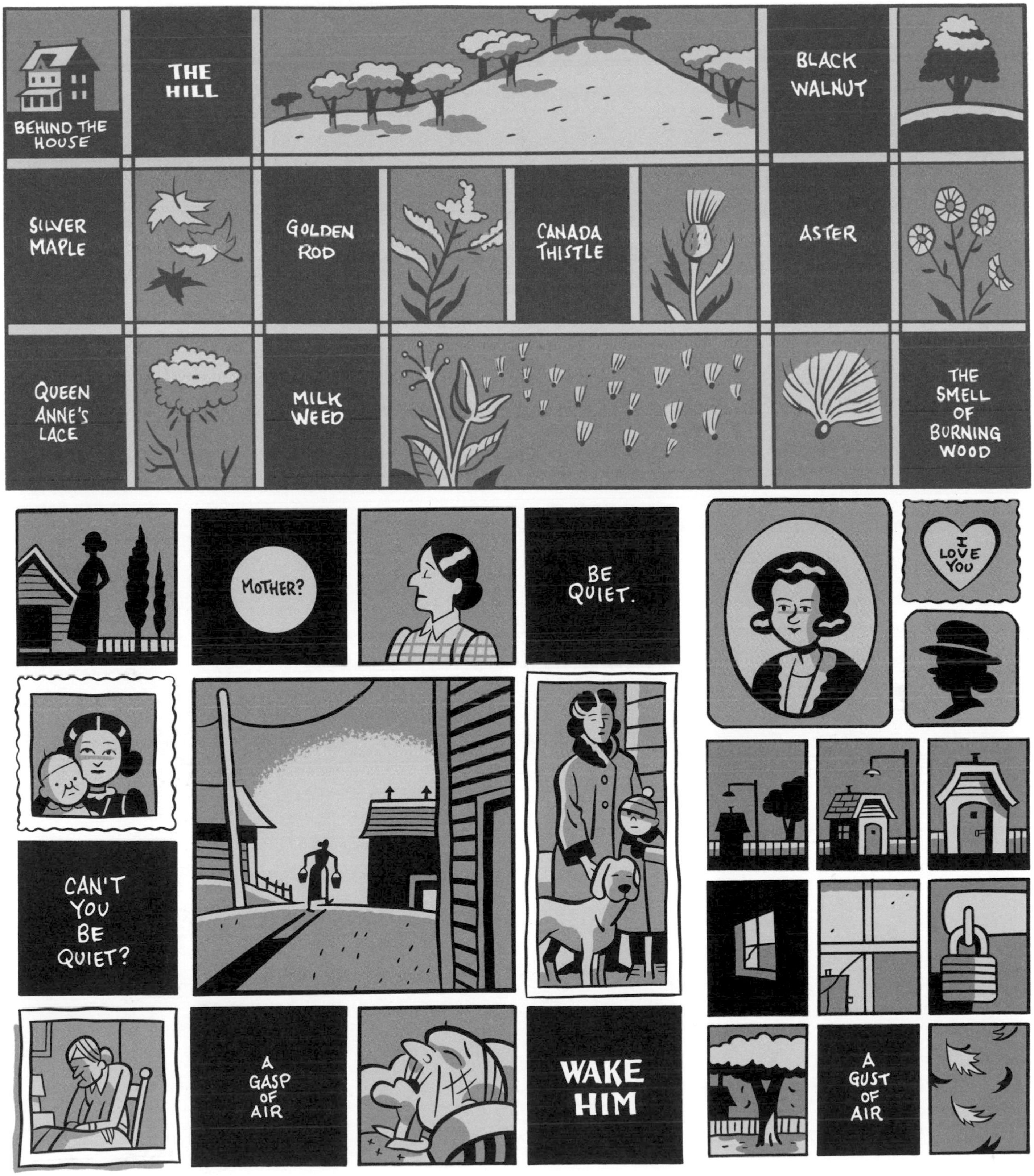
BEHIND THE HOUSE
THE HILL
BLACK WALNUT
SILVER MAPLE
GOLDEN ROD
CANADA THISTLE
ASTER
QUEEN ANNE'S LACE
MILK WEED
THE SMELL OF BURNING WOOD
MOTHER?
BE QUIET.
I LOVE YOU
CAN'T YOU BE QUIET?
A GASP OF AIR
WAKE HIM
A GUST OF AIR

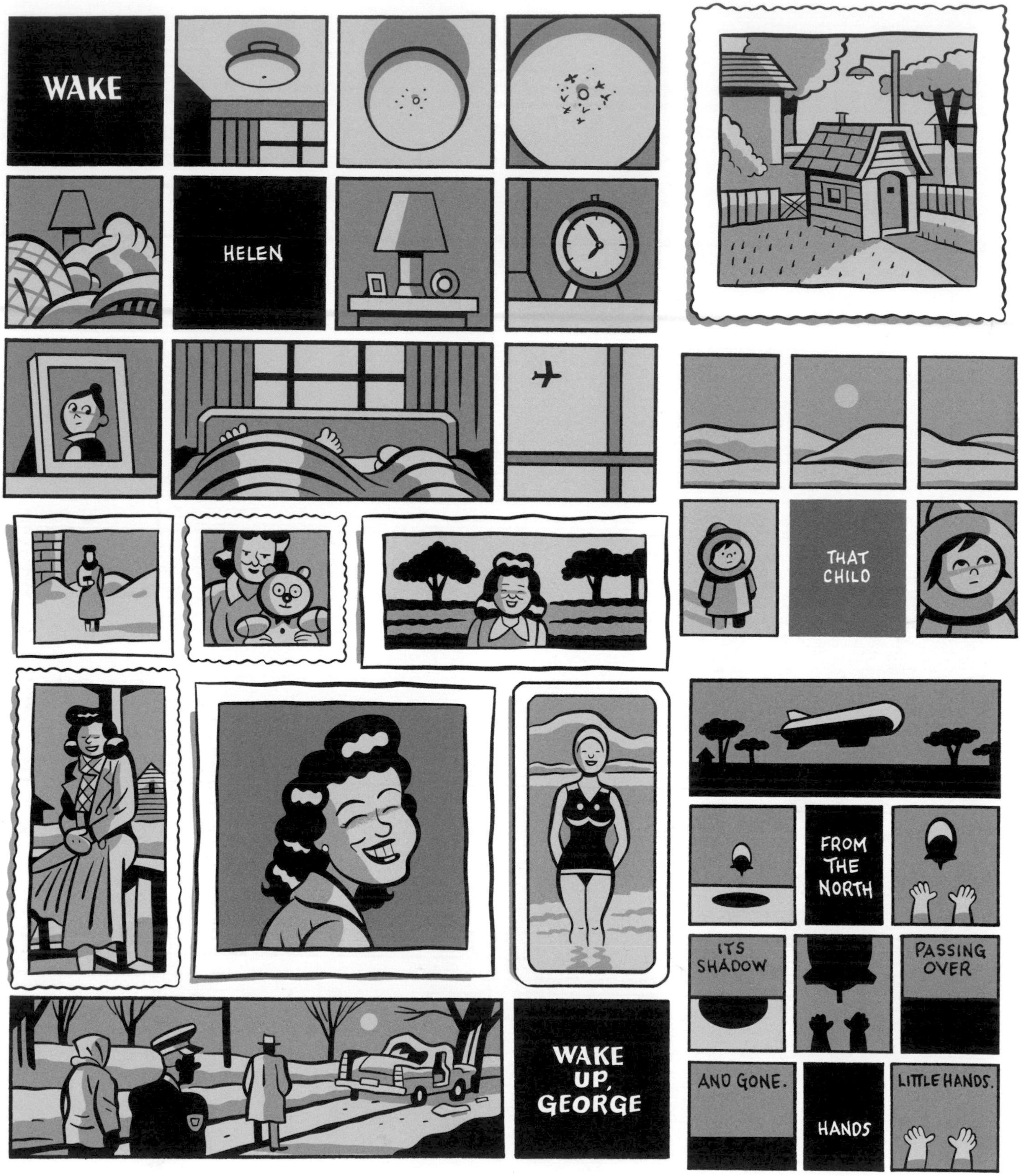
WAKE
HELEN
THAT CHILD
FROM THE NORTH
ITS SHADOW
PASSING OVER
AND GONE.
HANDS
LITTLE HANDS.
WAKE UP, GEORGE

UNFOLD→

WAKE

MY ROOM

THE CRACKED WINDOW

THAT PICTURE

THAT BALL

THAT TOY

THAT BIG SPIDER

ONE SUMMER.

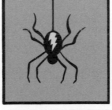

AND THAT BIRD

WAKE

THE SOUND OF TELEVISION SNOW

THAT GOT IN.

I REMEMBER

DAMN. SHOW'S OVER.

CLICK

THE SOUND OF A SNOWPLOW

THE SMELL OF OIL

DEEP IN THE NIGHT

OH, TO BE SOMEWHERE WARM.

EH, GEORGE?

THAT CHILD

WHAT'S THAT, GEORGE?

THAT CHILD

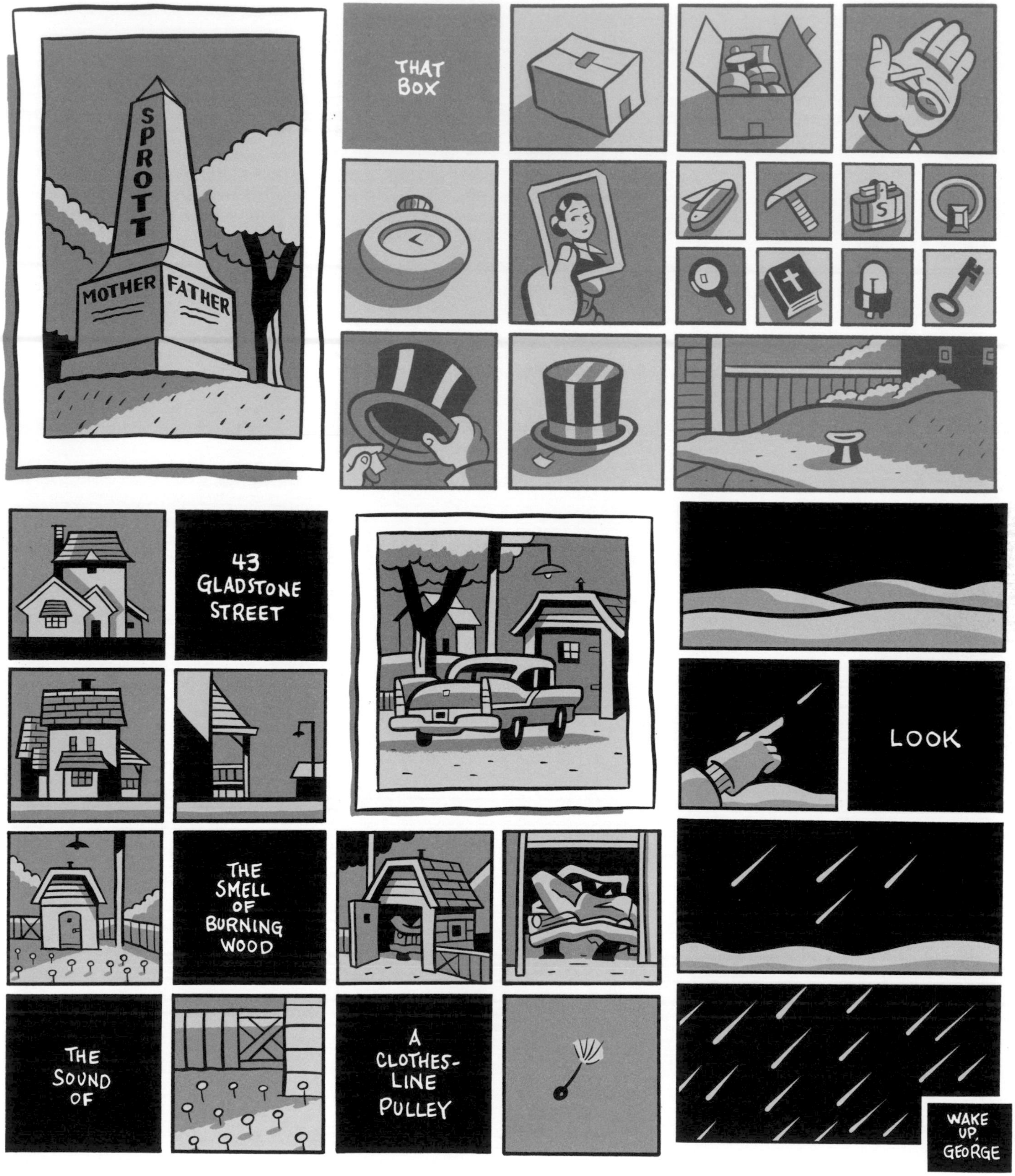
SPROTT
MOTHER
FATHER
THAT BOX
43 GLADSTONE STREET
THE SMELL OF BURNING WOOD
THE SOUND OF
A CLOTHES-LINE PULLEY
LOOK
WAKE UP, GEORGE

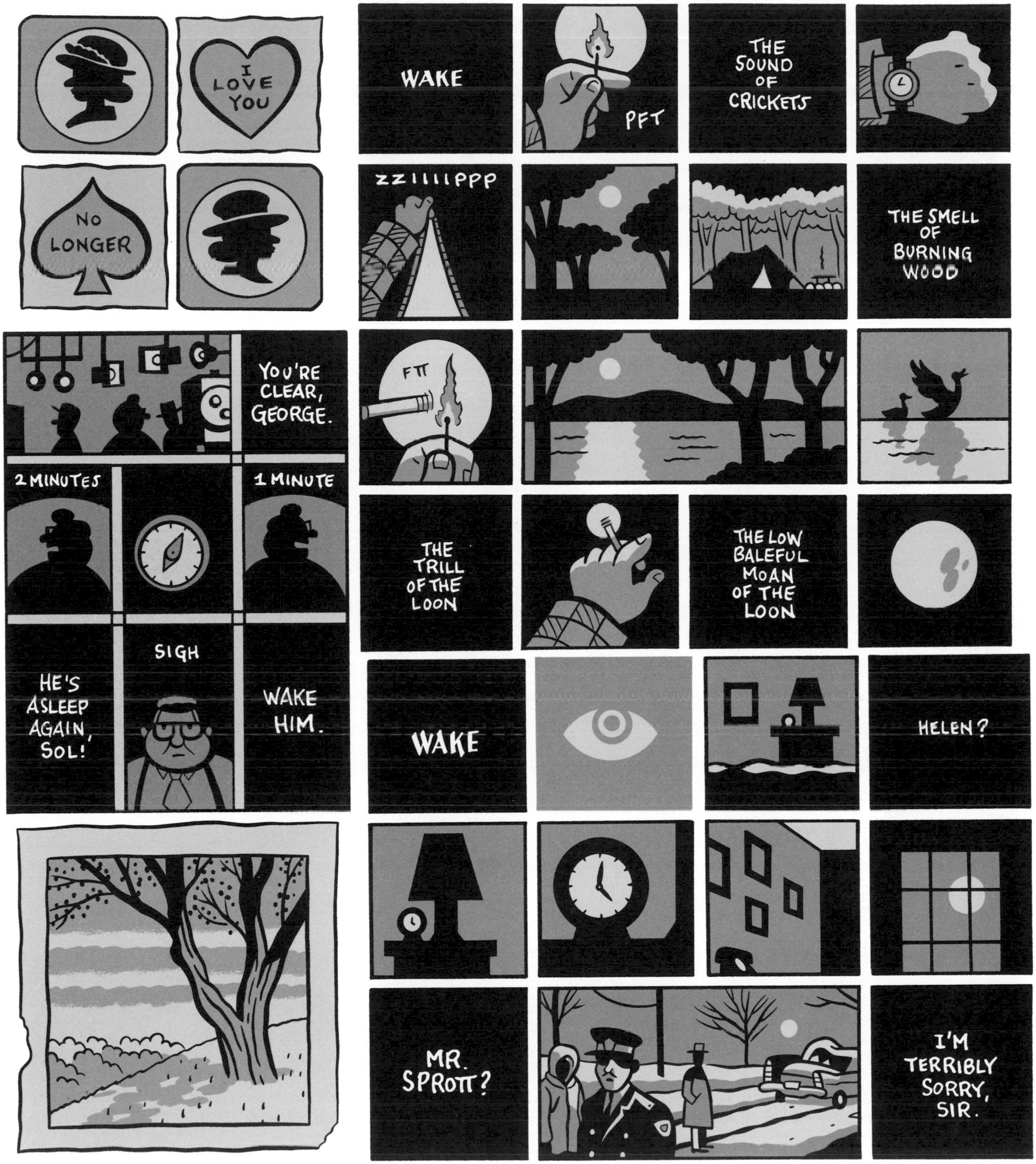
I LOVE YOU
NO LONGER
YOU'RE CLEAR, GEORGE.
2 MINUTES
1 MINUTE
HE'S ASLEEP AGAIN, SOL!
SIGH
WAKE HIM.
WAKE
PFT
THE SOUND OF CRICKETS
ZZIIIIPPP
THE SMELL OF BURNING WOOD
FTT
THE TRILL OF THE LOON
THE LOW BALEFUL MOAN OF THE LOON
WAKE
HELEN?
MR. SPROTT?
I'M TERRIBLY SORRY, SIR.

MORE FROM THE MAN HIMSELF

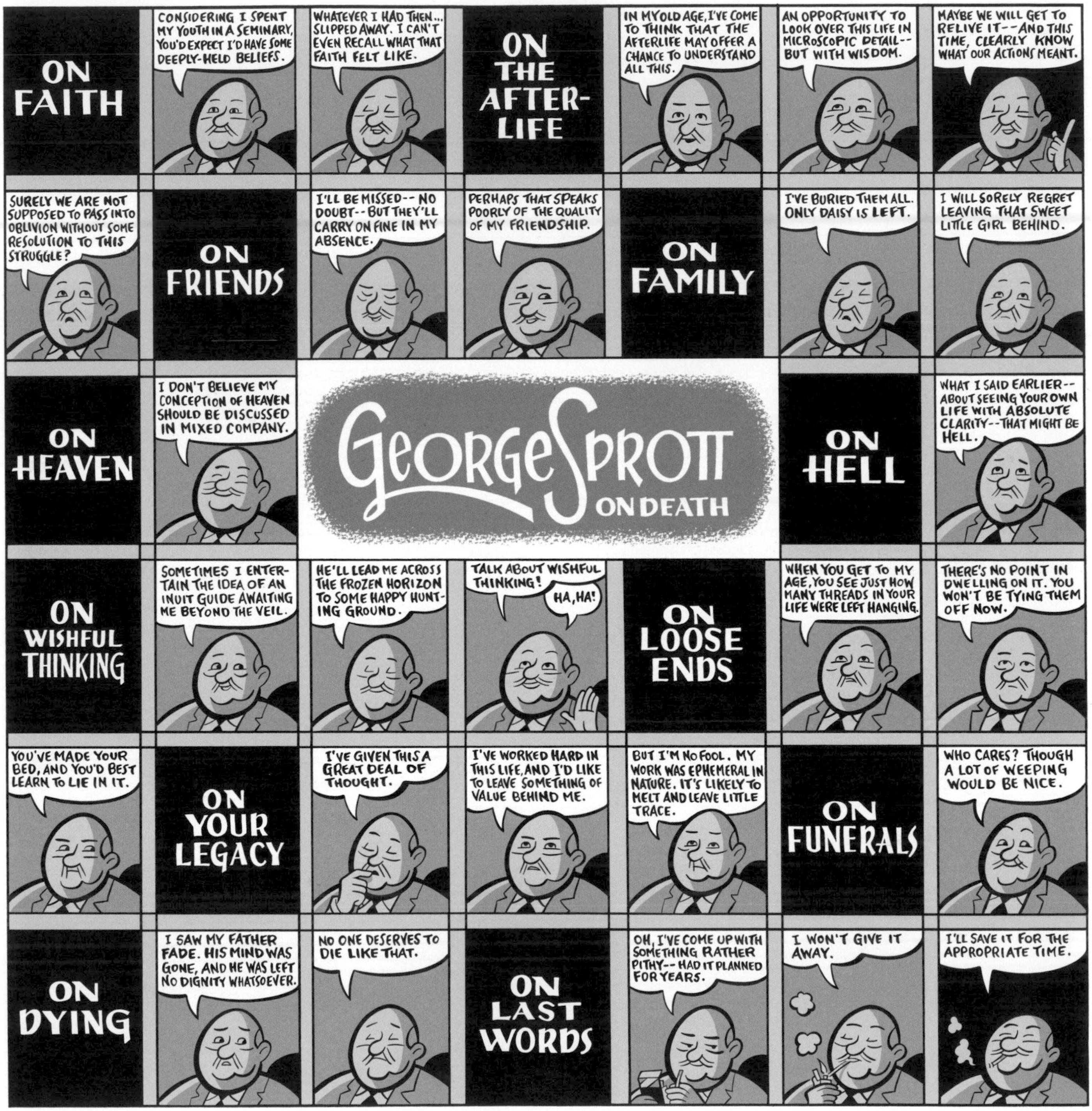
ON FAITH
CONSIDERING I SPENT MY YOUTH IN A SEMINARY, YOU'D EXPECT I'D HAVE SOME DEEPLY-HELD BELIEFS.
WHATEVER I HAD THEN... SLIPPED AWAY. I CAN'T EVEN RECALL WHAT THAT FAITH FELT LIKE.
ON THE AFTER-LIFE
IN MY OLD AGE, I'VE COME TO THINK THAT THE AFTERLIFE MAY OFFER A CHANCE TO UNDERSTAND ALL THIS.
AN OPPORTUNITY TO LOOK OVER THIS LIFE IN MICROSCOPIC DETAIL-- BUT WITH WISDOM.
MAYBE WE WILL GET TO RELIVE IT--AND THIS TIME, CLEARLY KNOW WHAT OUR ACTIONS MEANT.
SURELY WE ARE NOT SUPPOSED TO PASS INTO OBLIVION WITHOUT SOME RESOLUTION TO THIS STRUGGLE?
ON FRIENDS
I'LL BE MISSED-- NO DOUBT-- BUT THEY'LL CARRY ON FINE IN MY ABSENCE.
PERHAPS THAT SPEAKS POORLY OF THE QUALITY OF MY FRIENDSHIP.
ON FAMILY
I'VE BURIED THEM ALL. ONLY DAISY IS LEFT.
I WILL SORELY REGRET LEAVING THAT SWEET LITTLE GIRL BEHIND.
ON HEAVEN
I DON'T BELIEVE MY CONCEPTION OF HEAVEN SHOULD BE DISCUSSED IN MIXED COMPANY.
GEORGE SPROTT ON DEATH
ON HELL
WHAT I SAID EARLIER-- ABOUT SEEING YOUR OWN LIFE WITH ABSOLUTE CLARITY--THAT MIGHT BE HELL.
ON WISHFUL THINKING
SOMETIMES I ENTERTAIN THE IDEA OF AN INUIT GUIDE AWAITING ME BEYOND THE VEIL.
HE'LL LEAD ME ACROSS THE FROZEN HORIZON TO SOME HAPPY HUNTING GROUND.
TALK ABOUT WISHFUL THINKING!
HA, HA!
ON LOOSE ENDS
WHEN YOU GET TO MY AGE, YOU SEE JUST HOW MANY THREADS IN YOUR LIFE WERE LEFT HANGING.
THERE'S NO POINT IN DWELLING ON IT. YOU WON'T BE TYING THEM OFF NOW.
YOU'VE MADE YOUR BED, AND YOU'D BEST LEARN TO LIE IN IT.
ON YOUR LEGACY
I'VE GIVEN THIS A GREAT DEAL OF THOUGHT.
I'VE WORKED HARD IN THIS LIFE, AND I'D LIKE TO LEAVE SOMETHING OF VALUE BEHIND ME.
BUT I'M NO FOOL. MY WORK WAS EPHEMERAL IN NATURE. IT'S LIKELY TO MELT AND LEAVE LITTLE TRACE.
ON FUNERALS
WHO CARES? THOUGH A LOT OF WEEPING WOULD BE NICE.
ON DYING
I SAW MY FATHER FADE. HIS MIND WAS GONE, AND HE WAS LEFT NO DIGNITY WHATSOEVER.
NO ONE DESERVES TO DIE LIKE THAT.
ON LAST WORDS
OH, I'VE COME UP WITH SOMETHING RATHER PITHY-- HAD IT PLANNED FOR YEARS.
I WON'T GIVE IT AWAY.
I'LL SAVE IT FOR THE APPROPRIATE TIME.

LIFE IS BUT A DREAM

WHAT BECAME OF GEORGE SPROTT WHEN HE DEPARTED THIS LIFE?

EVEN AS AN OMNISCIENT NARRATOR, I DON'T HAVE AN ANSWER TO THAT QUESTION.

I CAN TELL YOU THIS, THOUGH...

AS MUCH AS HE FANCIED THE IDEA, THERE WAS NO INUIT SPIRIT GUIDE WAITING FOR HIM ON THE OTHER SIDE.

AS POETIC AS THAT MIGHT HAVE BEEN--NO ONE WALKED HIM INTO A DAZZLING ARCTIC LANDSCAPE.

PERHAPS HE IS STILL HOVERING ON THE EDGE OF THIS LIFE.

IF YOU BELIEVE IN GHOSTS, THERE ARE A FEW SPOTS YOU MIGHT LOOK FOR HIM.

YOU MIGHT TRY THE SMALL WOOD ON THE EDGE OF THE CREEK WHERE HE PLAYED AS A BOY.

OR YOU MIGHT LOOK INSIDE THE BROKEN HULK OF THE MELODY GRILL.

ESPECIALLY BY THE BAR, WHERE HE ALWAYS HELD COURT.

OR YOU MIGHT HEAD FAR NORTH.

OUT ON THE TUNDRA, AT THE SITE OF A GROUPING OF ANCIENT STONE HOUSES,

HE ONCE SPENT A GLORIOUS NIGHT THERE ALONE, UNDER THE NORTHERN LIGHTS,

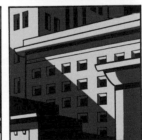

THESE WERE THE PLACES WHERE HE WAS THE HAPPIEST.

PERHAPS A GHOST CAN BE IN MORE THAN ONE SPOT--HE MIGHT BE FOUND AT ALL THREE.

I DON'T HAVE A SATISFYING ANSWER FOR YOU ON THAT MATTER.

I DO KNOW THAT FOR A FEW MONTHS AFTER GEORGE DIED, THOSE WHO KNEW HIM WELL COULD STILL STRONGLY FEEL HIM NEARBY.

BUT NOW, ALL THESE YEARS LATER...

THEY DO NOT FEEL HIS PRESENCE IN THE WORLD ANYMORE.

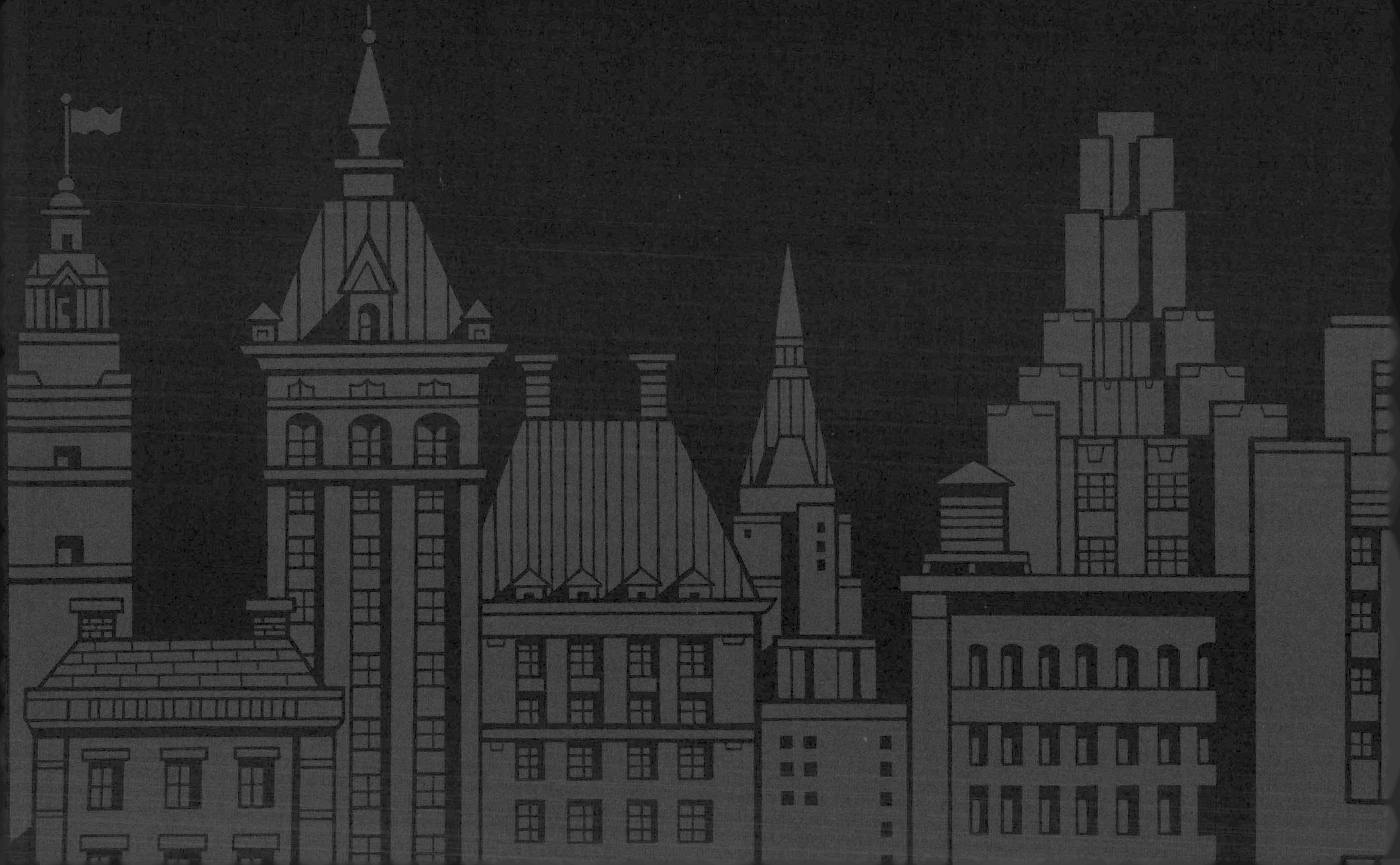

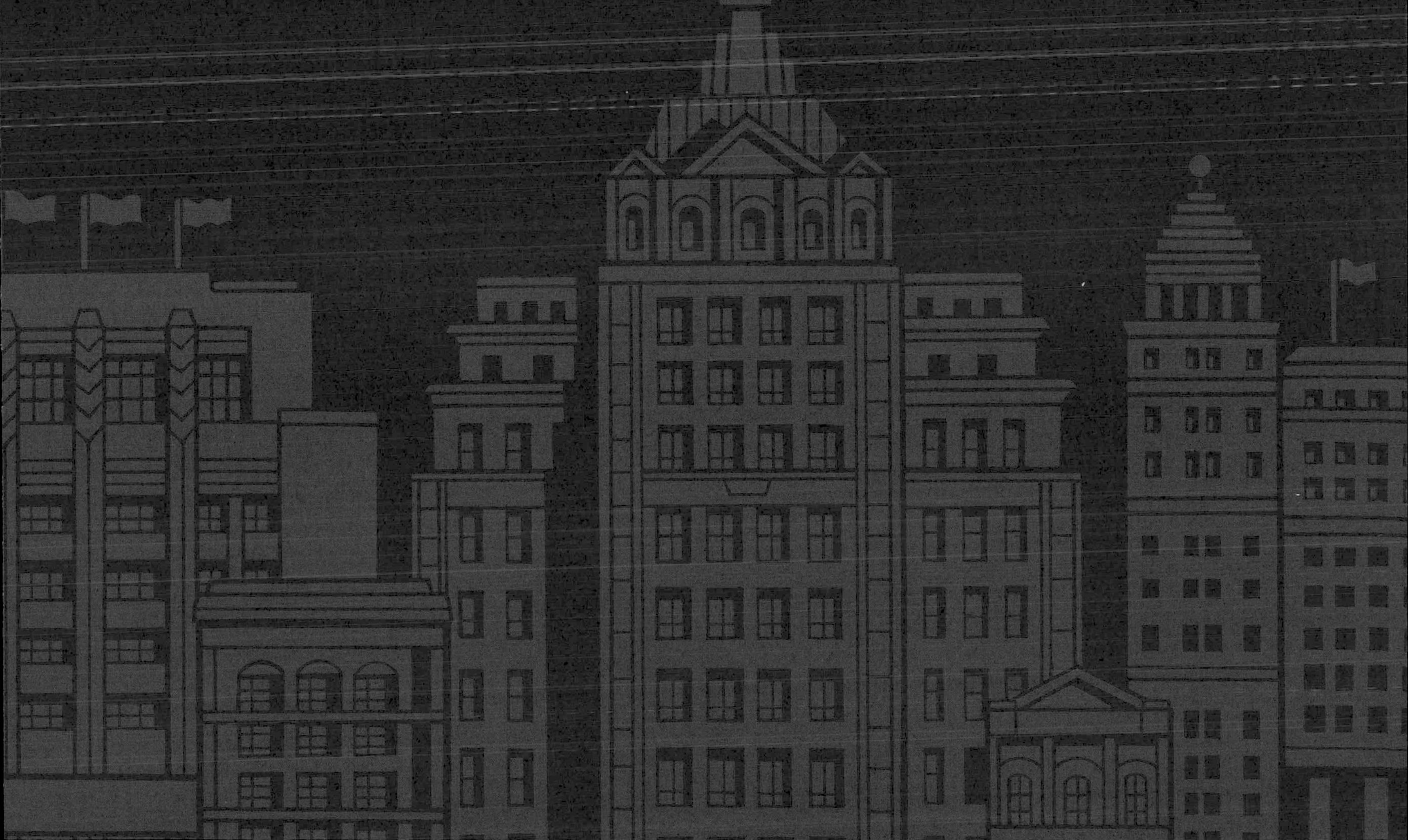

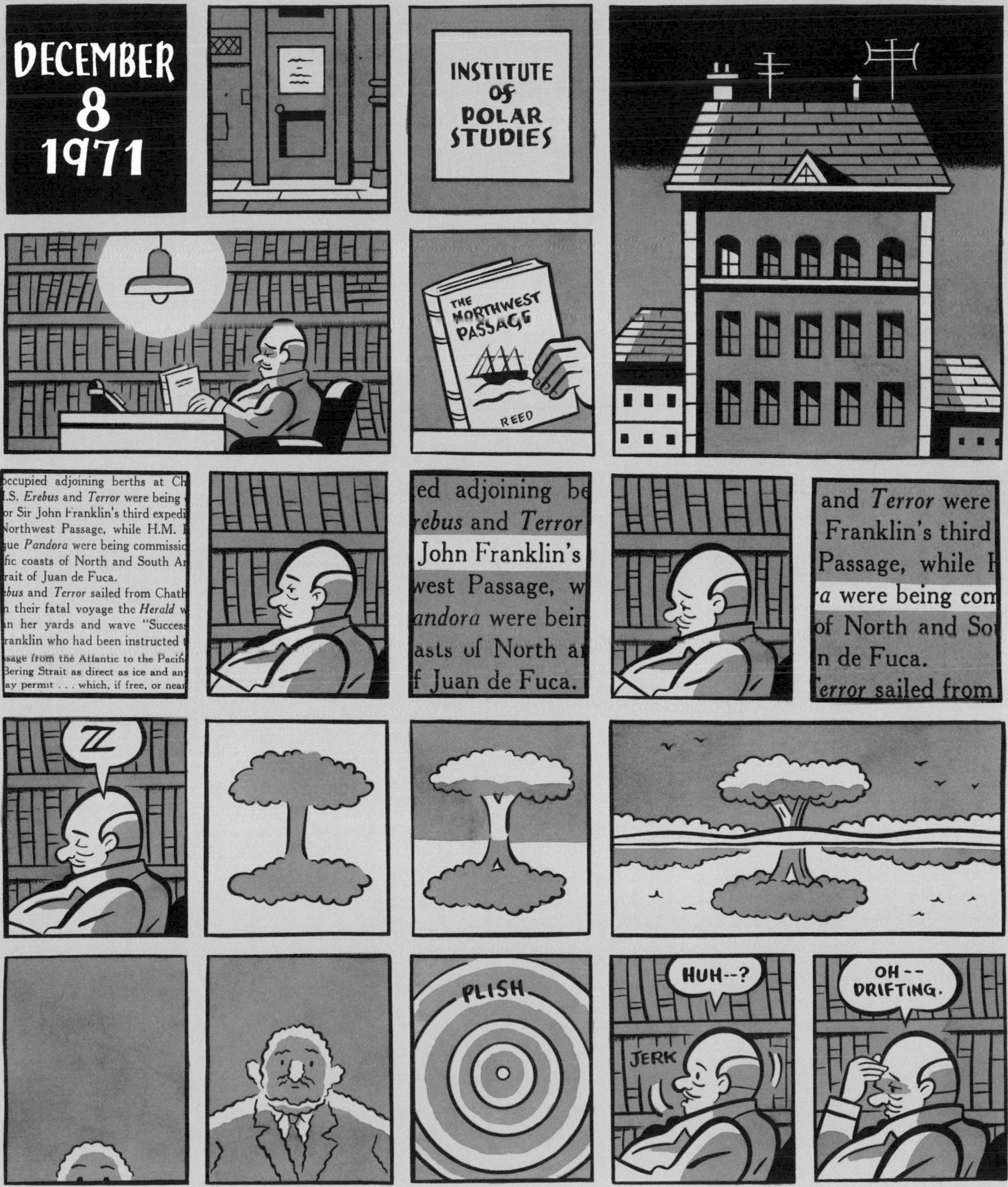
DECEMBER 8 1971
INSTITUTE OF POLAR STUDIES
THE NORTHWEST PASSAGE
REED
occupied adjoining berths at Ch
.S. *Erebus* and *Terror* were being
or Sir John Franklin's third expedi
Northwest Passage, while H.M.
ue *Pandora* were being commissio
fic coasts of North and South A
rait of Juan de Fuca.
ebus and *Terror* sailed from Chath
n their fatal voyage the *Herald* w
n her yards and wave "Success
ranklin who had been instructed
ssage from the Atlantic to the Pacifi
Bering Strait as direct as ice and an
ay permit . . . which, if free, or near
ed adjoining be
rebus and *Terror*
John Franklin's
west Passage, w
andora were bein
asts of North a
f Juan de Fuca.
and *Terror* were
Franklin's third
Passage, while
a were being com
of North and So
n de Fuca.
Terror sailed from
Z
PLISH
HUH--?
JERK
OH -- DRIFTING.

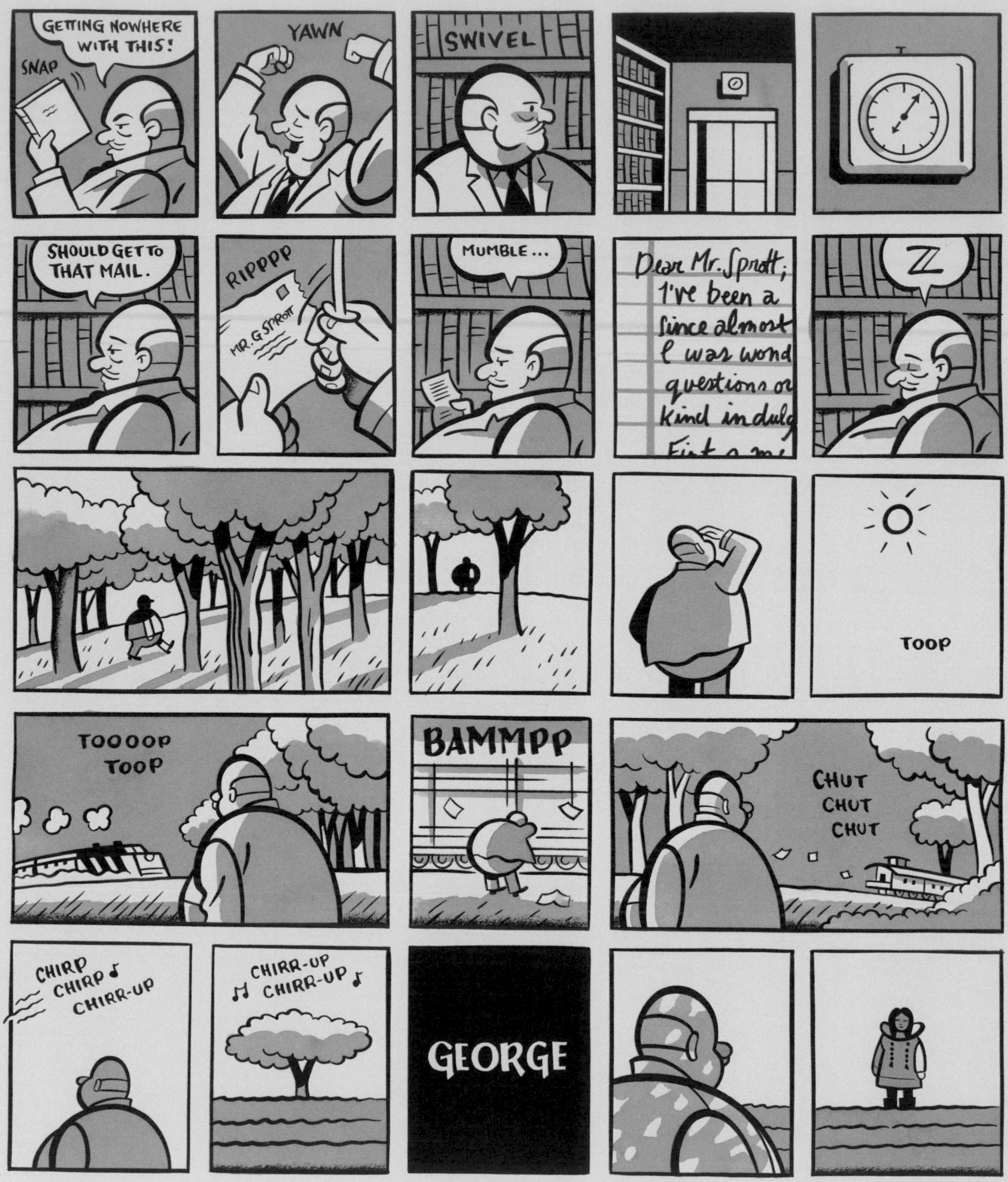
GETTING NOWHERE WITH THIS!
SNAP
YAWN
SWIVEL
SHOULD GET TO THAT MAIL.
RIPPPP
MR. G. SPROTT
MUMBLE...
Dear Mr. Sprott;
I've been a
since almost
I was wond
questions or
kind indulg
Z
TOOP
TOOOOP
TOOP
BAMMPP
CHUT
CHUT
CHUT
CHIRP
CHIRP
CHIRR-UP
CHIRR-UP
CHIRR-UP
GEORGE

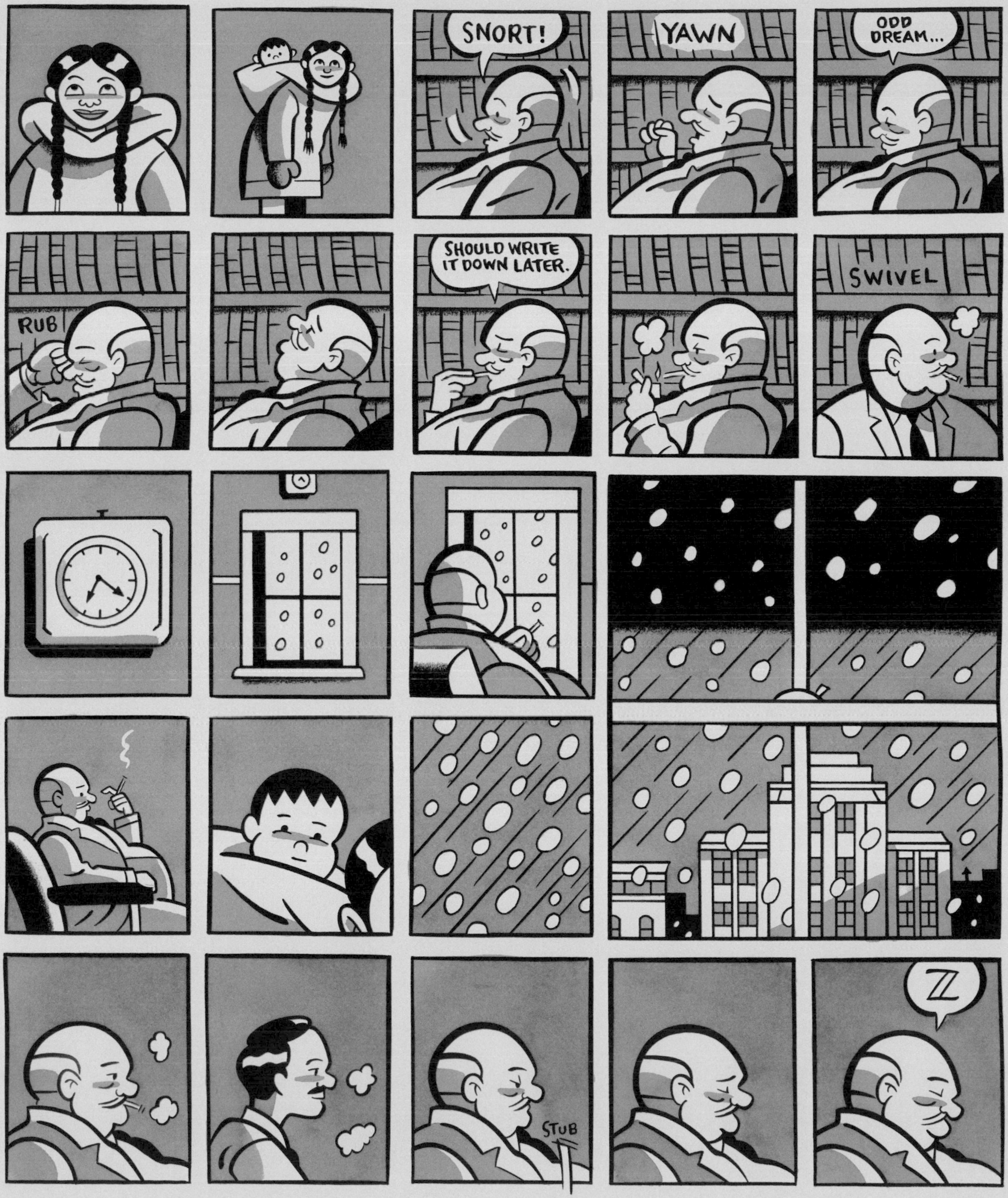
SNORT!
YAWN
ODD DREAM...
RUB
SHOULD WRITE IT DOWN LATER.
SWIVEL
STUB
Z

EPILOGUE

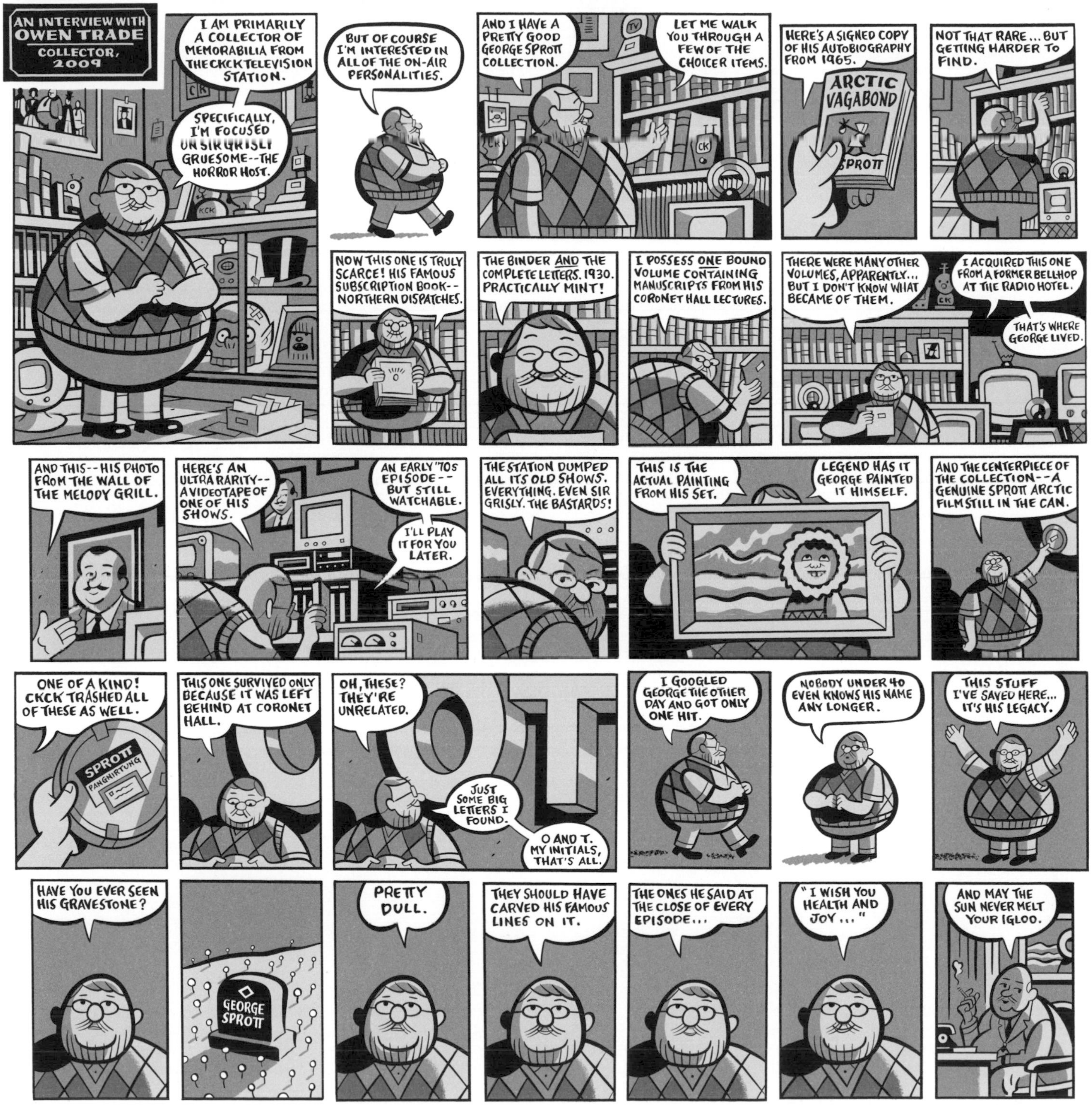
AN INTERVIEW WITH
OWEN TRADE
COLLECTOR, 2009
I AM PRIMARILY A COLLECTOR OF MEMORABILIA FROM THE CKCK TELEVISION STATION.
SPECIFICALLY, I'M FOCUSED ON SIR GRISLY GRUESOME--THE HORROR HOST.
BUT OF COURSE I'M INTERESTED IN ALL OF THE ON-AIR PERSONALITIES.
AND I HAVE A PRETTY GOOD GEORGE SPROTT COLLECTION.
LET ME WALK YOU THROUGH A FEW OF THE CHOICER ITEMS.
HERE'S A SIGNED COPY OF HIS AUTOBIOGRAPHY FROM 1965.
ARCTIC VAGABOND
SPROTT
NOT THAT RARE... BUT GETTING HARDER TO FIND.
NOW THIS ONE IS TRULY SCARCE! HIS FAMOUS SUBSCRIPTION BOOK--NORTHERN DISPATCHES.
THE BINDER AND THE COMPLETE LETTERS. 1930. PRACTICALLY MINT!
I POSSESS ONE BOUND VOLUME CONTAINING MANUSCRIPTS FROM HIS CORONET HALL LECTURES.
THERE WERE MANY OTHER VOLUMES, APPARENTLY... BUT I DON'T KNOW WHAT BECAME OF THEM.
I ACQUIRED THIS ONE FROM A FORMER BELLHOP AT THE RADIO HOTEL.
THAT'S WHERE GEORGE LIVED.
AND THIS--HIS PHOTO FROM THE WALL OF THE MELODY GRILL.
HERE'S AN ULTRA RARITY--A VIDEOTAPE OF ONE OF HIS SHOWS.
AN EARLY '70S EPISODE--BUT STILL WATCHABLE.
I'LL PLAY IT FOR YOU LATER.
THE STATION DUMPED ALL ITS OLD SHOWS. EVERYTHING. EVEN SIR GRISLY. THE BASTARDS!
THIS IS THE ACTUAL PAINTING FROM HIS SET.
LEGEND HAS IT GEORGE PAINTED IT HIMSELF.
AND THE CENTERPIECE OF THE COLLECTION--A GENUINE SPROTT ARCTIC FILM STILL IN THE CAN.
ONE OF A KIND! CKCK TRASHED ALL OF THESE AS WELL.
SPROTT
PANGNIRTUNG
THIS ONE SURVIVED ONLY BECAUSE IT WAS LEFT BEHIND AT CORONET HALL.
OH, THESE? THEY'RE UNRELATED.
JUST SOME BIG LETTERS I FOUND.
O AND T. MY INITIALS, THAT'S ALL.
I GOOGLED GEORGE THE OTHER DAY AND GOT ONLY ONE HIT.
NOBODY UNDER 40 EVEN KNOWS HIS NAME ANY LONGER.
THIS STUFF I'VE SAVED HERE... IT'S HIS LEGACY.
HAVE YOU EVER SEEN HIS GRAVESTONE?
GEORGE SPROTT
PRETTY DULL.
THEY SHOULD HAVE CARVED HIS FAMOUS LINES ON IT.
THE ONES HE SAID AT THE CLOSE OF EVERY EPISODE...
"I WISH YOU HEALTH AND JOY..."
AND MAY THE SUN NEVER MELT YOUR IGLOO.

The End

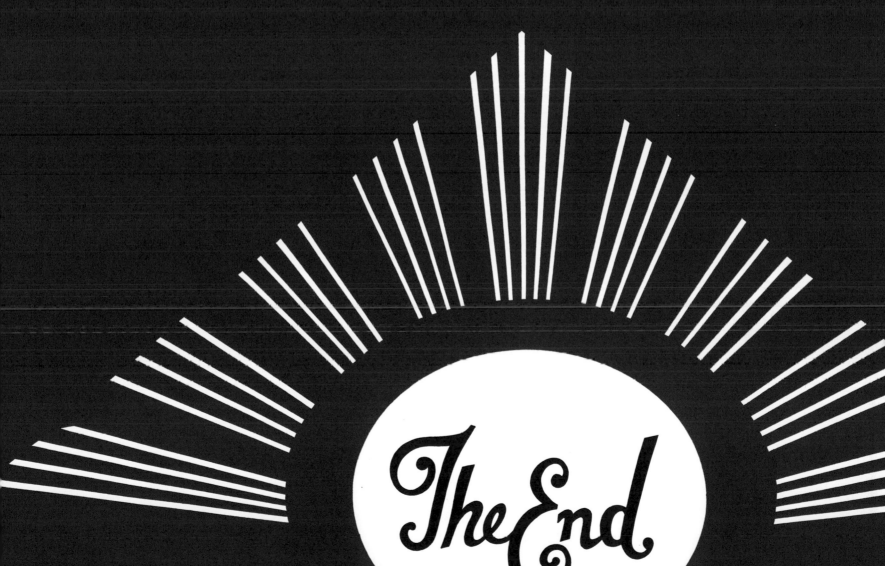

SIGN

THIS CONCLUDES ANOTHER TELECAST DAY FROM CKCK TELEVISION...

CKCK Television

THE BROADCAST SERVICE OF THE CANADA-KAMPF BROADCASTING SYSTEM.

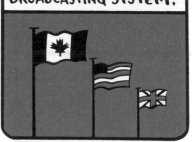

WITH STUDIOS LOCATED AT 85 OAK ROAD IN LAKESIDE, ONTARIO...

AND AT THE NATIONAL PRESS CENTRE IN OTTAWA.

CKCK PROGRAMMING IS SIMULTANEOUSLY BROADCAST

ACROSS NORTHERN ONTARIO ON DIFFERENT CHANNELS

VIA A NETWORK OF REGIONAL TX TRANSMITTERS

LICENCED BY THE CANADIAN RADIO-TELEVISION COMMISSION.

IN DOMINION, CKCK IS SEEN ON CHANNEL 10...

FROM OUR TRANSMITTER IN RELIANCE WITH A POWER OF 370,000 WATTS.

THROUGHOUT THE TUKTUK REGION, YOU SEE CKCK ON CHANNEL 6...

FROM OUR TRANSMITTER IN BRIDGEWATER WITH A POWER OF 100,000 WATTS.

OFF

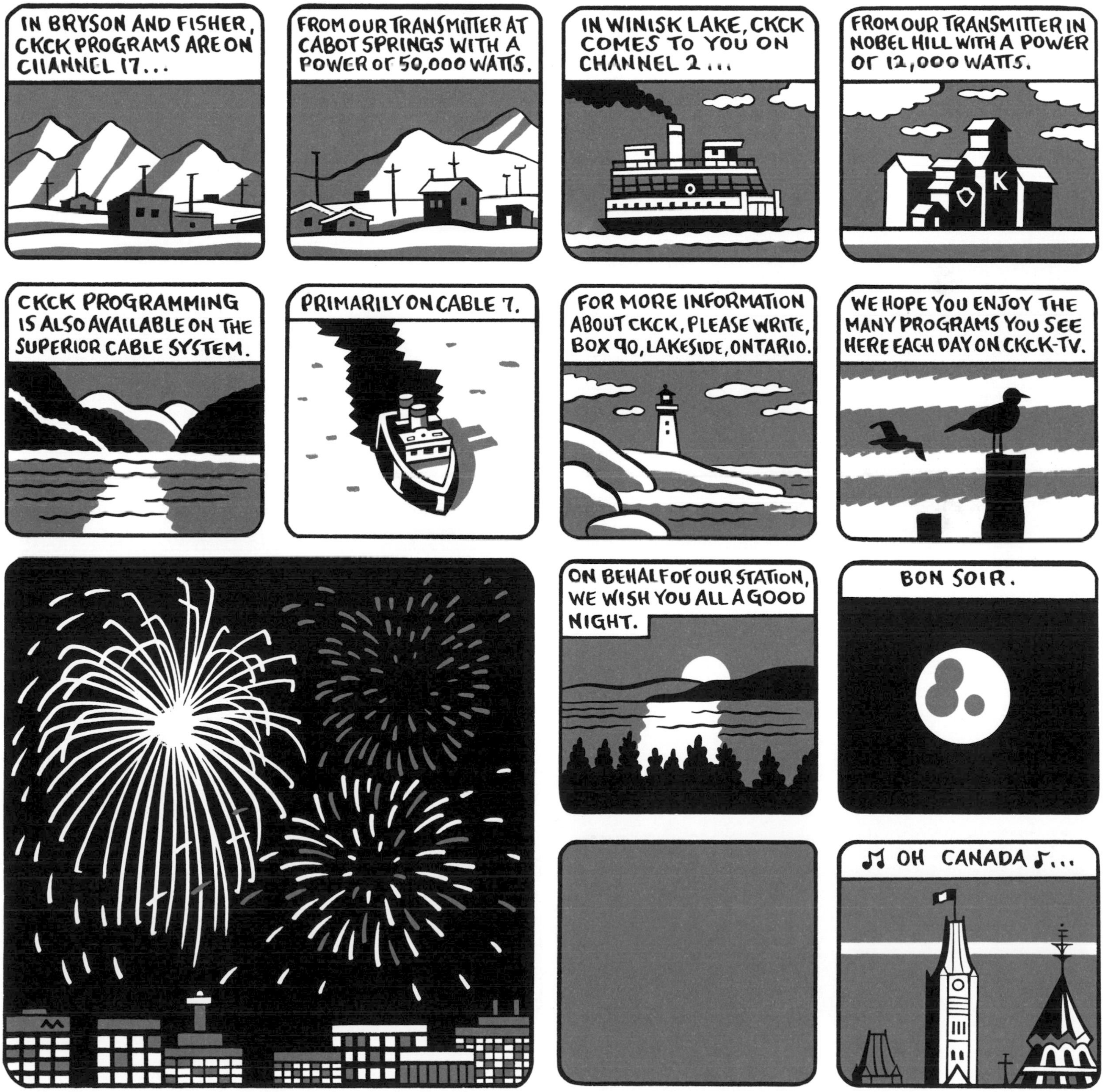
IN BRYSON AND FISHER, CKCK PROGRAMS ARE ON CHANNEL 17...
FROM OUR TRANSMITTER AT CABOT SPRINGS WITH A POWER OF 50,000 WATTS.
IN WINISK LAKE, CKCK COMES TO YOU ON CHANNEL 2...
FROM OUR TRANSMITTER IN NOBEL HILL WITH A POWER OF 12,000 WATTS.
CKCK PROGRAMMING IS ALSO AVAILABLE ON THE SUPERIOR CABLE SYSTEM.
PRIMARILY ON CABLE 7.
FOR MORE INFORMATION ABOUT CKCK, PLEASE WRITE, BOX 90, LAKESIDE, ONTARIO.
WE HOPE YOU ENJOY THE MANY PROGRAMS YOU SEE HERE EACH DAY ON CKCK-TV.
ON BEHALF OF OUR STATION, WE WISH YOU ALL A GOOD NIGHT.
BON SOIR.
♫ OH CANADA ♪...

SPECIAL THANKS
TO SHEILA GLASER, FOR MAKING MY
STINT AT THE NY TIMES SUCH A JOY
& TO TOM DEVLIN, FOR DOING
ALL THE HARD, THANKLESS STUFF.

Published by Jonathan Cape

2 4 6 8 10 9 7 5 3 1

Copyright © Seth 2010

Seth has asserted his right under the Copyright, Designs
and Patents Act 1988 to be identified as the author of this work

Parts of this book were serialized in a different form
in The New York Times Magazine
Photographs by: David Briggs Photography

First published in Great Britain in 2010 by
Jonathan Cape
Random House, 20 Vauxhall Bridge Road,
London SW1V 2SA

www.rbooks.co.uk

Addresses for companies within The Random House Group Limited can be found at:
www.randomhouse.co.uk/offices.htm

The Random House Group Limited Reg. No. 954009

A CIP catalogue record for this book is available from the British Library

ISBN 9780224089982

The Random House Group Limited makes every effort to ensure that the papers used in its books are
made from trees that have been legally sourced from well-managed and credibly certified forests. Our
paper procurement policy can be found at: www.randomhouse.co.uk/paper.htm

Printed and bound in China by C & C Offset Printing Co., Ltd